BIBLIOTHEKEN UND VERLAGE ALS TRÄGER DER INFORMATIONSGESELLSCHAFT

BIBLIOTHEKEN UND VERLAGE ALS TRÄGER DER INFORMATIONSGESELLSCHAFT

VORTRÄGE DES 4. EUROPÄISCHEN BIELEFELD KOLLOQUIUMS 10.-12. FEBRUAR 1998

Herausgegeben von
Karl Wilhelm Neubauer und W. Robert Müller

VITTORIO KLOSTERMANN · FRANKFURT AM MAIN

ZEITSCHRIFT FÜR BIBLIOTHEKSWESEN UND BIBLIOGRAPHIE
SONDERHEFTE
Herausgegeben von Jürgen Hering

SONDERHEFT 74

Die Deutsche Bibliothek – CIP-Einheitsaufnahme

[Zeitschrift für Bibliothekswesen und Bibliographie / Sonderhefte]
Zeitschrift für Bibliothekswesen und Bibliographie. Sonderhefte. –
Frankfurt am Main : Klostermann.
Früher Schriftenreihe. – Früher angezeigt u.d.T.: Zeitschrift für
Bibliothekswesen und Bibliographie / Sonderheft
Teilw. u.d.T.: Zeitschrift für Bibliothekswesen und Bibliographie /
Sonderheft
Reihe Sonderhefte zu: Zeitschrift für Bibliothekswesen und
Bibliographie
ISSN 0514-6364
74. Bibliotheken und Verlage als Träger der Informationsgesellschaft. – 1999
Bibliotheken und Verlage als Träger der Informationsgesellschaft
: Vorträge des 4. Europäischen Bielefeld-Kolloquiums, 10. - 12.
Februar 1998 / hrsg. von Karl Wilhelm Neubauer und W. Robert
Müller. – Frankfurt am Main : Klostermann, 1999
(Zeitschrift für Bibliothekswesen und Bibliographie : Sonderhefte ; 74)
ISBN 3-465-02781-7

Satz: Fotosatz L. Huhn, Maintal-Bischofsheim
Druck: Hubert & Co., Göttingen
Gedruckt auf alterungsbeständigem Papier ∞ ISO 9706
Printed in Germany

Inhalt

NEUE DIENSTLEISTUNGEN DER BIBLIOTHEKEN

ELEKTRONISCHES URHEBERRECHT – NÄCHSTE SCHRITTE

METADATEN

BIBLIOTHEKEN IN DER INFORMATIONSGESELLSCHAFT – NATIONALE INITIATIVEN

EFFEKTIVE AUS- UND WEITERBILDUNG ALS VORAUSSETZUNG FÜR DIE MEISTERUNG DER NEUEN HERAUSFORDERUNGEN

GRUSSWORTE

Die Konferenz über Bibliotheken und Verlage als Träger der Informationsgesellschaft ist eine inhaltlich gewichtige und zugleich umfang- und facettenreiche Veranstaltung mit gesamteuropäischem Charakter. Ich danke dem British Council und der Buchhändler-Vereinigung, daß sie sich bereitgefunden haben, zusammen mit unserer Universitätsbibliothek die Tagung zu organisieren, auf der dieser Band beruht.

Der Sprung in die elektronisch bestimmte Informationsgesellschaft stellt Bibliotheken und Verlage vor die wahrscheinlich größten Herausforderungen ihrer Geschichte, denn noch nie haben sich die technologischen Rahmenbedingungen für ihre Aufgaben in derart rasender Geschwindigkeit und zugleich geradezu revolutionär verändert. Vor allem hinsichtlich der Verlage, die ja, anders als die Bibliotheken, auch notwendig profitorientierte Unternehmen sind, konnte dies einen mit Sorge erfüllen. Würden die erforderlichen Investitionen nicht zu einer weiteren Konzentration im Verlagswesen und damit zu einem Verlust der Vielfalt führen? Bringen neue und gewiß nicht triviale urheberrechtliche Fragen die Verlage nicht in erhebliche Bedrängnis, und würde das traditionelle Medium Buch nicht über kurz oder lang aus dem Zentrum der Verlagsarbeit verschwinden? Inzwischen hat man als unbeteiligter Laie den Eindruck, daß den Verlagen die Umstellung besser, als mancher befürchtet hat, gelingt. Zugleich sieht man, daß das Buch sich trotz allem weiter neben den modernen Datenträgern behauptet und daß es Bereiche gibt, in denen es sicher weiter unersetzlich sein wird. Um einmal ganz lebensweltlich zu argumentieren: wer nimmt schon gern statt eines Krimis in Papierform seinen Laptop mit ins Bett? – Aber selbst an dieser Stelle können wir angesichts der grenzenlosen Kreativität der Ingenieure nicht ganz sicher sein.

Die gewaltigen Vorteile, die Digitalisierung und Vernetzung mit sich bringen, hat inzwischen jeder, der auf wissenschaftliche Informationen angewiesen ist, selbst erlebt. Der weltweite Zugriff auf Datenbanken, neue Möglichkeiten des electronic publishing oder auch erheblich verkürzte Wartezeichen im Fernleihbetrieb bedeuten Arbeitserleichterungen, von denen man vor wenigen Jahren nur träumen konnte. Gleichzeitig steigt allerdings auch die Menge des Datenmülls, dessen man sich auch im wissenschaftlichen Bereich erwehren muß, in zuvor ungeahnte Dimensionen an. Auch für die öffentlichen Bibliotheken bedeutet die digitale Revolution ein hohes Maß an Herausforderung.

Neben der Bereitschaft, wahrscheinlich nicht selten im Kopf vorhandene Barrieren zu beseitigen und sich auf diese neuen Herausforderungen wirklich einzulassen, spielt dabei einmal mehr das Geld eine herausragende Rolle. An dieser Stelle können wir uns in Nordrhein Westfalen für den großzügigen Ausbau der Hochschulbibliotheken nur bedanken. Bei der Informationsgesellschaft handelt es sich aber selbstverständlich um nichts, was an Landesgrenzen stehen bleiben kann. Die Formel vom „global village" ist inzwischen zwar schon etwas viel strapaziert, wird dadurch aber längst noch nicht falsch. Erfreulicherweise laufen auch auf europäischer Ebene zahlreiche Projekte, die eine noch engere internationale und regionale Kooperation im Bibliothekswesen ermöglichen sollen. Daß der Europagedanke allerdings auch seine Kehrseite haben kann, haben wir an der gerade wieder aufgeflammten Diskussion um die Buchpreisbindung gesehen. Ich glaube, wir sollten bei allem Verständnis für Belange der europäischen Einigung als Wissenschaftler und Betreiber von Bibliotheken, aber auch als pluralistisch denkende Bürger, ein großes Interesse an einer möglichst vielfältigen Verlags- und Buchhandlungslandschaft haben!

Der Weg in die Informationsgesellschaft wirft viele spannende Fragen auf. Dabei ist für uns von außerordentlich großem Interesse, aus erster Hand zu erfahren, wie sich die Entwicklung in den Nachbarländern darstellt, Länder nämlich, die Deutschland im Multimedia-Einsatz im Hochschulbereich zum Teil erheblich voraus sind.

Prof. Dr. Gert Rickheit
Rektor der Universität Bielefeld

Das 4. Europäische Bielefelder Kolloquium vom 10.-12. Februar 1998 wird auch in diesem Jahr von den Veranstaltungspartnern Bibliothek der Universität Bielefeld, Buchhändler-Vereinigung GmbH und The British Council veranstaltet. Mit dem Titel des diesjährigen Kolloquiums „Bibliotheken und Verlage als Träger der Informationsgesellschaft" knüpfen die drei Veranstaltungspartner an die Thematik an, mit welcher sie vor sechs Jahren das Kolloquium ins Leben gerufen haben: Elektronische Vermittlung von Fachinformationen. Blickt man allerdings zurück auf das Thema des 1. Kolloquiums „CD-ROM-Netze in Bibliotheken", so läßt sich am diesjährigen Programm die rasante Weiterentwicklung im Bereich elektronisches Publizieren ablesen. Doch soll den Teilnehmern des Kolloquiums auch die Möglichkeit gegeben werden, Themen, die bereits in den letzten Kolloquien aufgezeigt wurden, erneut aufzugreifen und fortzuschreiben, weil die erforderlichen und gewünschten Lösungen noch nicht erreicht sind.

Die Internationalisierung der Teilnehmer des diesjährigen Kolloquiums läßt erkennen, daß die Probleme des elektronischen Publizierens und des elektronischen Vermittelns von Fachinformationen durchaus nicht als nationale Angelegenheit zu betrachten sind. Die Thematik ist vielmehr von grenzüberschreitender Bedeutung, die internationale Zusammenarbeit und Lösungen erfordert.

Dies wird bereits durch den Titel des 4. Europäischen Bielefelder Kolloquiums zum Ausdruck gebracht. Die Entwicklung der Informationsmärkte vollzieht sich sehr schnell und ist in der Gesamtheit nicht abzuschätzen. Doch stellt gerade diese Tatsache eine Herausforderung sowohl für Verlage als auch für Bibliotheken dar. Es bietet sich zur Zeit die Chance, sich durch innovatives Handeln und gezielte Investitionen im Bereich elektronische Publikationen als Träger der Informationsgesellschaft zu etablieren. Es liegt zwar in der Natur der Sache, daß Spannungsfelder zwischen Verlagen und Bibliotheken bestehen, doch dient das Kolloquium dazu, die Zusammenarbeit auf dem Weg an die Spitze der Informationsgesellschaft zu fördern. Denn diese Zusammenarbeit ist unerläßlich. Die Buchhändler-Vereinigung GmbH engagiert sich zusammen mit den anderen beiden Partnern für den Ideen- und Infomationsaustausch zum Thema elektronische Publikationen, weil das elektronische Vermitteln von Fachinfomationen nicht ohne die Verlage als Inhaber der Rechte zur Vervielfältigung und Verbreitung möglich ist.

Die sich permanent wandelnde Informationsgesellschaft verstärkt zudem die Notwendigkeit der Zusammenarbeit zwischen Verlagen und Bibliotheken, da beide ihre Rolle innerhalb dieser veränderten Gesellschaft neu definieren müssen, um auch in Zukunft ihre Position im Informationsgefüge zu behaupten. Es geht jedoch nicht nur um die eigene Rolle gegenüber der Öffentlichkeit, sondern auch darum, die eigene Strategie als Unternehmen bzw. als öffentliche Institution an den sich neu entwickelnden Strukturen der Informationsgesellschaft auszurichten.

Der Einfluß elektronischer Medien auf die Gesellschaft löst in zunehmendem Maße Handlungsbedarf auch auf politischer Ebene aus. Die Verpflichtung der Regierung, eine flächendeckende Informationsversorgung der Gesellschaft sicherzustellen, erfordert eine intensive Auseinandersetzung der politischen Entscheidungsträger mit neuen elektronischen Medien. Daher wird bei dem diesjährigen Kolloquium die Verantwortung der Politik für die Förderung der Informationsgesellschaft thematisiert. Es kann nur im Interesse aller Beteiligten sein, wenn sich Verlage und Bibliotheken mit politischen Vertretern über die Zukunft der Informationsgesellschaft austauschen, um Probleme gemeinsam anzugehen und zukünftig an einem Strang zu ziehen.

Auf dem Weg zu einer immer stärker von elektronischen Medien geprägten Gesellschaft bietet sich im Bereich elektronische Publikationen sowohl für Verlage als auch Bibliotheken die einmalige Chance, sich durch Kooperation zu den entscheidenden Trägern der Informationsgesellschaft zu entwickeln. Ziel des 4. Europäischen Bielefelder Kolloquiums ist es, nationalen und internationalen Verlagen und Bibliotheken ein Forum für diese Kooperation zu bieten.

W. Robert Müller
Buchhändler-Vereinigung GmbH, Frankfurt am Main

Many developments in the field of electronic information systems and information provision have taken place over the last two years. Many of the topics of the last colloquium's programme published in *Elektronisches Publizieren und Bibliotheken,* ZfBB Sonderheft 65, – like search mechanisms in the internet, textcentres for information provision, integrity of electronic documents or database tools – did not mean a lot to me then. Today no organisation can afford to be unaware of the latest technological developments, and every organisation has to evaluate their importance for its own work, and identify mechanisms for the successful integration of the new communication and information technologies into its activities. And libraries are ideally placed to carry these developments forward.

The first theme of this volume, based on the 1998 colloquium, is the responsibility of politics for the support of the information society. You will also hear a paper about recent initiatives of the new British government, of which I will mention just a few: The *Library and Information Commission*, which was established to provide the government with a national focus of expertise in the field of library and information services, presented only a couple of weeks ago a proposal for a nationally co-ordinated strategic approach to research, development and innovation for library and information services for the United Kingdom, where appropriate in co-operation with European and other international partners.

The *Dearing report „Higher education in the learning society"*, which was published in July 1997, also makes recommendations to the government for the development of the higher education system over the next twenty years. The recommendations for the improvement of teaching and learning, the use of communication and information technology as well as the administration of universities are of direct relevance to library services. Dearing recommends for example that every institution should have a detailed communication and information strategy in place, that electronic networks and the electronic libraries programme should be further developed and that all students should have access to networked computers.

This colloquium and its results in this volume are mainly for academic libraries serving the higher education community, but governments have the responsibility to ensure that every citizen can benefit from the developments in information technology and will have access to information. Public libraries, as the Library and Information Commission argues in its report: *New Library: The People's Network*, should become the hubs of the information community connecting everyone to the Internet, so that society does not risk becoming divided between information 'haves' and 'have-nots'. The report identifies three important areas of interest: the consumer – or user – of library services; content, i.e. what is actually available through the networks; and training, both of the librarians and of the users. I find all of these aspects reflected in this volume, which suggests that these are areas of equal relevance to academic and public libraries.

Our collaboration for the fourth time in the organising of the colloquium demonstrates the British Council's commitment to international relations in the field of information and library work. Information work for us is an important element of cultural diplomacy and supports understanding between people. Many colleagues in Germany will have participated in one or the other way in our activities, be it the work-exchange programme, a study tour, participation at an Anglo-German conference or seminar, or in one of our specialist courses „English for librarians".

We see the support for British-German events also as a building stone for wider international relations within the European context, as this colloquium shows particularly well. Many of the partners now collaborating in multinational European projects are building on their earlier experience in bi-lateral British-German activities. And we are also proud to be one of the partners of the new European project EXPLOIT, which will encourage and support the exploitation of project results of the EU telematics for libraries programme, and to which we can bring our unique network of offices and information professionals in all European countries.

I believe that the publications in this volume will develop further the links between information specialists and publishers, will inform all of us about leading-edge developments and will help to strengthen European co-operation in this field.

W. Keith Dobson OBE
Director Germany
The British Council

KARL WILHELM NEUBAUER

Einführung

Die technische Entwicklung geht bekanntlich sehr rasch voran und beschleunigt sich immer mehr. Die Entwicklung der Märkte, der menschlichen Organisation, der auf dem Markt durchsetzungsfähigen Produkte, neuer Anbieterstrukturen und Mitspieler vollzieht sich hingegen oft vergleichsweise langsam. Dies zeigt sich auch bei diesem vor sechs Jahren erstmals und heute zum vierten Mal durchgeführten Kolloquium. Einerseits hat sich seit damals auch auf dem Markt einiges bewegt. Andererseits aber haben sich die seit langem angekündigten und erwarteten neuen Strukturen, neuen Rollenverteilungen der Hauptakteure, neuen Player im Bereich der elektronischen Informationsversorgung noch längst nicht grundlegend positioniert. Dies gilt sowohl für die elektronische Informationsversorgung selbst wie auch den Übergang von gedruckter zu elektronischer Information.

Es gibt viele Ansätze, aber viele Bereiche sind letzten Endes noch nicht über das Teststadium hinausgekommen. Neue Techniken sind hinzugekommen, vor allem in den letzten Jahren die großen Internet-Suchmaschinen mit neuen z.T. kommerziell tätigen Dienstleistern. Die Verlage ringen aber immer noch um die besten Strategien zur Sicherung ihrer Umsätze und Gewinne beim Übergang auf die elektronische Information. Die Bibliotheken haben noch längst nicht das Dienstleistungsspektrum und die dafür erforderliche Kooperation erreicht, die vor sechs Jahren bereits diskutiert und mit eindrucksvollen Szenarien entwickelt wurden. Die virtuelle Bibliothek, die natürlich nicht nur aus Bibliotheken im traditionellen Sinn bestehen kann, ist in vielen Ländern im Rahmen großer Programme in Entwicklung, natürlich auch in Programmen der Europäischen Union. Mangelt es hier häufig noch an der erforderlichen nationalen Kooperation, so fehlt weitgehend der große Wurf der letztendlich anzustrebenden internationalen bzw. weltweiten Kooperation im Zeitalter der weltweiten Netze. Die offene Struktur von Internet hat eine weltweite wissenschaftliche Kommunikation in früher unerwartetem Ausmaß angeschoben, aber gleichzeitig auch gezeigt, daß für qualifizierte Information und Kommunikation noch ein großes Bündel an Problemen zu lösen sein wird und immer neue Anforderungen erwachsen. Andererseits ist die gute alte CD-ROM, das Thema des ersten Kolloquiums, immer noch nicht tot. Erstaunlicherweise werden an Universitäten und anderen wissenschaftlichen Einrichtungen immer noch große CD-ROM-Netze unterhalten.

Die früher von vielen Propheten erwartete mehr oder weniger redundanzfreie Datenhaltung auf weltweit agierenden Hosts ist nicht eingetroffen. Im Gegenteil, parallel zu den großen Hosts und den vielen öffentlich zugänglichen Servern in der Welt werden viele Daten der wissenschaftlichen Information ganz bewußt auch lokal oder regional gespeichert, um sie in die jeweilige Umgebung besser einbinden zu können und der lokalen bzw. regionalen Gestaltung besser zur Verfügung zu stellen.

In den letzten Jahren ist – vor allem angeregt durch die Einsatzmöglichkeiten der großen Suchmaschinen – die Diskussion der Metadaten zur besseren Auffindbarkeit von Daten und Dokumenten im Internet auf breiter Ebene in Gang gekommen. Früher galt dieses Thema weitgehend als Reservat der Bibliothekare. Nun waren es gerade Informationsindustrie, Verlage und Fachgesellschaften, die diese Problematik im Hinblick auf eine vernünftige Wiederauffindbarkeit der Daten im Internet in den Vordergrund gestellt haben. Eine einigermaßen einsatzfähige und tragfähige Basis, die sich schon weltweit als Standard durchgesetzt hätte, gibt es auch hier noch nicht.

Fortschritte in der praktischen Realisierung sind inzwischen bei den E-Journals, bei den elektronischen Zeitschriften, erkennbar. Große wissenschaftliche Verlage bieten in der Zwischenzeit große Pakete elektronischer Zeitschriften, die bisher nur gedruckt vorlagen, den Bibliotheken und der Scientific Community an. Aber auch hier handelt es sich vorerst noch um ein Abtasten des Marktes. Wie der Zeitschriftenmarkt in fünf bis zehn Jahren aussehen wird, ist heute immer noch schwer vorauszusagen. Die Diskussion über die kommerzielle Herstellung von Zeitschriften und das Angebot von Zeitschriften und Zeitschriftenartikeln über das Internet durch die Wissenschaftler und Wissenschaftlerinnen selbst ist inzwischen differenzierter geworden. Es ist deutlich, daß es hier wohl kein Entweder-Oder, sondern ein Miteinander geben wird.

Auch der in den letzten Jahren heiß erwartete Einsatz von Multimedia in der Wissenschaft kommt nur schwer voran. Die Herstellung guter Multimedia ist sehr teuer und aufwendig. Das kommerzielle Marktpotential dafür ist noch wenig bekannt. Bei den daraus entstehenden Risiken tun sich die Anbieter noch schwer.

In Anbetracht der immer langsam mahlenden Mühlen der Gesetzgebungsmaschinerie und der gerade bei elektronischen Medien besonders ausgeprägten internationalen Verflechtung ist es vielleicht am wenigsten verwunderlich, daß die Neugestaltung des Urheberrechts noch erhebliche Anstrengungen erfordert. Daran wird aber national, in der Europäischen Union und weltweit hart gearbeitet. Darum gibt es durchaus Unterschiede im Fortschritt der gesetzlichen Regelungen in einzelnen Ländern, gerade auch im Vergleich zu den USA.

Dieser kurze Überblick sollte nur deutlich machen, daß die in diesem Band angesprochenen Themenblöcke einen hohen Aktualitätsgrad haben und einige der Themen, über die wir bereits vor sechs Jahren diskutiert haben, trotz teilweiser großer Fortschritte immer noch hohe Aktualität besitzen. Es ist nach wie vor viel zu tun. Packen wir's an.

DIE VERANTWORTUNG DER POLITIK FÜR DIE FÖRDERUNG DER INFORMATIONSGESELLSCHAFT

NICK MOORE

The British National Information Strategy

The last few years have seen an unprecedented effort throughout the world to assemble policy frameworks that will enable countries to manage their transition into information-intensive societies. This activity is a direct response to the major changes that are being brought about by developments in information and communications technology.

This pursuit of information policy has taken place in large countries like the USA and Japan, in small countries like Singapore and Luxembourg; in developed countries like Australia and Sweden, and in developing countries like Thailand and Malaysia. It is a feature of capitalist regimes like Canada and Korea as well as socialist countries like China and Vietnam. All these countries have, during the last five years, tried to put in place sets of policies that have two broad purposes in common: to ensure that the country is able to take full advantage of the opportunities that are offered by technological change, while at the same time avoiding the undesirable consequences that might arise from the developments.

The Approach

The approach adopted by different countries has also been remarkably consistent, usually involving three distinct stages. The first task is to investigate the problem: to assess the magnitude of the changes that are taking place, identifying the country's weaknesses and the opportunities that might be opening up. Then it becomes possible to articulate a vision of the kind of society and economy to which the country can aspire. Here it is worth noting that in many countries the most senior politicians have been intimately involved in articulating the vision. The final stage is to identify the actions that will be required to achieve the vision.

While the approaches adopted have distinct similarities, the mechanisms used for developing the policy frameworks have differed. Some countries have carried out the task within the executive branch of government: examples are Denmark, Finland, the Netherlands and Norway in Europe and Japan and Singapore further afield. Here the work is carried out by inter-departmental groups of civil servants and ministers, often under the chairmanship of the prime minister.

Other countries have delegated the task to an advisory body of experts drawn from the different sectors that will be most affected by the changes. Sweden, Australia and Canada are good examples of this approach, with the report of the Canadian taskforce (Information Highway Advisory Council, 1995) possibly being the best example of a single document that defines the problem, articulates a vision and specifies a desired list of actions.

A third group have combined both of these approaches, drawing on the expertise of appointed advisory bodies but retaining responsibility for developing policy within the executive. This is the approach used by the European Union with the Bangemann Group (European Commission, 1994) and, more recently, the High Level Expert Group on the Information Society (European Commission, 1996 and European Commission, 1997) and the associated Information Society Forum (European Commission, 1996b). It is also the approach adopted in the USA with the Advisory Council on the National Information Infrastructure providing expert advice to the National Information Task Force (Advisory Council on the National Information Infrastructure, 1996).

The British Approach

We, in Britain, find the formal approach to policy formulation a little uncomfortable – a little too prescriptive and rigid. Instead we prefer a more evolutionary approach, one that involves the development of a range of strategies, actions and responses to specific issues that can be observed, evaluated and adapted in the light of changing requirements. The kind of pragmatic, rooted approach to policy development that Charles Lindblom elegantly described as 'the science of muddling through' (Lindblom, 1968).

One consequence of this informal approach to policy is that it is not possible to point to a single document that describes what the British national information policy encompasses. Instead, we must consider a range of activities and aspirations across a fairly wide canvass. The question is how to identify what is going on? One tool that we can use in our trawl of policy actions is the information policy matrix that was drawn up to assist the European Commission develop its policy in the information content sector (Moore, 1993).

The Information policy Matrix

We can first identify three distinct levels of policy: industrial, organisational and social.

Industrial
The industrial level is concerned with the information sector of the economy. Here the concern is to ensure that we have an information sector that can respond effectively to the growing demand for information within Britain and which can compete effectively in the rapidly expanding global market for information.

The information sector itself needs further definition. It is possible to divide the overall sector into three segments: content, delivery and processing. The information content segment is concerned with the creation, development and exploitation of intellectual property. Essentially, it is the production and publishing industry. The information delivery segment is concerned with the transmission of data and information and comprises the telecommunications and broadcasting industry. The information processing segment is concerned with hardware, software and computer services.

Organisational
The organisational level of information policy is concerned with the use of information as a corporate resource within organisations in both the public and private sectors. In the private sector, information is widely perceived as offering the potential for raising levels of productivity and, more generally improving a firm's competitive position. It can contribute in a number of ways. Automation can greatly reduce administration costs; better use of information can stimulate innovation and accelerate product development; market research and intelligence can enable firms to position and promote their products more effectively; and information about customer behaviour can be used to reduce risk, particularly in the financial services sector.

Information use can also make a significant contribution in the public sector, enabling organisations to reduce cost and improve quality and effectiveness.

The extent to which a nation's corporate bodies improve efficiency and effectiveness determines, to a very great extent, the country's overall level of international competitiveness.

Social

At the social level we are concerned with the way in which people can use information to improve the quality of their daily lives. Some of the issues raised at this level are of national significance, such as the level of access to the information required to allow democratic processes to function effectively. Others are more individual, such as the labelling of food products so that people can select those that are best for their health.

Essentially, social information is needed so that individuals can exercise choice; can hold corporate bodies to account; can obtain the benefits that are due to them as members of society and, at the most fundamental level, can participate fully in democratic processes.

At each of these three levels it is possible to identify four cross-cutting elements that need to be considered: information technology, information markets, human resources and legislation and regulation.

Information technology

Information technology is clearly pervasive. It underlies developments at all levels. Probably the most fundamental issue is concerned with the question of universal access to the technology, particularly telecommunications. Secondary questions concern the development of navigation tools and other software to enable us to make most effective use of the technology – is this an issue that should be left to the market or should the government be sponsoring research and development?

Information markets

The concept of information markets implies more than the buying and selling of information. The policy issues are concerned with the broader question of the exchange of information: the interface between the provider and the consumer. Much information, it is true, is traded commercially – it is generally thought that the annual value of information traded this way within Europe is over 150 billion ECU – but even greater volumes are exchanged in circumstances where the information is 'free at the point of use'. The information that is provided by libraries, citizens advice bureaux, government departments, hospitals and many other individuals and organisations provides an essential ingredient of organisational and social life and we require policies to ensure that this information system operates effectively.

Human resources

People are a key factor in the development of an information society. Whether it is ensuring that the information industries have access to adequate numbers of appropriately trained individuals; or that managers are able to cope with the increased flows of information, or that individuals can properly interpret the latest batch of statistics about school examination results, the human factor will be a critical determinant of the success or failure of Britain as an information society.

Legislation and regulation

Legislation and regulation is needed to provide the formal structure within which an information society operates. In some cases we need to bring existing legislation up-to-date so that it accommodates changed circumstances. In others it is a question of developing new legislation to strengthen the move towards an information society. At the social level, it is possible to identify the emergence of intellectual rights as a fourth right of citizenship (Moore, 1998).

Increasingly legislative and regulatory questions have an international dimension.

Information policy matrix

By putting these levels and cross-cutting elements together it is possible to construct a matrix which can be used as a tool to analyse existing policies, to specify inconsistencies and conflicts and to identify gaps.

	Information technology	Information markets	Human resources	Legislation regulation
Industrial				
Organisational				
Social				

In this case, we can use it to identify the patchwork of policies and initiatives that, together, constitute the British information policy framework.

The industrial Level

Here policy is concerned with developing and supporting the information sector of the national economy. Very broadly, the aim is to ensure that the sector can meet the demands for information that arise from other parts of the economy and that it can compete successfully in global markets, generating a balance of trade surplus.

The legacy of the Conservative government is such that we do not have a strong industrial development framework in Britain, having preferred to leave such matters to private capital and the market. We do, however, have certain strengths. The early privatisation of British Telecom, even though it was carried out for other reasons, has provided us with an efficient telecommunications system and a company that is able to compete successfully in world markets. In marked contrast, we have very little competitive strength in the hardware industries and we are almost wholly reliant on imports to meet our hardware requirements.

There has also been relatively little support for the development of the information content industries. True, the BBC is regarded as one of the world's leading television production companies, thanks largely to a tradition of public service broadcasting. But the success of our publishing and financial data companies is attributable to the ubiquity of the English language and the centrality of London's financial markets and the international acumen of the publishing fraternity rather than to any official support.

Things are changing and we are likely to see a stronger industrial policy developing in the future. There are signs that the Department of Trade and Industry is becoming more active through its programme to support the communications and information industries (Department of Trade and Industry, 1998) and, it is to be hoped that support for the information sector will feature more significantly in the future.

Even now there are signs that the need for support is being acknowledged; the recent Green Paper on Crown Copyright (Office for Public Service, 1998) for example, refers to the desirability of relaxing crown copyright so that information and data might be made more readily available to the publishing industry for exploitation by them. There is also the work of the Library and Information Commission which, though it is primarily concerned with the public sector of the industry, has defined a national research strategy (Library and Information Commission, 1997b) and has set out a clear vision of what is required from libraries and information services in an information society (Library and Information Commission 1997c).

On the whole, however, there is relatively little that can be identified as policy to support the development of what is likely to become one of the most critical elements of our future industrial structure.

The organisational Level

Here the aim is to encourage organisations in both the public and private sectors to become more information-intensive so that they use information as a resource to raise productivity levels, to improve quality and to meet consumer needs more effectively. In part, this involves encouraging greater use of information technology but it is really about supporting the use of information as a management resource.

The government has done more to support development at this level. The highest-profile activity has been the Information Society Initiative (Department of Trade and Industry, 1996a) launched by the previous government but continued by the present one. It is a programme with ambitious aims to stimulate the take-up of information and communications technology, particularly in small and medium-sized enterprises. While the aims are ambitious, the budget is not, representing only a tiny proportion of the total amount spent on information technology and the impact is, therefore, unlikely to be significant.

The Information Society Initiative is supported by a programme called IT for All (Department of Trade and Industry, 1996b). This aims to encourage the take-up of information technology by individuals and community groups.

In 1996 the government published a Green Paper setting out its plans to deliver government services electronically (Central Information Technology Unit, 1996). The consultation period has now closed and the government is laying the groundwork for a major process of service development which will have a significant impact on businesses and their dealings with the state (Parliamentary Office for Science and Technology, 1998).

Programmes such as these, though, can only be a beginning. What is required is a change in organisational culture and this will take time and considerable effort to achieve.

The social Level

As societies become more complex they become more reliant on information. People need to use information to make choices as consumers. Increasingly this applies to their consumption of public goods as public services like health and education are re-engineered to offer greater degrees of choice to consumers. People also need information about their rights and responsibilities so that they can claim their entitlements and play a full part in society. In addition, they need information as citizens in a democracy – information to enable democratic choices, as well as the information required to hold politicians and service providers to account.

The IT for All programme (Department of Trade and Industry, 1996b) seeks in part, to support this function within society. It aims to raise awareness of information technology applications particularly within community groups and in the voluntary sector.

The government's programme to develop electronic service delivery will also stimulate awareness of the role of information in social life and should go some way towards breaking down some of the barriers created by unfamiliarity with technology.

More recently the Library and Information Commission published a far-reaching plan to develop the public library service as an information network to meet a range of social information needs (Library and Information Commission 1997a). The report calls for a level of public investment that is unlikely to be forthcoming, but the vision that was articulated was important.

We also have in Britain a unique resource in the network of independent advice services like citizens advice bureaux. No other country has such a well-developed network of agencies that can meet social information needs. Local branches of the network are supported by local authorities, while the National Association of Citizens Advice Bureaux is grant-aided by the Department of Trade and Industry.

Again, however, we need to bring about a major cultural change in both the provision and use of information at the social level. And such change must be carried out effectively throughout society if we are avoid creating a class of people who are disenfranchised by their inability to make use of information.

Information Technology

Here the government seeks to achieve two goals: to create an effective technological infrastructure and to ensure that the technology is used to greatest effect.

Many commentators appear to be arguing that the infrastructural problems have largely been overcome. Despite reservations from some quarters, notably the House of Lords Select Committee (House of Lords, 1996), there appears to be little demand for government action to strengthen the infrastructure.

Hardware is readily available. Prices continue to drop steadily as capacity expands. Software is increasingly becoming regarded as a commodity that can be purchased cheaply off the shelf rather than produced expensively to meet the specific requirements of individual organisations. We might be concerned that few British companies are key players in these markets, but that concern is usually over-ridden by the ubiquity of cheap imports.

The telecommunications infrastructure is also fairly robust and capable of meeting most requirements. The privatisation of British Telecom and the encouragement of cable companies has done much to stimulate investment in the telecommunications infrastructure. There is likely to be a continuing demand for greater capacity but the existing providers seem likely to be able to respond appropriately without significant government intervention.

In the light of this situation, attention has shifted to the application of the technology. Here the Technology Foresight Panel has done much to create a climate of critical review and perceptive prediction (Office for Science and Technology, 1995). On a more practical level, the Information Society Initiative (Department of Trade and Industry, 1996a) and the IT for All programme (Department of Trade and Industry, 1996b) has sought to stimulate take-up of the technologies.

Human Resources

Changing the culture of information use and developing people's capacity to use information is, arguably, the most important element in forging an information society. Here attention needs to be focused on the education and training systems.

At the primary and secondary levels, a considerable amount has been achieved through the work of agencies such as the National Council for Educational Technology (from April 1998 re-named as the British Educational Communications and Technology Agency), building on the early efforts to introduce computers into schools. Clearly, schools are still constrained financially. They do not have – and probably never will have – sufficient numbers of up-to-date computers and many schools, despite the best efforts of the Department for Education and Employment to develop Internet access (Department for Education and Employment, 1997b), still cannot afford the cost of constant access to the Internet. But the basic provision exists and is being built upon.

The future efforts will focus on the development of information processing, as distinct from IT, skills. Here there are signs that the national curriculum has been modified to support the development of information handling, evaluation and analysis skills (see, for example Department for Education and Employment, 1997c). We can be reasonably confident that future generations will emerge from the school system at ease with information technology and with a basic understanding of information processing.

Similarly, great progress has been made at the tertiary level. The Follett Report (Joint Funding Council, 1993) has stimulated a far-reaching programme to support the creation of digital libraries, as a result of which, universities and colleges of higher education have greatly improved their capacity to handle digital information. Similarly the Dearing Report (Department for Education and Employment, 1997a) emphasised the need to develop high-level information processing skills.

There is, however, a continuing need to address those who have already left school and college. There is a widespread recognition, articulated well by the European Commission's High Level Group of Experts (European Commission, 1997), that an information society must also be a learning society. To this end it is encouraging to see large-scale development projects like the Education Department's superhighways initiative (Department for Education and Employment, 1997b), to be followed by the National Grid for Learning (Department for Education and Employment, 1997d) which is designed to link up all schools and other education establishment and to provide access to people undertaking continuing education. These initiatives with others outside the formal system, such as the University for Industry (University for Industry, 1998) which will do much to provide the continuing education and retraining services that will be required in the future.

The take-up of services such as these will be stimulated by programmes emanating from the government's plans to develop the National Lottery (Department of Culture Media and Sport, 1997). The proposal is to develop two new sources of funds that can support the development of human resources in an information society. The New Opportunities Fund will provide substantial sums of money to fund information technology training for librarians and teachers, while the National Endowment for Science, Technology and the Arts is intended to stimulate employment and training in the creative industries.

We have, therefore, a good start with the formal education system and strong signs that the non-formal sector is expanding its capacity to cope with future demand.

Markets

The aim is to have an information market that is fair; that avoids domination by one or two key players; that supports enterprise; that encourages new entrants and that operates in the consumer interest. The record here in the past has not been very good.

There are several examples where pressure exerted by key players in the market has resulted in changes to policies that were originally introduced to protect broad consumer interests. Probably the best example is the over-turning of resale price maintenance in the book market: a step that will favour the big publishers and booksellers at the expense of the small and which will, quite probably, lead to reduced consumer choice. Similar examples can be found in the history of the exercise of monopolies and mergers legislation with respect to media ownership. The position on cross-media ownership in Britain is also one which would not be tolerated in many other countries.

In contrast, our record on the regulation of telecommunications and broadcasting industries is impressive. Our early privatisation of British Telecommunications meant that we had to learn quite quickly how to regulate the industry to stimulate competition and to encourage new entrants into the market while operating in the consumer interest. We may not have got it completely right but many of the lesson learned in Britain are now being applied in the opening telecommunications market in Europe. It is likely that our steps towards the convergence of regulators (OFTEL, 1998) will be similarly copied.

The Green Paper on copyright Office for Public Service, 1998) is an attempt to sort out the relationship between the holders of public information assets and the information industry and, as such, represents a step forward in resolving what many have seen as an impediment to the development of the information market.

Legislation and Regulation

The development of an information society calls for the creation of a framework of laws and regulations that will make the whole system function effectively. The information industry needs efficient intellectual property right legislation; organisations need to operate within clear data protection laws and, increasingly, will require a legal framework within which electronic commerce can operate. Individuals need a set of intellectual rights that will give effect to citizenship in an advanced information society.

Here there has been considerable activity in recent years, particularly since the change of government in May 1997.

Intellectual property rights law has been revised to accommodate the changing requirements imposed by technology (Statutory Instrument, 1997). There will be a need for continuous revision but much progress has been made.

Similarly, the Data Protection Act is under revision to take account of a changed technological environment (Home Office, 1997). The concept of data protection was first developed within the Council of Europe and that Council's Convention of Human Rights embodies a number of individual rights that will shape individual rights as the Convention is adopted by the government. Chief of these will be a right to privacy.

There have also been considerable changes in attitudes towards rights of access to official information. In the 1980s we were given rights of access to personal information held by health services and some branches of local government. We were also given rights of access to local government information generally. Now, in the late 1990s we can look forward to the introduction of legislation that will give us similar rights of access to information held by central government (Office for Public Service, 1997).

Together these newly-acquired rights constitute a fourth set of citizenship rights, which define the relationship between individuals and the state in an information society (Moore, 1998).

It is also likely that the forthcoming White Paper on better government will have much to say on the relationship between individuals and public services and on ways in which this relationship – essentially one of information exchange – can be improved in the future.

What does it all add up To? The first thing that becomes apparent from this brief review of information policy development is that it represents a very British approach to policy making. We are far from having a wide-ranging vision which sets the tone for the subsequent coordinated development of a coherent policy framework. Rather, what we can observe is a fragmented set of policy responses to issues and problems. There is little coordination and little sense of overall direction. It is also hard to see how any single element fits into the overall picture or what impact it will have on other parts of the system.

There is also an enduring belief in the value of market forces in shaping the development of the British information society. One need look no further than the policies concerning broadcasting – we have probably the best public service broadcasting system in the world, yet market forces have been the driving force behind recent developments in broadcasting policy, with the result that the public service ethos is grave in danger of being lost.

There are, however, signs of change. The present government is less emotionally attached to the private sector and to the power of the market. There are also signs that the Cabinet Office is becoming more effective at coordinating the development and harmonisation of policy. We are also beginning to benefit from a more positive stance towards Europe. The European Commission has clearly given a high priority to the development of an information society and this is likely to feature more and more prominently in the development of the Union in the years to come. This will undoubtedly provide a stimulus for the continuing development of a framework of information policies in Britain.

Addendum

In April 1998, two months after this paper was presented at the Bielefeld Colloquium, the British Government published „Our Information Age: the Government's vision“ This draws together many of the initiatives described in the paper and sets out a development plan based on five principles:

1. Transforming education to harness new technology so that all can gain the knowledge and skills they need for the information age.
2. Widening access to ensure that the benefits of the information age are open to all, with no split between the information haves and have-nots.
3. Promoting competition and competitiveness to help business harness change and prosper, for the benefit of customers, jobs and the wider economy.
4. Fostering quality to ensure that the content of new services matches and exceeds the best available today.
5. Modernising government to ensure that the government uses new technology to deliver better, more convenient services.

The full text of the vision statement can be found at
http://www.number-10.gov.uk/public/info/releases/publications/finalver.zip

References

Advisory Council on the National Information Infrastructure (1996) A nation of opportunity: final report of the United States Advisory Council on the National Information Infrastructure (1996)

Central Information Technology Unit (1996) government.direct. HMSO

Department of Culture Media and Sport (1997) The People's Lottery. The Stationery Office <www.culture.gov.uk/WHITEPAP.HTM>

Department for Education and Employment (1997a) Higher education in a learning society: report of the national committee of enquiry into higher education (The Dearing Report). The Stationery Office

Department for Education and Employment (1997b) Preparing for the information age: synoptic report of the Education Department's Superhighways Initiative.

The Stationery Office <www.open.gov/dfee/dfeehome.htm>

Department for Education and Employment (1997c) Information technology in the National Curriculum.. <www.open.gov.uk/nc/itindex.html>

Department for Education and Employment (1997d) A National Grid for Learning. <www.open.gov.uk/dfee/grid/index.htm>

Department of Trade and Industry (1996a) The Information Society Initiative. <www.isi.gov.uk>

Department of Trade and Industry (1996b) IT for All. <www.itforall.org.uk>

Department of Trade and Industry (1998) The communications and Information Programme. <www.dti.gov.uk/comms.html>

European Commission (1994) Europe and the global information society: recommendations to the European Council .(The Bangemann Report)

European Commission (1996a) Building the European information society for us all: first reflections of the High Level Group of Experts.

European Commission (1996b) Networks for people and their communities: making the most of the information society in the European Union. (First Annual report of the Information Society Forum) Information Society Project Office.

European Commission (1997) Building the European information society for us all: Final report of the High Level Expert Group Information Society Projects Office 1997 <www.ispo.cec.be/hleg/Building.html> Home Office (1997) Data Protection: the government's proposals. <www.homeoffice.-gov.uk/datap1.htm>

House of Lords (1996) Information society: an agenda for action in the UK. Select Committee on Science and Technology

Information Highway Advisory Council (1995) Connectivity, community, content: the challenge of the information highway. Final report of the Information Highway Advisory Council. Ministry of Supply and Services, Canada <http://info.ic.gc.ca/info-highway/if.html>

Joint Funding Council (1993) Libraries review: The Follett Report. Higher and Further Education Funding Council for England <www.-ukoln.ac.uk/follett/report>

Library and Information Commission (1997a) New library: the people's network

Library and Information Commission (1997b) Prospects: a strategy for action.

Library and Information Commission (1997c) 2020 vision.

Lindblom, Charles (1968) The policy-making process. Prentice Hall

Moore, Nick (1993) Information policy and strategic development: a framework for the analysis of policy objectives. Aslib Proceedings 45 (11/12) pp 281-285

Moore, Nick (1998) Rights and responsibilities in an information society. Journal of Information Law and Technology 1998 (1) <http://elj.warwick.ac.uk/jilt/infosoc/98_1moor/> Office for Public Service (1997) Your right to know. The Stationery Office

Office for Public Service (1998) Crown copyright in an information age: a con-

sultation document on access to public sector information (1998) The Stationery Office
Office for Science and Technology (1995) Progress through partnership: report of the steering group of the Technology Foresight Panel. HMSO 1995
OFTEL (1998) Press release on regulation in a time of technological convergence.
<www.coi.gov.uk/coi/depts/GOT/coi9239d.ok>
Parliamentary Office for Science and Technology (1998) Electronic government: information technologies and the citizen. <www.parliament.uk/post/-home.htm>
Statutory Instrument (1997) The copyright and rights in databases regulations, 1997. <www.hmso.gov.uk/si/si1997/06511001.htm>
University for Industry (1998) Programme description <www.ufi.org.uk>

FRIEDRICH BODE

Die Weiterentwicklung der wissenschaftlichen Informationsversorgung auf regionaler Ebene – wichtiger Baustein für die Informationsgesellschaft in Europa

Dieser Bericht gilt der Informationsversorgung im Land Nordrhein-Westfalen. Es liegt nahe, daß ich dazu aus der Perspektive des zuständigen Ministeriums für Wissenschaft und Forschung in Düsseldorf berichte. In den über 50 Hochschulen in NRW leisten die elektronischen Medien einen zunehmend wichtigen Beitrag zur Informationsversorgung. Die Technik bietet enorme Übertragungs- und Speicherkapazitäten, die die digitale Bereitstellung von riesigen Informationsbeständen ermöglichen. Der Zugriff auf immer mehr Volltextdatenbanken und elektronische Zeitschriften im Hochschulnetz oder übers Internet gehört in unseren Hochschulen zum Alltag. Voraussetzung für den Online-Zugang zu diesen Medien ist die gute flächendeckende Vernetzung, die wir mit dem NRWWissWeb, unserem Anschluß an das Breitband-Wissenschaftsnetz, erreicht haben.

Angesichts des zunehmend vielfältigen Angebots an elektronischen Medien drängt sich die Frage auf, wie unsere Bibliotheken die Informationsflut dieser neuen Medien bewältigen, wie sie digitale Informationen beschaffen, bereitstellen und online verbreiten, und wie sie das riesige weltweite Angebot ordnen und strukturieren. Und schließlich muß gefragt werden: Wie ist der zeit- und ortsunabhängige Zugriff für die Nutzer, ob Studierende oder Wissenschaftler, auf diese neue Medienwelt gestaltet?

Um Antworten auf die genannten Fragen zu finden, hat Frau Ministerin Brunn – übrigens bereits vor Beginn der aktuellen Diskussion um die Verbesserung der Studienbedingungen – die Hochschulbibliotheken gebeten, einen Statusbericht über ihren Umgang mit den elektronischen Medien vorzulegen. Der daraufhin erarbeitete Bericht liegt nunmehr – übrigens auch online – vor und heißt:

„Die Digitale Bibliothek NRW" (abrufbar unter http://www.wissenschaft.nrw.de).

Dieser Werkstattbericht belegt, daß unsere Bibliotheken auf die Verbreitung der elektronischen Medien nicht bloß reagieren, sondern auf vielen Gebieten bereits in hervorragender Weise die Initiative übernommen haben. Aus den zahlreichen Aktivitäten und Projekten an vielen Standorten sind landesweit einheitliche und regelmäßige Dienstleistungen hervorgegangen, die bereits deutliche Konturen der von uns angestrebten „verteilten digitalen Bibliothek" erkennen lassen.

Diese virtuelle Bibliothek entsteht real in lokalen Kompentenzzentren an vielen Hochschulen, sie basiert auf vielfältigen Kooperationsformen, und sie erzeugt – wie wir im Hochschulalltag oder sogar online von Zuhause aus erleben können – enorme Synergieeffekte.

Ich meine, daß diese „verteilte digitale Bibliothek" als Modell für die Bibliotheken der Zukunft im Europa der Regionen angesehen werden kann.

Diese landesweite „digitale Bibliothek" ist ein Eckpfeiler unserer gemeinsamen Multimedia-Initiative, für die seit 1996 erhebliche Mittel der Hochschulen und aus dem Hochschulsonderprogramm eingesetzt wurden. Wir konnten bei den Verhandlungen zum Hochschulsonderprogramm III des Bundes und der Länder bis zum Jahr 2000 Sondermittel in Höhe von knapp 50 Mio. DM reservieren, vielleicht werden es noch mehr. Mit Hilfe dieses Multimedia-Aktionsprogramms können wir die Bibliotheken als Lernort und Informationsagentur ihrer Hochschule auf die Zukunft ausrichten.

In den kommenden Monaten und Jahren werden wir die Entwicklung, Bereitstellung und Verbreitung elektronischer Medien in den Hochschulbibliotheken forcieren und die äußerst fruchtbare landesweite Zusammenarbeit auf diesem Gebiet fördern. Ich erwarte vom schnellen und einfachen Online-Zugriff auf Texte, Bilder, Daten und andere Informationen vor allem die Optimierung von Lern- und Lehrprozessen und eine Steigerung der Leistungsfähigkeit von Wissenschaft und Forschung.

Durch Absprachen und Arbeitsteilung zwischen den Hochschulen und ihren Infrastruktureinrichtungen sollte dieses Dienstleistungsangebot im Sinne einer „verteilten kooperativen Zuständigkeit" von Bibliotheken, Rechenzentren und Medienzentren gemeinsam realisiert werden. Dazu gehört auch, daß wir das breite Angebot von Multimedia-Produkten landesweit und unter einer einheitlichen Oberfläche zugänglich machen.

Die online-Nutzung kann natürlich nur eine weitere Facette, eine zusätzliche Erscheinungsform einer Bibliothek sein, kann über Engpässe in der Beschaffung hinweghelfen, wenn ein Buch auch online abgerufen werden kann. Sie kann Informationen in greifbare Nähe rücken, die man noch gestern nur durch monatelange Auslandsaufenthalte bekommen hätte. Die Aufgaben der realen Bibliothek werden sich sicherlich verändern, es werden andere Aufgaben auf sie zukommen, neue Schwerpunkte bilden sich schon heute heraus. Hierzu wird auch gehören, die Bibliothek nicht nur als Ort des Lernens, sondern auch als Ort der Begegnung, als Ort der Kommunikation zu begreifen.

Mit der Diskussion um die virtuelle Bibliothek, die die digitalen Dokumente vorhält, beginnt ein neuer Abschnitt in der Hochschulgeschichte, und dessen sollten wir uns bewußt sein, wenn über die Möglichkeiten für elektronische Informationsversorgung der Wissenschaft diskutiert wird.

Ich habe vom Werkstattbericht „Die Digitale Bibliothek NRW" berichtet. Er war gerade erschienen, da haben Bund und Länder beschlossen, noch für dieses Jahr jeweils weitere 40 Mio. DM für die Bibliotheken bereitzustellen, also insgesamt 80 Mio DM. Ziel ist nicht die einmalige Verbesserung von Lehrbuchsammlungen – jedenfalls nicht in NRW. Darüber sind wir längst hinaus. Wir wissen, daß es heute nicht mehr ausreichend, geschweige denn zufriedenstellend ist, Bücher en masse in die Bibliotheken zu stellen. Die Hochschulen sollen mit Hilfe dieses Programms, das der Bund erst auf Drängen der studentischen Proteste aufgelegt hat, in den nächsten Jahren in die Lage versetzt werden, ihre Rolle, die wir heute für die Bibliotheken diskutieren, ernsthaft und erfolgreich auszufüllen. Ich will dabei allerdings nicht von den Bibliotheken als „Träger" der Informationsgesellschaft sprechen – die Gesellschaft darf nicht getragen werden, sie muß sich selbst bewegen, muß sich verändern und sich den Neuen Techniken und Diensten öffnen. Gerade an dieser Öffnung sind die Bibliotheken maßgeblich beteiligt. Sie vermitteln das Wissen, den Umgang mit dem Wissen, und sie ermöglichen den Zugang zum Wissen, das sie auch wahren.

Das Programm soll folgende Bereiche unterstützen:

- Beschaffung neuer Literatur.
- verstärkte Nutzung von elektronischen Medien.
- Verbesserung der Informationsdienstleistungen der Hochschulbibliotheken.
- Maßnahmen zur Verbesserung der Nutzung vorhandener Bestände im Interesse der Studierenden.

Soweit die Bund-Länder-Vereinbarung, die am 12.2.1998 in der BLK abgestimmt wird. Diese Ziele sind sehr allgemein gehalten, um den Ländern eine bedarfsorientierte Verbesserung der Medien-Versorgung in den Hochschulen zu ermöglichen.

Was wollen wir in NRW daraus machen?

Wir werden in NRW einen Hochschulentwicklungsplan für „Information, Kommunikation und Multimedia" erarbeiten. Auf dieser Grundlage werden wir mit diesen Mitteln – von den 80 Mio. DM erhält NRW 17,6 Mio. DM – folgende Dienstleistungen und Medienangebote unterstützen:

Ausbau der digitalen Bibliothek, insbesondere mit dem *Schwerpunkt einer Studienbibliothek* (für Studierende im Grundstudium)
Das heißt konkret: Ausbau des Informations-Managements für Beschaffung,

Produktion, Erschließung, Bereitstellung und Vermittlung sowie Archivierung von Informationen, Dokumenten, Fakten und Quellen.

Hierzu gehören vor allem:

- Zugriff auf Online-Literatur durch Kauf, Erwerb von Lizenzen oder Speicherung vor Ort bzw. den einmaligen Bezug im Bedarfsfall.
- Bedarfsgerechte Digitalisierung von Druckwerken vor Ort und ggf. in Verbünden und ihre Bereitstellung über das Netz.
- Nachweis von Dokumenten durch Metadaten.
- Dauerhafte Archivierung und Recherchemöglichkeiten im Datenbestand
- Förderung des „elektronischen Publizierens“ und neuer Publikationsformen in den Hochschulen
- Beratung zur Nutzung der Dienste, Informationen und Dokumente
- Entwicklung eines Kostenmanagements – ich denke da z.B. an interne Verrechnungssysteme oder an neue Mehrwertdienste.

Die Bibliotheken leisten hierzu einen zentralen Beitrag, insbesondere im Bereich der Informationsversorgung und Beschaffung. Andere Fragen des Einsatzes neuer Medien, Techniken und Dienste in der Hochschule werden von den Rechenzentren und Medienzentren kompetent beantwortet. Und das beste: Diese drei zentralen Einrichtungen der Hochschulen stimmen sich untereinander ab und entwickeln Perspektiven, wie sie sich ihren Beitrag hierzu vorstellen. In wenigen Tagen wird hierzu ein bundesweit erarbeitetes Thesenpapier veröffentlicht, das Sie auch online abrufen können. Dieses Papier zeigt: Es werden neue Anforderungen an das Personal, an den Zuschnitt der Aufgabenbereiche und an die Dynamik in den Hochschulen gestellt. Es zeigt auch: Der Weg in die Informationsgesellschaft ist kein lokaler oder regionaler; die Hochschulen stehen vielmehr in einem internationalen Wettbewerb, für den wir sie gemeinsam heute wappnen müssen. Wissenschaftliche Informationsversorgung regional – für Nordrhein-Westfalen heißt das nicht zuletzt deshalb auch: wissenschaftliche Informationsversorgung in Europa.

Das Ministerium für Wissenschaft und Forschung will insbesondere durch seine Förderung von Beziehungen zu ausländischen Hochschulen einen Schwerpunkt in seiner Politik setzen. Hierfür haben wir bereits für dieses Jahr die Mittel fast verdreifacht, für das kommende Jahr haben wir sie im Haushalt festgeschrieben und noch einmal verdreifacht. Dabei beschränken wir uns nicht auf den Blick über die nahen Grenzen in den Westen. Beispiele hierfür sind bekannt: wie die Zentralbibliothek für Landbauwissenschaften in Bonn, die u.a. mit Wageningen, Budapest kooperiert; oder die Bibliothek der Universität Duisburg, die einen Schwerpunkt mit England pflegt. Aber wir legen auch besonderen Wert auf den Blick nach Osten, d.h. die Zusammenarbeit der Universität Köln mit Bukarest, mit Cluj, Sofia, Prag und weiteren Hochschulen in der Mitte und im Osten Europas. Wir legen Wert auf die Aktivitäten der Universität Bochum, die ein JASON-Projekt mit Zagreb plant. Gleiches gilt für die Kooperationen der Bibliothek der UGH Wuppertal mit Kosice, Budapest, Wien, ihre Büchergaben nach Minsk und Nishni Nowgorod – und natürlich die Kooperationen der Universität Bielefeld mit den Universitäts- und der Nationalbibliothek in Bratislava und Kosice. Jüngste Herausforderung ist eine Kooperation mit den Hochschulen in den palästinensischen Gebieten und im Gazastreifen. Ich kann für fast jede Hochschule ein solches Kooperationsprojekt nennen, und darüber freue ich mich.

Auch die Europäische Kommission, der Europäische Rat befassen sich mit dieser Frage, und ich denke, wenn wir hier Staatsgrenzen einmal überschritten haben, sollten wir auch die weitere Diskussion international, eben bezogen auf ganz Europa führen. Die Europäische Kommission hat gerade im Oktober eine Liste von 24 Projekten beschlossen, die im Bereich Telematik und Bibliotheken mit Mitteln in Höhe von 10 Mio. ECU gefördert werden sollen. Sie stellte übrigens bei der Auswertung der bisherigen Projekte im Sektor Telematik für die Bibliotheken Europas fest, daß 42% aller Projekte von Hochschulbibliotheken konzipiert waren – auch das macht stolz.

Würden Sie noch vor vielleicht 10 Jahren jemandem geglaubt haben, der Ihnen all dies vorhergesagt hätte?

Uns allen ist die unglaubliche Dynamik und Bedeutung des Themas bewußt. Manchmal werden Zweifel laut, die eine Technikbegeisterung befürchten, die Neue Techniken und Dienste um ihrer selbst willen fördert. Ich halte das eine wie das andere Extrem für falsch. Schon heute sehen wir, welche immensen Vorteile der Einsatz neuer Informationswege bringt. Bei der Antwort auf die Frage, wie sie optimal zu nutzen sind, sollten wir uns nicht allzu getrieben fühlen: Es hat fast 200 Jahre gedauert, bis erkannt wurde, wofür der Buchdruck außer zur Vervielfältigung der Bibel genutzt werden konnte: weltliche Bücher, dann Zeitungen und später Flugblätter kamen so viel später, daß wir uns bei der Entwicklung unserer Visionen für die Nutzung der neuen Technologien nicht allzu getrieben fühlen sollten*. Ich denke wir sind auf einem guten Weg. Nichtsdestotrotz möchte ich die Gelegenheit nutzen, und abschließend unseren Standort auf diesem Weg bestimmen – und bitte um Verständnis, wenn dieser Standort in NRW liegt:

* Dr. Antonius Jammers, Generaldirektor der Staatsbibliothek Berlin und mein Vorgänger im Amt, hat dazu angemerkt: Um 1500 war unter der gedruckten Literatur 1% Bibeln, aber 30 % religiöse Schriften.

1. Die nordrhein-westfälischen Bibliotheken engagieren sich aktiv für den Einsatz neuer Informations- und Kommunikationstechnologien in der Wissenschaft – diese Veranstaltung ist ein greifbarer Beweis.
2. In NRW wurde europaweit das erste große europäische Konsortium mit einer beeindruckend großen Zahl elektronischer Zeitschriften gegründet. Ich möchte bei dieser Gelegenheit auch dem Vertragspartner Elsevier danken, der hieran nicht nur als weltweit größter Verlag für wissenschaftliche Zeitschriften beteiligt ist, sondern auch sein europäisches Engagement plastisch dokumentiert.
3. NRW bleibt hier nicht stehen; Verhandlungen mit anderen großen Anbietern elektronischer wissenschaftlicher Zeitschriften sind geplant bzw. schon angelaufen. So werden alle Zeitschriften des größten deutschen Anbieters in einem Test z.Zt. von einigen nordrhein-westfälischen Bibliotheken der jeweiligen Campus-Klientel kostenlos angeboten.
4. Es ist ganz wesentlich, daß die elektronischen Zeitschriften auch zum Zweck der Fernleihe zur Verfügung stehen, da damit Arbeitsgänge beschleunigt werden können. Dies muß zumindest für die Titel möglich sein, die sowohl gedruckt als auch elektronisch vorgehalten werden. Ohne Einbezug der Elektronischen Volltexte in den Fernleihverkehr werde ich keine Projektmittel bereitstellen.
5. Ebenso wichtig ist es, daß alle Nutzungsdaten den Bibliotheken zur Auswertung zur Verfügung stehen. Das muß unabhängig davon sein, ob die Texte lokal oder auf einem Verlags-Server zur Verfügung gestellt werden.
6. Heute stellen manche Verlage ihre Texte den Bibliotheken lokal bereit, während andere ihre Texte selbst auf eigenen Servern vorhalten. Hieran sollte erprobt werden, welches Verfahren unter Nutzer- aber auch unter Kostenaspekten wie zu beurteilen ist. Dies muß Projektinhalt sein.
7. In der heutigen Etatsituation muß es unser Ziel sein, aus der Preisentwicklung für Zeitschrifteninhalte herauszubrechen. Elektronische Zeitschriften könnten ein Weg dahin sein, wenn es andere Finanzierungsmodelle als das des jährlichen Abonnements gäbe. Interessant unter Kosten-Nutzen-Aspekten wäre der Kauf von Zugriffskontingenten oder die Variante Pay-per-View für selten benutzte Zeitschriften. Für die häufig genutzten Zeitschriften bleibt die Variante Abonnement interessant.
8. Die Verlagskooperationen sind für mich ein Test. Geht dieser Test nicht zufriedenstellen aus, beabsichtige ich, das visionäre Projekt „Universitätsverlag NRW“ anzupacken.

Ich rechne also durchaus mit unruhigen Zeiten. Sie sehen: Wir haben viel geschafft, und vieles, was wir heute noch gar nicht bestimmen können, bleibt zu tun – in NRW und in Europa. Wir sind auf dem richtigen Weg.

ELEKTRONISCHE DOKUMENTE IM SPANNUNGSFELD ZWISCHEN BIBLIOTHEKEN UND VERLAGEN

KLAUS-DIETER LEHMANN

Das elektronische Pflichtexemplar – die Rolle der Nationalbibliothek

Die Faszination der schnellen und globalen Verfügbarkeit digitaler Publikationen, hier insbesondere von Netzpublikationen, läßt häufig vergessen, daß die Wissenschaft und Forschung nicht nur davon lebt, daß ihre neuesten Ergebnisse eine rasche Verbreitung erfahren, sondern mindestens genauso davon, daß ihre Ergebnisse auch langfristig zugänglich bleiben. Langzeitverfügbarkeit ist in unserer schnellebigen digitalen Zeit mit ihrer ausgeprägten Wegwerfmentalität in der öffentlichen Diskussion nicht sehr präsent. Langzeitsicherung erscheint teuer und unwirtschaftlich, mit technischen und rechtlichen Problemen behaftet und reduziert sich in den Augen der dominierenden Naturwissenschaft als ein Nischenproblem der Wissenschaft, speziell der Geisteswissenschaft.

Dabei hat schon Leopold von Ranke, der Begründer der modernen Geschichtswissenschaft, festgestellt, daß die Vermehrung der Erkenntnis nicht nur darin besteht, noch unbekannte Informationen über die Tatsachen zu ergründen und mitzuteilen, sondern auch – und vielleicht noch häufiger – eine neue Auffassung des schon Bekannten aufzustellen.

So wie unser Jahr aus vier Jahreszeiten besteht, so wird unser Wissen, unsere Erkenntnis aus vier Quellen gespeist:

1. Die Weiterentwicklung von Wissen durch die Forschung
2. Die Vermittlung von Wissen durch die Lehre
3. Die Verbreitung von Wissen durch das Publizieren
4. Die Erhaltung von Wissen in den Sammlungen der Archive, Bibliotheken und Museen

Dieses Bild soll verdeutlichen, wie gleichrangig die intellektuelle und kulturelle Überlieferung Wissen und Erkenntnis trägt.

Welche Rolle ein Land kulturell und wissenschaftlich spielt, wird nicht zuletzt auch davon abhängen, wie kompetent es intellektuell und institutionell mit seiner kulturellen Überlieferung umgeht, wie kreativ und offensiv es diese vermittelt, welche Chancen es zur Zusammenarbeit nutzt.

Für die Langzeitsicherung im traditionellen Publikationswesen gibt es nahezu in allen Kulturstaaten gesetzliche Regelungen zur Pflichtablieferung an eine nationale Depotbibliothek, hinzu kommen regionale Bestimmungen. Letztlich übernehmen auch die wissenschaftlichen Bibliotheken mit historischer Dimension Verantwortung zur langfristigen Verfügbarkeit ihrer Sammlungen. Mit dem Aufkommen der digitalen Publikationen hat sich viel geändert – technisch, organisatorisch und auch strukturell. Dazu kommt, daß diese dynamische Veränderung anhält und damit die Konsequenzen noch nicht konkret überblickt werden können.

Die Probleme beziehen sich insbesondere auf den physischen Verfall digitaler Informationen, Änderungen von Codierung und Formaten, schneller Wechsel der Software- und Betriebssysteme und der Hardware. Gefährdung der Authenzität durch Manipulierbarkeit, unsichere Referenzierbarkeit. Aber auch die Informationsinfrastruktur der Bibliotheken selbst bleibt von ständiger Anpassung nicht verschont.

Der Wechsel zu einem neuen System garantiert nicht immer die Kompatibilität zu den bis dahin eingesetzten Archivierungs- und Bereitstellungssystemen.

Der physische Verfall digitaler Informationen kann durch das Umkopieren auf einen Träger gleichen Typs verhindert werden oder durch das Konvertieren auf einen anderen stabileren Träger. Die Rückübertragung auf Papier mag zwar in diesem Zusammenhang auf den ersten Blick attraktiv erscheinen, sie ist aber nicht zu empfehlen. Wichtige Multimediaeigenschaften können dabei verloren gehen.

Digitale Publikationen sind im Vergleich zu den Druckmedien weder homogen noch statisch. Sie sind jeweils eingebunden in eine spezifische systemabhängige Umgebung. Änderungen der Systemumgebung ändern auch die Präsentation. Präsentationsform und Inhalt sind nicht immer zu trennen, sondern bilden häufig erst das gemeinsame Informationsprodukt. Es ist mehr als die Rohdaten. Netzangebote mit Hyperlinks entziehen sich einer eindeutigen Zuordnung. Hier müssen die Grenzen der Publikation jeweils neu definiert werden. Das sind nur einige Problemaspekte.

Die Tatsache, daß die Langzeitarchivierung digitaler Publikationen erheblich größere Schwierigkeiten verursacht als herkömmliche Publikationen, darf aber kaum zum Maßstab einer Entscheidung „ob oder ob nicht" gemacht werden, sondern sollte Ansatz für die Entwicklung geeigneter Verfahren sein. Digitale Publikationen müssen in die Regelungen der Langzeitarchivierung einbezogen werden. Dabei muß von Anfang an Zugriff und Verfügbarkeit berücksichtigt werden.

Die Deutsche Bibliothek ist per Gesetz verpflichtet, die in Deutschland erscheinenden Veröffentlichungen (Bild, Ton und Text) und die deutschsprachigen Veröffentlichungen des Auslandes vollständig zu sammeln, dauerhaft aufzubewahren, nach nationalbibliographischen Grundsätzen zu verzeichnen und öffentlich der Benutzung zur Verfügung zu stellen. Es ist nur konsequent, den Auftrag auf die Langzeitarchivierung digitaler Publikationen zu erweitern.

Die jetzige gesetzliche Regelung, die in den §§ 3 und 18 eine Pflichtablieferung für Veröffentlichungen festlegt, ermöglicht die Einbeziehung von digitalen Publikationen auf physischen Trägern (CD-ROM, Disketten, Magnetbänder usw.) nicht jedoch die Pflichtablieferung von Netzpublikationen. Hierfür ist eine Novellierung des geltenden Gesetzes erforderlich. Derzeit gehen pro Jahr ca. 6000 digitale Publikationen auf physischen Datenträgern ein. Sie werden in der Nationalbibliographie angezeigt.

Die Deutsche Bibliothek hat die Vorbereitungen dazu getroffen und in verschiedenen Hearings mit Bibliothekaren, Verlegern und Regierungsvertretern sowie den Gremien der Deutschen Bibliothek ihre Vorschläge diskutiert. Als Ergebnis dieser Hearings ist festzuhalten, daß übereinstimmend die Auffassung bestand, daß Die Deutsche Bibliothek digitale Publikationen in ihren Sammelauftrag einbeziehen muß, unabhängig davon, ob sie auf einen Datenträger oder als Netzpublikationen vorliegen.

Netzpublikationen (Nichtkörperliche Medienwerke) im Sinne des Sammelauftrags sind alle Darstellungen in Schrift, Bild und Ton, die zur Verbreitung über Datennetze bestimmt sind. Folgende Aspekte wurden definiert:

Die Netzpublikationen sind grundsätzlich über Datennetze abzuliefern. Auf Anforderung der Bibliothek sind sie auf einem elektronischen Datenträger abzuliefern. Netzpublikationen in verschiedenen Formaten (Datenstruktur) sind in dem von der Bibliothek gewünschten Format abzuliefern.

Werden inhaltlich identische Medienwerke gleichzeitig in physischer Form und als Netzpublikation verbreitet, sind beide Formen abzuliefern. Ist die physische Form ein elektronischer Datenträger, ist nur dieser abzuliefern.

Werden inhaltlich identische Netzpublikationen von mehreren Anbietern gleichzeitig verbreitet, sind sie nur einmal abzuliefern.

Nicht ablieferungspflichtig sind insbesondere:

- öffentliche Kommunikation und Nachrichten (e-mail, listserver)
- Mitteilungen, Meinungsforen
- verteilte Netzpublikationen (Hyperlinks)

- Werbung; Publikationen, die nur gewerblichen, geschäftlichen und innerbetrieblichen Zwecken dienen

Der Bibliothek ist gestattet, eine Kopie der digitalen Publikationen für Zwecke der Langzeitarchivierung herzustellen. Dabei ist die Authenzität des Inhalts zu wahren.

Während über diese grundsätzlichen Definitionen und Verfahren kaum unterschiedliche Meinungen bestanden, zeigte sich, daß der signifikant andere Charakter von Netzpublikationen, der rasche technologische Wandel und Überlegungen zu sinnvollen Absprachen bei der Aufgabenverteilung zwischen den Partnern der Informationskette es ratsam erscheinen ließen, zunächst mit einer Vereinbarung anstatt mit einem Gesetz für die Ablieferung von Netzpublikationen zu beginnen. Vor einer gesetzlichen Regelung sollten gesicherte Erkenntnisse über Inhalt und Umfang des neuen Pflichtbereichs vorliegen.

Würde man eine möglichst allgemein formulierte Gesetzesnovellierung vorsehen, bestünde weder auf der Seite der Verleger noch auf der Seite der Bibliothek eine ausreichende Sicherheit über die Konsequenzen. Würde man eine möglichst eng formulierte Gesetzesnovellierung vorsehen, bestünde die Gefahr, ständig Anpassungen an den technologischen Wandel vornehmen zu müssen. So einigte man sich einvernehmlich auf ein Verfahren, das die freiwillige Ablieferung von Belegexemplaren durch Verleger und Produzenten vorsieht, Online-Hochschulschriften eingeschlossen. Der Probelauf unter Echtbedingungen soll, beginnend mit 1998 in einem Zeitraum von 3-5 Jahren gesicherte Erkenntnisse für eine dauerhafte gesetzliche Regelung bringen. Diese Empfehlung wurde förmlich vom Verlegerausschuß des Börsenvereins des Deutschen Buchhandels im Juni 1997 bestätigt und lautet:

„Da im Bereich der elektronischen Publikationen bisher nur physisch verbreitete Datenträger wie CD-ROM oder Disketten abgabepflichtig sind, empfiehlt der Verlegerausschuß den Verlagen bis zu einer gesetzlichen Regelung, ihre Netz-(Online-) Publikationen der Deutschen Bibliothek freiwillig abzugeben bzw. zugänglich zu machen. Der Verlegerausschuß befürwortet die Einbeziehung auch dieser Publikationen in den Aufgabenbereich Der Deutschen Bibliothek. Er umfaßt die Archivierung und Verfahren zur Langzeitsicherung, die Erschließung und die kostenfreie Nutzung (lesender Zugriff) im Lesesaal.

Die darüber hinausgehende Nutzung – elektronische Übernahme und Weiternutzung der Daten sowie Nutzung durch externe Nutzer erfolgt gemäß entsprechender Vereinbarungen mit Verlagen.

Die dabei gewonnenen Erfahrungen werden von Der Deutschen Bibliothek mit dem Ziel ausgewertet, einen Rahmenvertrag vorzulegen, in dem weitergehende Nutzungsmöglichkeiten von Netzpublikationen geregelt werden.“

Damit läßt sich ein Phasenkonzept sowohl im Hinblick auf die Menge und Art der Publikationen, die Produktgruppen, die Migrationsverfahren, die Regelung der Zugriffs- und Benutzungsrechte und die Kosten definieren.

Aber es bieten sich auch Chancen, aus der Kooperation von Verlagen und Bibliothek Schnittstellen für den Datenbezug gemeinsam festzulegen und den Bezug von digitalen Publikationen für die Langzeitarchivierung aus verschiedenen Phasen des Produktionsprozesses zu prüfen, z. B. aus einem Autorensystem oder einem Nutzungssystem, über Formate und Dokumenttypen und den sich daraus ergebenden Konsequenzen gemeinsam nachzudenken usw.

Das vom BMBF initiierte Programm Global Info, das Verlage, Wissenschaftseinrichtungen, Fachgesellschaften und Bibliotheken zusammenführt, ist für diese Fragestellung ein interessantes Forum. Die Deutsche Bibliothek wird deshalb im Schwerpunkt I / Arbeitsgruppe Dokumenttypen, Formate, Archivierung aktiv mitarbeiten und ihre Lösungsansätze gemeinsam mit den anderen in der Arbeitsgruppe beteiligten Bibliotheken und Verlagen entwickeln.

Derzeit sind wir dabei, mit den Verlagen die Kooperation abzustimmen, Dokumenttypen und Formate für ein erstes Archivierungskonzept zusammenzustellen und Zugangsverfahren zu digitalen Publikationen auf Archivservern (Metadaten) zu entwickeln.

Die Langzeitsicherung digitaler Publikationen kann nur erfolgreich sein, wenn mit einer sicheren Technologie ein möglichst einheitliches Archivierungskonzept gefunden wird, das sich durch Reformatierung und Konversion aus der jeweiligen Distributions- und Nutzungsform ergibt.

Beim Neubau für Die Deutsche Bibliothek in Frankfurt am Main konzentrierte sich die Aufmerksamkeit deshalb auch besonders auf eine leistungsfähige Informationsinfrastruktur. Es wurde praktisch für alle Anwendungsgebiete eine neue technische Plattform definiert:

- neues Kommunikationsnetz mit ATM-Technologie
- neue Endgeräteausstattung (multimediafähig)
- Ablösung der Großrechneranlage
- neues Bibliographiesystem
- Multimedia-Bereitstellungssystem

ATM kommt nicht nur im Server- und Backbonebereich zum Einsatz, sondern wird bis zu den Endgeräten geführt. Damit können im Haus circa 900 passive Anschlüsse, 50 Multimedia-PCs und circa 600 Endgeräte realisiert werden. Die Standorte Deutsche Bücherei Leipzig und Deutsches Musikarchiv Berlin werden über ein logisches ATM-Hochgeschwindigkeitsnetz einbezogen.

Zugänge über offene Kommunikationsschnittstellen (Z 39.50) erleichtern das Arbeiten und die globale Suche.

Für die Erfassung, Verwaltung, Recherche, Präsentation und Langzeitsicherung von digitalen Publikationen ist das Multimedia-Bereitstellungssystem (MMB) von besonderer Bedeutung. Es wurde gemeinsam mit CSC Ploenzke entwickelt und bietet folgende Funktionen:

- den Zugang zum Online-Katalog, zu digitalen Publikationen und zum Internet
- die Kopplung von Online-Katalog und digitalen Publikationen
- das Arbeiten in einer WWW-Umgebung (Internet und Intranet)
- die Nutzung vom System vorinstallierter Publikationen
- den Ausdruck oder das Herunterladen von Arbeitsergebnissen
- die Konvertierung digitaler Publikationen in eine Archivversion zur Langzeitsicherung

Die Oberfläche ist intranet-typisch als Web-Browser ausgeführt. Die Benutzer haben auf nahezu selbsterklärende Weise Zugriff auf alle Funktionen unter einer standardisierten Benutzeroberfläche, die Arbeitsabläufe laufen vollautomatisch im Hintergrund ab – ohne Zutun und Kenntnis des Benutzers. Diese ganze umfängliche Installation verfügt auch über Benutzerverwaltungs- und Abrechnungsverfahren, um urheberrechtlichen und lizenz-rechtlichen Vorschriften gerecht zu werden.

Die digitalen Publikationen, die künftig von Der Deutschen Bibliothek archiviert und verfügbar gehalten werden müssen, sind:

- digitale Publikationen auf physischen Datenträgern
- online verfügbare Publikationen (Netzpublikationen)
- konvertierte digitale Publikationen
- transformierte analoge Objekte

Die Deutsche Bibliothek bietet ihren Nutzern zwei Formen der Nutzung des MMB:

1. Anonyme Benutzer: Sie erhalten im Rahmen der Bibliotheksbenutzung Zugriff auf das MMB einschl. Exportmöglichkeiten.
2. Eingetragene Benutzer: Sie erhalten für einen bestimmten Zeitraum eine Arbeitsumgebung, die auch die Nutzung des Internets und Bestellfunktionen für digitale Publikationen enthält sowie die Speicherung von Auszügen aus Publikationen und – in einer späteren Ausbaustufe – die Anlage und Bearbeitung eigener Dokumente erlaubt.

Die besondere Problematik des MMB liegt darin, daß es derzeit für Multimedia-Publikationen keinerlei technische Standards oder Konventionen gibt. Während die von uns selbst digitalisierten Archivalien einheitlich aufbereitet werden können, bringen vor allem Veröffentlichungen auf CD-ROM ihre eigene Präsentationssoftware mit und stellen sehr unterschiedliche Anforderungen an Betriebssystem, Treiberausstattung und Hardware der Arbeitsplatzrechner.

Zur Lösung dieser Problematik wurde ein Verfahren entwickelt, das die Installation und Deinstallation automatisch steuert. Dazu wird bei der Ersterfassung einer digitalen Publikation ein Installationsskript erstellt. Damit kann dann später bei Aufruf des Dokuments der Arbeitsplatzrechner des Benutzers exakt mit den erforderlichen Modulen und Dateien ausgestattet werden.

Für die Bereitstellung der digitalen Publikationen innerhalb des MMB wird ein gemischtes technisches Verfahren zur Speicherung angewandt.

1. Die am häufigsten angeforderten Publikationen werden als Images in ein Raid-System importiert (derzeit 80 GB). Das MMB-System übernimmt dabei die Aufgabe, die Daten vom ursprünglichen Datenträger in das Speichersystem zu überführen.
2. Weitere oft gebrauchte CD-ROMs können in Jukeboxen im ständigen Zugriff gehalten werden (bis zu 1000 CDs).
3. Individuell gewünschte Publikationen werden auf Anforderung per Hand aus dem Magazin entnommen und in das jeweils geeignete Medienserver-Subsystem importiert und über das Neutz zur Verfügung gestellt.
4. Publikationen, die sich – z. B. auf Grund von Kopierschutzmechanismen oder mangelnder Netzfähigkeit – der Installation und Wiedergabe innerhalb des Systems entziehen, werden den Nutzern an Einzelarbeitsplätzen zur Verfügung gestellt.

Es ist selbstverständlich, daß urheberrechtliche Bestimmungen und Lizenzverwertungsrechte beachtet werden. Ebenso wird darauf geachtet, daß die digitalen Publikationen nicht „physisch" in die Hände des Nutzers gelangen, sondern über das System zur Verfügung gestellt werden. Dadurch sollen Manipulation, Beschädigung oder sonstige mißbräuchliche Benutzung verhindert werden.

Für die technische Langzeitsicherung der digitalen Objekte (DO) – das sind Medien und Nutzdaten des MMB-Systems wird ein Verfahren eingesetzt, das das Kopieren von kompletten DO-Inhalten vom Plattenspeicher auf CDRs vorsieht. Die Archivierung erfolgt durch Markierung der DOs, die archiviert werden sollen und einem zeitversetzten Archivierungslauf, bei dem alle zur Archivierung markierten DOs auf CDRs gebrannt werden. Archivierte DOs werden ausgelagert, d. h. der DO-Inhalt wird vom Plattenspeicher gelöscht, das Verzeichnis bleibt erhalten. Ausgelagerte DOs können wieder hergestellt werden. Darunter versteht man die Möglichkeit, den DO-

Inhalt von der zuletzt erstellten Archiv-CDR auf dem Plattenspeicher wiederherzustellen.

Die Aktivitäten des Archivierungsprozesses werden in einer Logdatei protokolliert. Sie enthält die Attribute Datum/Zeit, DO-ID, Archiv-ID und Ereignis.

Diese Maßnahmen sind für technische Überlegungen zur Sicherung durchaus praktikabel, für eine Langzeitsicherung sind jedoch nicht nur technische Aspekte zu berücksichtigen; erforderlich ist ein ganzes Maßnahmebündel im Sinn eines strategischen Vorgehens.

Aus diesem Grund beteiligt sich Die Deutsche Bibliothek an einem europäischen Projekt zur Langzeitarchivierung digitaler Publikationen im Rahmen des Telematics-Programm der Europäischen Union. Sie ist der Auffassung, daß Verfahren und Strukturen für einen so komplexen Anwendungsbereich von Anfang an möglichst international (europäisch) angelegt sein müssen, um keine isolierten Strukturen zu schaffen. Sie ist ferner der Auffassung, daß von Anfang an Verlage und Softwarehäuser einbezogen werden sollten. Definiert worden ist deshalb das NEDLIB-Projekt (Networked European Deposit Library)!

Durch NEDLIB sollen Mechanismen entwickelt werden, die die Aufgaben von Nationalbibliotheken und -archiven auf dem Gebiet der Langzeitsicherung durch eine geeignete Infrastruktur unterstützen.

Die Infrastruktur umfaßt generische Modelle und Werkzeuge, Standards und nachnutzbare Verfahren. Entstehen soll so die Basis für eine verteilte und vernetzte europäische Archivbibliothek. Die entwickelte System-Architektur, unabhängig von deren Herkunft, Trägermedium und Datenformat, soll digitale Publikationen speicher- und zugriffsfähig für Endnutzer und für Institutionen machen. Gleichzeitig sollen kommerzielle und Copyright-Interessen der Produzenten und Verleger durch Zugriffskontroll-Verfahren berücksichtigt werden.

Die Kooperation mit Verlegern ist vorgesehen, ebenso eine laufende Rückkopplung der Ergebnisse. Wo immer möglich sollen existierende Standards und Technologien verwendet werden.

Der Nutzen von NEDLIB liegt vor allem darin, daß praktisch nutzbare Instrumente (toolbox) zum Management eines Archivsystems für digitale Publikationen entwickelt werden, die mit der Infrastruktur der beteiligten Partner kompatibel sein sollen, in unserem Fall zum MMB-System. Die Ergebnisse sind anderen Bibliotheken, die ebenfalls Aufgaben zur Langzeitarchivierung wahrnehmen, zugänglich. Über die Kontakte zwischen Verlegern und Produzenten digitaler Publikationen und den NEDLIB-Projektpartnern wird ein intensiver Dialog über Herstellungs-, Nutzungs- und Archivierungsbedingungen zustandekommen.

Zusammenfassend sind die Projektziele so zu definieren:

- Sicherung und langfristige Verfügbarkeit digitaler Publikationen
- Infrastrukturmaßnahmen für den Aufbau einer vernetzten europäischen Depotbibliothek
- Definition von Modellen, Standards, Werkzeugen und Verfahren
- Kooperation mit Verlagen zur Abstimmung von Schnittstellen zwischen Ablieferern und Depotbibliotheken
- Bereitstellung der Projektergebnisse in Form von Prototypen

Beteiligt sind die Nationalbibliotheken in den Niederlanden, in Frankreich, Norwegen, Finnland, Portugal, Deutschland und die Verlage Elsevier, Kluwer und Springer sowie die Softwarehäuser Level-7 Ltd., Großbritannien; INESC, Portugal, CSC Ploenzke, Deutschland. Assoziiert sind die Schweiz (Schweizerische Landesbibliothek Bern) und Italien (Nationalbibliothek Florenz). Das Projekt hat im Januar 1998 begonnen und endet im Dezember 2000.

Die Deutsche Bibliothek ist an vier Arbeitspaketen beteiligt:

- Spezifikation der Systemarchitektur, Standards, Grobdesign
- Herstellung und Text von Werkzeugen zur Aufnahme digitaler Publikationen in die Datenspeicher der Depotbibliotheken; hier werden Erfahrungen aus dem MMB-System genutzt
- Projektmanagement
- Informations- und Knowhow-Transfer, insbesondere auch Nachnutzungsmöglichkeiten für deutsche Bibliotheken.

Neben gesicherten Verfahren zur Archivierung müssen auch geeignete Zugriffsverfahren zur Verfügung gestellt werden.

Zur Zeit ermöglicht Die Deutsche Bibliothek internen Nutzern den Zugriff über den Web OPAC, externen Nutzern über das Z 39.50 Gateway auf den OPAC. Dieser Zugriff wird auch für die deponierten digitalen Publikationen die Grundlage bilden. Bei Netzpublikationen soll künftig die URL des Produzenten (PURL) dem Katalogeintrag hinzugefügt werden. PURL ist eine aktive Verbindung zum Verlagsserver, solange dort die Publikation aktuell vorgehalten wird.

Verglichen mit traditionellen Katalogeinträgen enthalten die Informationen über verfügbare digitale Publikationen zusätzliche Angaben, wie z. B. Publikationstyp, Datum der Evaluierung, Online-Verfügbarkeit früherer Ausgaben. Copyright-Angaben, ggf. Nutzungseinschränkungen, ggf. Hinweis auf dem Verlagsserver, Datenformat, empfohlener Browser und Präsentationssoftware, Art des Zugriffs (WWW), Hypertext Links usw.

Der nationalbibliographische Datensatz wird sich zusammensetzen aus den Metadaten des Produzenten und denen Der Deutschen Bibliothek.

Für die Realisierung des Zugriffs müssen die Daten der neuen Publikationen im Index der Suchmaschine ergänzt werden, die Software bereitgestellt werden und das jeweilige Format in das geeignete Format Der Deutschen Bibliothek überführt werden.

Das schnelle Anwachsen der Zahl von Netzpublikationen macht eine generelle Vorschrift zur bibliographischen Erschließung jeder einzelnen Publikation durch Katalogisierer utopisch. Andererseits hängt der Status einer digitalen Publikation als wissenschaftliche Quelle von ihrem eindeutigen Auffinden ab. Man wird Verfahren entwickeln müssen, die eine Überfrachtung mit Datenfeldern vermeiden, Erschließungsnormen international auf ein Metadatenformat von überschaubarem Umfang festlegen (Dublin Core Set) und dieses ggf. bei wissenschaftlichen Ansprüchen verknüpft mit ergänzenden nationalbibliographischen Daten. Die Deutsche Bibliothek führt derzeit gemeinsam mit der SUB Göttingen und der BSB München ein Projekt Meta-LIB durch. Die Deutsche Bibliothek hat dabei die Aufgabe übernommen, das Dublin Core Set durch nationalbibliographische Elemente aufzuwerten. Dazu sollen insbesondere die folgenden Verfahren untersucht werden:

1. bibliographische Erweiterung der Datenfelder
2. Verknüpfung mit Normdateien
3. Verknüpfung mit Numerierungsverfahren

Sie sind wiederum in Beziehung zu setzen zu bestimmten Gruppen von Publikationen (Niveaus). Das von der DFG finanzierte Förderprojekt hat wie NEDLIB im Januar 1998 begonnen und wird von Der Deutschen Bibliothek durchaus im Zusammenhang mit der Depotfunktion gesehen, auch wenn es darüber hinaus von allgemeinem Interesse für die Erschließung von digitalen Publikationen ist.

Digitale Kommunikation ist nicht allein ein Phänomen des globalen Netzes. Das Netz verteilt lediglich die Information. Entscheidend für Inhalt und Einfluß sind die Informationsquellen selbst, die Text- und Mediensammlungen. Deshalb wird für die Zukunft entscheidend sein, ob und wie lokale bzw. nationale Ressourcen des Wissens verfügbar gemacht werden, um mit den globalen Ressourcen verknüpft zu werden. Bei den digitalen Publikationen geht es um mehr als um Auswahl und Verwaltung durch Institutionen. Es geht um die Authentizität von Publikationen, um die Sicherung des geistigen Eigentums und um die Dauerhaftigkeit kurzlebiger Informationen.

So wichtig, wie das Bekenntnis zu den Büchern ist, so richtig ist die Erkenntnis, daß Bibliotheken, besonders auch Nationalbibliotheken – ohne Fortführung bzw. Transformation nicht gedacht werden können. Dabei ist entscheidend, daß sich ihre Entwicklung aus der kulturellen Mentalität und den wissenschaftlichen Bedürfnissen bestimmt. Es ist nur folgerichtig, daß Die Deutsche Bibliothek als nationale Archivbibliothek digitale Publikationen in ihren Sammelauftrag einbezieht. Ihre Funktionen werden bei der Archivierung künftig dadurch weniger statisch und mehr dynamisch sein, denn Archivierung bedeutet bei digitalen Publikationen immer auch Verfügbarkeit im Netz.

Es ist durchaus vorstellbar und auch anzustreben, daß sich Nationalbibliotheken künftig als Teil einer virtuellen Bibliothek verstehen und ihre Depotfunktion gegenseitig zum Transfer von Wissen und Information nutzen.

REINHARD ECKER

Technische Aspekte der Langzeitarchivierung von Daten

1. Einleitung

Seit einigen Jahren werden in zunehmendem Umfang elektronische Dokumente den Benutzern in aller Welt über Internet und andere Datennetze zur Verfügung gestellt. Wir stehen hier am Beginn einer Entwicklung, deren Ziel darin besteht, alle wichtigen Informationen jederzeit und von überall auf Knopfdruck abfragbar bereit zu halten.

Die Begeisterung, mit der Benutzer auf diese neue Art des Informationszuganges reagieren, wirkt als Katalysator für weitere Projekte und wird nach Meinung von Experten bereits in wenigen Jahren das Informationsverhalten entscheidend beeinflussen. Es besteht darüber hinaus kein Zweifel, daß tiefgreifende gesellschaftliche und ökonomische Veränderungen folgen werden.

Bibliotheken – traditionell eine der tragenden Säulen der konventionellen Informationsvermittlung – erkennen und nutzen die Chance, nun auch in der Bereitstellung elektronischer Informationen eine Führungsrolle zu übernehmen. Nationale und internationale öffentliche Einrichtungen, Firmen und private Förderer stellen erhebliche Mittel für Erfassung, Speicherung und Bereitstellung der Dokumente zur Verfügung.

Fehler in der Vergangenheit haben immer wieder dazu geführt, daß wertvolle Daten verloren gegangen, unbrauchbar oder wertlos geworden sind. In der Tat sind digitale Dokumente in vielfacher Hinsicht in ihrem Erhalt bedroht. Es ist daher an der Zeit, der langfristigen Sicherung der Daten besonderes Augenmerk zu widmen.

2. Lebensdauer von Speichermedien

Vom Standpunkt der gesicherten Lebensdauer ist Stein oder Ton das ideale Langzeitspeichermedium, denn die ältesten überlieferten Schriftdokumente befinden sich auf diesen Trägern. Auch Pergament und säurefreies Papier sind hervorragend stabile Materialien, ganz im Gegensatz zu säurehaltigem Papier, das sich tragischerweise zu spät als gänzlich ungeeignet erwiesen hat. Der Mikrofilm soll nach neuesten Hochrechnungen bis zu 500 Jahre halten.

Unbestritten stellt er einen bewährten analogen Langzeitspeicher hoher Dichte dar.

Weil elektronische Speicher relativ neu sind, kann es auch noch keine hinreichenden praktischen Erfahrungen in Bezug auf ihre Haltbarkeit geben. Zeitraffertests haben erbracht, daß optische Speicherplatten, wie die CD ROM oder die WORM-Disc, bei sorgfältiger Lagerung eine Haltbarkeit von über 100 Jahren erreichen sollten. Selbst Untersuchungsergebnisse über die Lebensdauer von Magnetbanddaten sprechen heute von mindesten 20 Jahren. Angesichts der einfachen Kopierbarkeit elektronischer Daten verliert damit die Frage der Lebensdauer des Mediums an Relevanz.

Auf Magnetplatten gespeicherte Daten gehen mit dem ersten Head-Crash verloren. Auf RAM-Speichern werden die Daten mit dem Abschalten des elektrischen Stroms gelöscht. Beide Medien sind daher für die Langzeitarchivierung denkbar ungeeignet.

3. Digitale und Digitalisierte Daten

Im Umfeld der digitalen Bibliothek unterscheiden wir Digitale Dokumente, die von vorne herein in elektronischer Form erstellt wurden, und Digitalisierte Dokumente, die durch elektronische Erfassung der analogen Version (zum Beispiel auf Papier gedruckt) erhalten wurden, sowie Mischformen.

Unter dem Gesichtspunkt der Langzeitarchivierung sind Digitale Dokumente problematisch, weil das bequeme Papieroriginal fehlt.

Obwohl zur Zeit bereits viele digitale Zeitschriften herausgegeben werden, es werden täglich mehr, ist die Frage ihrer Langzeitarchivierung und damit auch ihrer Zitierfähigkeit noch nicht geklärt. In wie weit ist das Datei-Format oder gar die Erstellungssoftware Bestandteil des Dokumentes, das es in seiner Identität zu erhalten gilt? Wer stellt die Archivierung sicher? Der Autor, der Verlag, Bibliotheken? Wer sorgt für die laufende Migration auf neue Datenträger, Hardware, Software? Dies sind jedoch weniger technische denn organisatorische Fragen.

Wesentlich komfortabler ist die Situation der Digitalisierten Dokumente, weil noch das Papier-Original vorhanden ist, auf das als zusätzliche Speicherform im Notfall zurückgegriffen werden kann. Aus der digitalen Kopie eines Papierdokumentes läßt sich auch eine originalgetreue Kopie in hoher Druckqualität erstellen, die dann an Stelle eines etwa durch Säurefraß vernichteten Originals treten könnte.

4. Kriterien der Langzeitarchivierung

Als relevant für die Langzeitarchivierung sehe ich folgende drei technische Kriterien, deren Wichtigkeit jedoch unterschiedlich bewertet wird:

- Wertbeständigkeit des Datenspeichers
- Wertbeständigkeit der Daten selbst
- Wertbeständigkeit der Metadaten

Unter Wertbeständigkeit verstehe ich hier, daß die technische Qualität des Systems und der Daten den langfristig erkennbaren Anforderungen gerecht wird.

4.1 Wertbeständigkeit des Datenspeichers

Für die Wertbeständigkeit des Datenspeichers gelten folgende Kriterien:

- Haltbarkeit des Speichermediums
- Verfügbarkeit von Abspielgeräten
- Verfügbarkeit der Lesesoftware

Die bereits zitierte Lebensdauer von 100 Jahren für optische Speicher halte ich für mehr als ausreichend. Wesentlich problematischer sehe ich die Verfügbarkeit von Abspielgeräten. Wir dürfen uns nicht von der relativ langen Formattreue von CD und CD ROM täuschen lassen. Nun sind mit der DVD neue Formate höherer Speicherdichte auf dem Markt und weitere Entwicklungen werden folgen. Als Faustregel darf man auch in Zukunft alle fünf Jahre einen Technologiewechsel erwarten. Bei den WORM-Platten beobachte ich sogar zur Zeit die Einführung der vierten Generation innerhalb von gut 10 Jahren. Die Anbieter von Abspielgeräten verfolgen zumeist die Regel, nicht mehr als zwei Gerätegenerationen parallel zu pflegen. Dies würde bedeuten, daß die gigantischen Datenmengen mit hohen Kosten im Rythmus von 10 Jahren umkopiert werden müßten. In der Tat sind heute frühe Anwender WORM-basierter Archivsysteme längst mit der Überspielung auf eine neue Datenträgergeneration befaßt.

Ähnliches, wie für die Abspielgeräte, gilt auch für die Lesesoftware zur Interpretation der gespeicherten Daten und ihrer Visualisierung am Bildschirm oder über Drucker. Auch ihre Pflege wird angesichts immer neuer Betriebssysteme nicht beliebig fortgeführt werden.

Hier wird deutlich, daß nicht die Haltbarkeit der Datenträger sondern die Lebensdauer der Abspielsysteme den bestimmenden Zeitfaktor in der Langzeitarchivierung darstellt.

4.2 Wertbeständigkeit der Daten selbst

Nicht jedes heute erzeugte Digitalisat wird in 10, 20 oder 100 Jahren noch den Ansprüchen der Benutzer in Hinblick auf technische Qualität und Standards genügen. Was können, was müssen wir tun, damit der Wert der digitalen Daten langfristig sichergestellt wird?

Digitale Dokumente sind hier eher unproblematisch, weil sie zumeist als codierte Texte in einem offenen Standardformat, das sich leicht konvertieren läßt, vorliegen.

Völlig anders stellt sich jedoch die Situation bei Digitalisierten Dokumenten dar. Um ein gedrucktes Buch über das Internet verfügbar zu machen, muß es in elektronischer Form erfaßt werden. Der zentrale Schritt besteht dabei in der Digitalisierung des Dokumentes mittels eines Scanners. Bei diesem Vorgang wird aus der Druckvorlage durch optische Abtastung ein Abbild in Form von vielen Bildpunkten erhalten. Dieses Abbild wird als Datei gespeichert.

Wichtige Kriterien für die Festlegung der Digitalisierungsparameter ergeben sich aus der Art der Vorlagen und der geplanten Nutzung der digitalen Daten.

In der Folge sind einige Beispiele für die Variationsbreite von Vorlagen aufgeführt:

- Papiervorlagen
  Gebunden – Einzelblätter – Karteikarten
  einseitig – doppelseitig bedruckt
  Übliches Seitenformat bis ca. DIN A4 – Kleinformate – Großformate bis A0 und größer
  Text – Graphiken – Halbton – Farbe etc.
- Filmvorlagen
  Mikrofilm
  Mikrofiche
  Filmlochkarte
  Diafilm
  großformatige Reprofilme etc.
- andere Vorlagen
  Gegenstände (dreidimensional) etc.

Die folgenden Beispiele zeigen einige der Möglichkeiten zur Nutzung und Weiterverarbeitung digitaler Images:

- Darstellung am Bildschirm
- Darstellung durch Ausgabe über einen Drucker
  Lokaler Ausdruck einzelner Seiten des Dokumentes
  Nachdruck des gesamten Dokumentes

Reproduktion des Dokumentes in professioneller Qualität
Erstellung von Postern in höchster Farbtreue und Druckauflösung

- Weiterverarbeitung
  Maschinelle Inhaltskategorisierung (z.B. Dokumenttyp-Analyse)
  Maschinelle Volltexterzeugung mittels OCR/ICR
  Maschinelle Vektorisierung von Strichgraphiken

Es ist unbestritten, daß es sehr schwierig sein wird, Qualitätsanforderungen für künftige Nutzungsarten eines digitalisierten Dokumentes realistisch abzuschätzen.

Für das Scannen beispielsweise eines Buches stehen folgende Vorgehensweisen zur Verfügung, deren Vor- und Nachteile im Einzelfall beurteilt werden:

- Direktscannen mittels Buchscanner
- Mikroverfilmen und Digitalisieren des Films per Filmscanner
- Aufschneiden des Buches und Scannen mit Einzugsscanner

Üblicherweise bewegt sich die Bandbreite für die Scanauflösung (Anzahl der Bildpunkte) zwischen 100 und 600 dpi, in besonderen Fällen auch bis 3000 dpi („dots per inch"), für die Bildtiefe bei Schwarz/Weiß-Vorlagen zwischen 1 und 12 Bit, bei Farbvorlagen bis zu 3 x 12 Bit.

Direkt proportional zu der gewählten Auflösung und Bildtiefe ist die Größe der Bilddatei. Während zum Beispiel eine DIN A4 Seite in der Standard Fax-Auflösung von 100 dpi mit 1 Bit Bildtiefe ein Speichervolumen von ca. 100 Kilobyte erfordert, erreicht die Dateigröße mit 600 dpi und 3 x 8 Bit Farbe annähernd 100 Megabyte.

Falls die direkt nach dem Scannen erzielbare Qualität nicht den an sie gestellten Anforderungen entspricht, kann durch Bildnachbearbeitung eine Qualitätsverbesserung versucht werden. Vom Grundsatz her sind den Möglichkeiten der Bildmanipulation keine technischen sondern höchstens finanzielle Grenzen gesteckt. Zu den typischen Beispielen billiger, weil in der Regel automatisierter, Nachbearbeitungsmethoden zählen:

- Trennen von Doppelseiten
- Entfernen von Rändern
- Seite lotrecht einstellen
- Kontrast steigern, Grauschleier entfernen
- Skalierung auf Originalgröße

4.3 Wertbeständigkeit der Metadaten

Die von einer Druckseite nach dem Scannen erhaltene Bilddatei beschreibt im Grunde nicht mehr als die graphische Darstellung dieser Druckseite. Damit diese „Images" verwaltet, recherchiert und wieder ausgegeben werden können, wird nun eine Indexierung als zusätzliche Erschließung der Seite oder eines aus einer Gruppe von Seiten bestehenden Dokumentes vorgenommen. Diese Erschließung erfolgt nach technischen, bibliographischen und inhaltlichen Gesichtspunkten und kann in fast beliebiger Tiefe bis hin zum recherchierbaren Volltext des Dokumentes gehen.

Metadaten werden – von wenigen Ausnahmen abgesehen – mit ihren zugehörigen Imageseiten in einer Datenbank verknüpft. Daher ist es auch grundsätzlich möglich, Metadaten zu einem späteren Zeitpunkt zu verändern. Dennoch ist es unumgänglich, die Dokumente bereits von Anfang an ausreichend zu erschließen.

5. Speicherung der Daten

Das bei dem Einscannen erhaltene Image bildet den sogenannten „Digitalen Master" in der höchsten Qualität. Als langfristig zu erhaltende Archiv-Version sollte der digitale Master in einem standardisierten Format unter verlustfreier Datenkompression auf einem langlebigen Datenträger gespeichert werden. Als Dateiformat für die Speicherung bitonaler Scans hat sich TIFF in Kombination mit dem Kompressionsalgorithmus nach CCITT G4 international durchgesetzt. Als weiteres Format wäre eventuell noch PNG zu nennen.

Von diesem digitalen Master können dann anwendungsspezifische Nutzungskopien, wie eine „Onlineversion" für die Bildschirmanzeige und eine „Downloadversion" für das Herunterladen auf den eigenen Rechner erstellt werden.

Für die Onlineversion genügt zumeist eine Auflösung in Bildschirmqualität, d.h. ca. 100 dpi. Hier eignen sich vor allem die Formate JPEG und GIF. TIFF wird von den meisten Web-Browsern noch nicht unterstützt. Als Formate für die Downloadversion eignen sich PDF und Postscript, bei kleineren Dokumenten auch HTML.

Bei den Speichermedien wird zur Zeit ein Trend weg von den großen optischen WORM-Platten hin zur kleineren CD-R (CD Recordable) als Langzeitspeicher für die Archiv-Version und zu schnellen Magnetplatten für die Speicherung der Nutzungskopie festgestellt. Es wird dringend empfohlen, mindestens eine weitere Sicherungskopie des digitalen Masters zu erstellen und räumlich entfernt von dem Original aufzubewahren.

Eine Übersicht der empfohlenen Parameter und Formate für digitalisierte Dokumente ist in den folgenden Tabellen wiedergegeben.

Texte, Strichgraphik

Scannen	(300)/400/600 dpi		1 Bit
Speichern		TIFF/CCITT G4	1 Bit
Viewing	70-120 dpi	GIF	1-4 Bit
Gallery/Thumbnails	15 dpi	GIF	1 Bit
Download	300/400/600 dpi	PDF	1 Bit

... aber, falls Vorlagen in altdeutscher Schrift einer OCR-Konversion unterzogen werden sollen, sind ca. 4 Bit Graustufen erforderlich.

S/W – Rasterabbildungen, Fotos

Scannen	300dpi		8 Bit
Speichern		TIFF unkomprimiert	8 Bit
Viewing	512x768 bis 1024x1536	JPEG	4 Bit
Gallery/Thumbnails	~ 100x150	JPEG	4 Bit
Download	2048x3072	JPEG	8 Bit

Manuskripte

Scannen	300dpi		8 Bit
Speichern		TIFF unkomprimiert	8 Bit
Viewing	512x768 bis 1024x1536	JPEG	1-4 Bit
Gallery/Thumbnails	~ 100x150	JPEG	<8 Bit
Download	2048x3072	JPEG	8 Bit

Farbige Abbildungen

Scannen	200-300dpi		3x8 Bit
Speichern		TIFF unkomprimiert Farbkeile!	3x8 Bit
Viewing	512x768 bis 1024x1536	JPEG	3x8 Bit
Gallery/Thumbnails	~ 100x150	JPEG	8 Bit
Download	2048x3072	JPEG	3x8 Bit

3-D Objekte → 2-D Darstellung

Scannen	200-300dpi		3x8 Bit
Speichern		TIFF unkomprimiert Farbkeile!	3x8 Bit
Viewing	512x768 bis 1024x1536	JPEG	3x8 Bit
Gallery/Thumbnails	~ 100x150	JPEG	8 Bit
Download	2048x3072	JPEG	3x8 Bit

Akzeptabe Kompression für JPEG-Files
Bei Graustufen: maximal 10:1
Bei Farbe: maximal 15:1

6. Bereitstellung der Daten im DMS

Die digitalen und die digitalisierten Dokumente werden auf Dokumentenservern abgelegt. Diese Server verfügen über große Massenspeicher sowie über ein Softwaresystem, das Speicherung, Verwaltung und Zugriff auf die Daten steuert.

Der Dokumentenserver verfügt über eine spezielle Schnittstelle, die dem Nutzer den Zugang zu den Daten per Internet ermöglicht.

Herzstück jedes digitalen Archivs ist das Dokumentenmanagementsystem (DMS), welches für die Verwaltung aller Daten und die Steuerung aller Abläufe zuständig ist.

Das DMS basiert in der Regel auf einer relationalen Datenbank. Es greift auf die Speichersysteme für die Dokumente, die bibliographischen (Katalog-) Daten und die inhaltserschließenden Daten (Volltexte, Inhaltsverzeichnisse, Register) zu. Für den automatisierten Datenimport aller drei Kategorien bestehen entsprechende Importschnittstellen. Die Software stellt sicher, daß die erforderlichen Nutzungskopien entweder direkt im Zuge des Datenimports oder später auf Anforderung („on the fly") formatgerecht erzeugt und die verschiedenen Header-Informationen eingetragen werden.

Der externe Zugriff wird über eine Internet/Intranetschnittstelle gewährleistet. Daneben besteht eine lokale Exportschnittstelle zur Ausgabe von Daten auf CD-R oder als elektronischer Auflagendruck. Für die interne Bearbeitung und Recherche sind ebenfalls geeignete Schnittstellen vorhanden.

ZUGANG ZU INFORMATIONEN – NEUE DIENSTLEISTUNGEN FÜR DEN ENDBENUTZER

NEUE DIENSTLEISTUNGEN DER FIRMEN

WIM LUIJENDIJK

Services Provided by the Journal Agencies

„The wise Gods cover with the darkness of night
the issues of the future
and they laugh
if a mortal is anxious beyond what is right"

Horatius

It is very clear that computer based information technologies will both enhance and alter the present communications system of scientific information. At present, we need to distinguish between modernization and transformation of scientific information. Modernization is defined as the use of a new technology to continue to do the same thing, but presumably in a more cost effective or efficient manner, whereas transformation is the use of a new technology to change a process in a fundamental way.

We are in the middle of an information revolution and the latest statistics show more than 125 million people worldwide have access to the Web. There are over 2 million home pages that enable shopping, reading of the daily news and the ability to search for an almost endless amount of information.

Librarians and academic officers began in the early 1990s to explore the capabilities of electronic technologies as solutions to the problem of scholarly communications in print form. The advantages of electronic publications are numerous and have been widely discussed, hence, we will only briefly enumerate them:

- Electronic journals can, in principle, be more current than print journals; their contents can be released to readers as soon as they are ready.
- Electronic journals can be accessed in a variety of innovative ways.
- They do not need to be bound or shelved.

- They make minimal demands on space.
- Missing issues and missing pages do not need to be replaced.
- Many individuals can use them simultaneously, eliminating the need for multiple subscriptions.

I would now like to comment on how the changing economics of the information industry are influencing publishers, subscription agencies and information aggregators and what this will mean for libraries and their consumers of scientific information.

Publishers

More and more publishers are making their paper journals electronically available and most publishers will allow subscription agencies to function as an intermediary. Two major STM publishers, Academic Press and Elsevier Science, so far prefer to deal directly with libraries. This strategy is based upon the fact that libraries all over the world are forming consortia, not only regional but also in some areas even national and most recently even transnational. We at EBSCO however believe that this policy sometime in the future will change as many individual libraries worldwide will remain that are no part of any consortium and rely on the banking function that subscription agencies historically have been offering. You all know that most publishers require payments in advance before any piece of information is being delivered. For those libraries that cannot pay in advance subscription agencies will do this for them and this will be no different in the world of electronic information. It is interesting to share with you some concerns which were raised by the University of Wisconsin-Madison which has signed an agreement with Elsevier. In the paper world they subscribe to about 600 of the 1,200 titles which Elsevier has offered via their Science Direct program to the University of Wisconsin in Madison. However, as I understand it rather than having access in electronic format to the 600 journals they used to subscribe to in paper they will get electronic access to all the 1,200 titles.

The cost will be based upon the number of Elsevier print subscriptions, calculated at the 1997 prices, plus an annual surcharge. The contract would run for three years. First year cost: 1997 list price plus 7.5%. Second year: cost of first year plus 9.5%. Third year: cost of second year plus 9.5%. In 1997 they paid Elsevier almost $850,000 for the 600 print subscriptions they take. The administration of the university estimates that this formula would result in a price in excess of one million dollars for the first year of the deal. Therefore, it appears that Elsevier would collect an additional $250,000 over the three year period. Moreover, the initial estimate for the cost to a library of mounting the database is between $70,000 to $100,000.

What's wrong with this Picture

It seems obvious that this deal is designed to carry Elsevier's enviable profit margins safely into the electronic era. Or, seen from the perspective of a librarian, it is a way to perpetuate the „serials crisis“ into the indefinite, electronic future. Admittedly, some universities might find this very seductive. Imagine! All that access and Elsevier locked into what might be considered modest increases for this publisher for three years.

But just how valuable is this access? The libraries should keep in mind that they are being asked to pay not only for the more successful titles that they have been forced to retain despite their mind boggling prices, but also for all the low-use, high-cost titles that many of them have canceled years ago. It seems that publishers have hit upon a brilliant, „back-to-the-future“ strategy, a return (via electronic vehicle) to the good old days of sum-sufficient serials budgets when librarians eagerly subscribed to every promising journal, knowing that the money would not come out of library budgets, but from some vaguely understood but seemingly limitless central library fund.

The publishers, of course, such as Elsevier and Academic Press, can hardly be blamed for wanting to make lots of money. They have only done what successful companies do: identify a promising new market (growing numbers of scholars/scientists who must publish to survive), devise a product to meet the need (new journals), and then charge as much as the market will bear.

Subscription Agencies

Every company is a collection of activities that are performed to design, market, deliver and support its products or services. All these activities we call a value chain and the way a company performs individual activities is a reflection of its history, its strategy, its approach to implementing its strategy and the underlying economics of the activities themselves.

The changing economics of information threaten to undermine established value chains in many sectors of the economy requiring virtually every company to rethink its strategy, not incrementally but fundamentally.

At EBSCO we have been making fundamental changes. Still many publishers are not thinking about electronic journals. Therefore, EBSCO has been working for over ten years now to obtain the rights from publishers to put their journals in an electronic file. At present we have over 3,100 journals which are not available directly from the publishers and therefore only available electronically via EBSCO. At present, we therefore differ from other subscription agencies who are operating globally, such as Blackwell's, Dawson and Swets.

Our historical competitors such as Swets and Blackwell's and Dawson so far have only made some incremental changes in developing an online journal system which offers access capabilities for end-users and administrative functions for librarians. However, EBSCO Online does the same but will give access to more, as through EBSCO Publishing we will have full text data which none of our historical subscription competitors will have.

The basic functions that an electronic journal subscription handling system will offer are:

- Integrating the library site's access to electronic journals via the World Wide Web
- Managing electronic licensing agreements with publishers
- Providing support and advice on electronic license definitions
- Dedicated customer support
- Dedicated technical support
- Product and software training materials for librarians and end users
- Combined invoicing for print and electronic journals (no period)
- Subject searching
- Keyword searching
- Browsing
- TOC services
- Alerting services
- Individual document printing

We already have technical complications here as so far there are no standards. At present basically three major software packages to obtain access are being used by the publishing community. Those are:

1. Acrobat from Adobe
2. IBM Tech Explorer
3. Real Page from Catchword

We are facing other practical problems as outlined by Richard Luce, Director of Carmel Los Alamos National Laboratory Research Library last year during an EBSCO seminar in Boston.

To give you an idea of the scope of what they are doing, they currently track 5,200 electronic based journals (some of these are self-published items from the Los Alamos physics community network). They have a database that includes 13.5 million citations, 95 million hyperlinks and 200 million cited references. The citations, hyperlinks and cited references are all linked together with their online catalog and this is done through robotically generated lines of software code from a program that they have developed. In developing these links they are guided and driven by the effort to build databases around how people need to get to the information. Everything is integrated with their catalog and citation databases and the bottom line for them is speed. He indicated that their customers (researchers) expect web access with links and integrated with the library catalog so that they have one place to go and one common user interface. They expect everything to be hyperlinked, with new associations and easy to view on the screen with printing capability. Their user community also wants an alerting service based upon their own personal interest profile and they expect to be able to search and retrieve full text from their databases regardless of who the publisher is. A checklist of concerns he reviewed are as follows:

- Inconsistent methods of access;
- Timeliness – receiving electronic versions at the same time or ahead of print versions;
- Unreliable service – poor response time;
- Usage data – indicated this is difficult to get from publishers so they are developing their own supplier software program in order to get the information they need;
- Article level identifier – this needs to be standardized and his preference is SICI (the Serial Item and Contribution Identifier); however, some publishers, among which are the American Chemical Society, the American Institute of Physics, and Elsevier Science, are heavily marketing PII, the Publisher Item Identifier, whilst lately the American Association of Publishers (AAP) issued a request for proposal to develop a scheme for identification of electronic articles and they call it the Digital Object Identifier (DOI). It seems though that we will now be having a standard as during the Frankfurt Book Fair in October 1997 DOI has been accepted by all the STM publishers.

Information Aggregators

An information aggregator signs individual agreements with publishers in order to obtain the rights for a particular journal to abstract, index and also to obtain the rights for full text. This can be obtained from the publisher if it is available or the information aggregator receives the permission from the publisher to convert the full text from print format into an electronic format. This information is then being packaged by subject and sold under different names to the marketplace worldwide. The major companies which are offering scientific information in packaged format are:

1. UMI
2. IAC
3. H.W. Wilson
4. SilverPlatter (only secondary databases and only abstracts and indexes)
5. OVID Technologies
6. EBSCO Publishing
7. OCLC

Those parallel developments are certainly very exciting but offer additional challenges to those companies which are either functioning as an intermediary or as a packager of information.

The packagers will have the full text of many a journal residing on their servers. The companies which are offering an online subscription service program most likely will have to link to numerous individual publisher servers in order to offer access to the information preferably to the end user from their workstations.

At EBSCO already we are matching the two together and in EBSCO's MEDLINE for instance, the new version which just came out, via the MEDLINE database we offer direct access to the full text of 61 journals in the medical sciences, all residing on our servers in Boston. Later this year we will link all other titles which are full text available from the various publishers and to which the library using this service has the rights to access the full text. One can imagine that this is not an easy job to accomplish as when a publisher's server is down the results cannot be obtained and we have to have systems in place to monitor this and to retrieve again what has not been submitted.

Last but not least, the problems of access as well as archiving if one looks at the tremendous volume of bits and bytes which will be accumulated on an annual basis, will not be easy to deal with.

If the information is stored on a floppy disk, optical disk or tape, one must first have the hardware and software to accommodate the medium such as an optical reader or system with appropriate disk-to-tape drives, and the correct version of the software program used to store the data. If the information is stored in a remote location, but is accessible through software, one must have the necessary software to locate and retrieve or download it. Additionally, one must have the necessary software to access or read the data. This introduces many problems and questions. Electronic journals, just like print journals, are produced with a variety of software programs that run on several different hardware platforms. As electronic journals become more sophisticated to include photos or graphics or even become multimedia, the number of formats will likely increase. Many programs or formats for these journals will come and go, just like word processing products have done and continue to do.

„Technology refreshing", whereby electronic information is transferred from one waning medium to an emerging one, will need to be practiced. It will be a challenging task for the group or person who wants to archive and provide easy, universal access over the long run.

The Information Age has done much to change the way we look at our industry and the library profession and the way in which we deliver information. Changing times call for a changing mind set.

But all the new technology which we are developing must be with the end user in mind as otherwise it will become useless. The problem we are facing at present is whether we can construct a system that users will find comfortable in making broad use of electronic journals as a substitute for printed ones, not only for today's information, but for all the information we have produced and will be producing from now onwards until many generations in the future.

If we are not successful in offering access to what has previously been recorded, I could end this presentation by using an interesting thesis from the book *Die Stadt hinter dem Strom* by Herman Kasack:

„Wäre das Gilgamesch Epos, wären die Gesänge der Upanishaden oder die Homers das Tao te King, oder die Göttliche Komödie um nur einige der alten Tafelwerke herauszugreifen nicht aufgezeichnet worden, so würde die Welt des Menschen sich heute von der Welt der Ameisen nicht mehr unterscheiden."

References

1. Malinconico, Michael. Electronic Documents and Research Libraries. IFLA Journal 22 (1996) 3.
2. Luijendijk, Wim. Archiving Electronic Journals: The Serial Information Provider's Perspective. IFLA Journal 22 (1996) 3.
3. Luce, Richard. Acquiring, Accessing and Managing Online Journals. Presentation at EBSCO's Academic Seminar, The Netherlands, March 1997.
4. Lynch, Clifford. Technology and its Implications for Serials Acquisition. Against the Grain, February 1997.
5. Rouse, Ken. The Serials Crisis in the Age of Electronic Access. Newsletter on Serials Pricing Issues, No. 177 (May 1997)
6. Kasack, Herman. Die Stadt hinter dem Strom (1946)

THOMAS RAKOW

Die Online-Dienstleistungen der Springer-Verlagsgruppe

Der wissenschaftliche Springer-Verlag setzt weniger als 1% seines Umsatzes direkt mit elektronischen Produkten um. Allerdings sind die Buch- und Zeitschriften eng mit elektronischen Medien (EM) verbunden. Einige Bücher werden von CD-ROMS begleitet, erscheinen in der Statistik aber nur als einfaches Buch. Mehr als 300 der den größten Teil des Umsatzes repräsentierenden Zeitschriften sind in einer elektronischen Version online verfügbar. Im Springer-Verlag und seinen Tochterunternehmen in aller Welt wächst also immer mehr die Bedeutung elektronischer Medien.

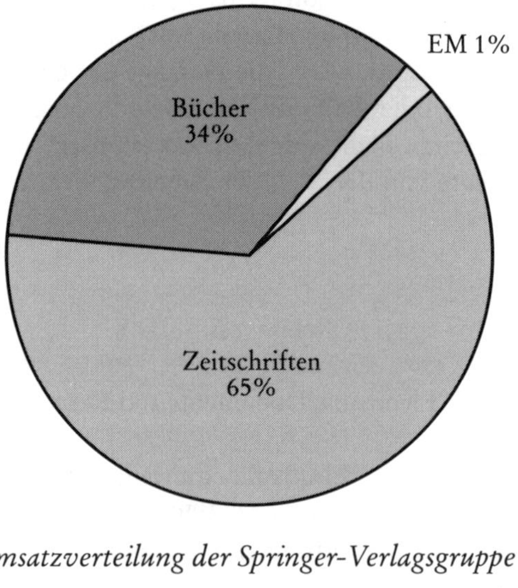

Umsatzverteilung der Springer-Verlagsgruppe 1996

Wie inzwischen jede Firma ist auch der Springer-Verlag im Internet mit seinen Webservern vertreten. Produktinformationen liegen hier suchbar und auch ‚push'-bar vor. Gemäß einem individuellen Interessengebiet können aktuelle Produktinformationen direkt nach Erscheinen dem Interessenten mitgeteilt werden. Deren multimedialen Beschreibungen erlauben beispielsweise bei der CD-ROM ‚*Albert*' Versuche aus der Physik anschaulich zu demonstrieren und zum Test auch auf den heimischen PC laden zu lassen. Die Audio- und Videosequenzen der ,*Vögel Europas*' sagen mehr als die 1000 Worte eines Textes über diese CD-ROM.

Die Merkmale wissenschaftlichen Publizierens garantiert ein Verlag dem Leser auch im Web. Wissenschaftliche Beiträge durchlaufen vor ihrer Veröffentlichung in der Regel einen Begut-achtungsprozeß (Peer-Review). Die Publikation in einer im jeweilgen Fachgebiet anerkannten Zeitschrift erlaubt dem Leser, sich auf die inhaltliche und technische Qualität der Information verlassen zu können. Insbesondere Eigenschaften wie Lesbarkeit, Zitierbarkeit und Archivierbarkeit dürfen im Web nicht aufgegeben werden. Wertvolle Erfahrungen hat der Springer-Verlag hierzu im BMBF-gefördertem Projekt ,*Medoc*' gesammelt.

Das gesamte wissenschaftliche Zeitschriftenprogramm umfaßt über 400 Titel in der Springer-Gruppe, mehr als 300 von ihnen sind zusätzlich zur gedruckten Ausgabe inzwischen auch online im *LINK Informationsservice* verfügbar. Abonnenten bekommen die elektronische Version als Basiszugang für drei simultane Nutzer kostenlos in der Volltextausgabe. Wissenschaftler profitieren davon direkt an ihrem Arbeitsplatz. Der LINK-Informationsdienst besitzt einen Webserver in Heidelberg und einen über eine Standleitung verbundenen Webserver in New York. Anhand eines Nutzernamens und Paßworts, bei institutionellen Nutzern auch anhand der IP-Adresse wird die Autorisierung überprüft. Jeder Webserver besitzt eine Kopie der Zugriffsrechte aller Kunden, so daß sich beispielsweise australische Nutzer den besten Zugang aussuchen können.

Die Weiterentwicklung der Online-Dienstleistungen erfolgt auch über gemeinsame Forschungs- und Entwicklungsprojekte mit deutschen und europäischen Institutionen. In ,*Global-Info*' wird der elektronische Publikationsprozeß durch Universitäten, Verlage, Abstracting-Dienste, Bibliotheken und Fachgesellschaften weiterentwickelt. Das multimediale Buch wird in drei Projekten entwickelt. In ,*OpenMath*' werden mathematische Formeln zum Leben erweckt: ,Mathematics comes alive!'

Die Kooperation mit anderen Online-Services ist eine wesentliche Zielsetzung von LINK. Für die Verlinkung sollen nicht kurzlebige URL eingesetzt, sondern Digital Object Identifier (DOI) verwendet werden. Das DOI-System besteht aus der Definition eines Nummernsystems zur eindeutigen Identifizierung von Objekten im Internet und aus einer Rechnerinfrastruktur zu dessen Unterstützung für Online-Services. Eine Reihe von Verlagen, unter ihnen auch der Springer-Verlag, haben das DOI-System in Prototypen getestet und erste positive Erfahrungen gesammelt. Bestehende Nummernsysteme werden integriert und auch das Problem von ins Leere zeigenden Verweisen in Webseiten wird gelöst. Hierfür wird von der DOI-Foundation ein Handle-Server betrieben, der einer DOI eine URL (Universal Resource Locator) als Webadresse zuordnet. Diese Zuordnung kann jederzeit aktualisiert werden, so auch beim Rechteverkauf und damit dem Umzug eines Objektes von einem Rechner zu einem anderen. Der DOI ändert sich dabei nicht, die URL wird vom neuen Besitzer geändert! Im LINK-Service ‚*Online First*' werden für einige wissenschaftliche Zeitschriften Beiträge vor dem Erscheinen der gedruckten Ausgabe im Internet mit ihrer DOI publiziert. Sie können damit von der Fachöffentlichkeit einige Wochen vor der gedruckten Ausgabe gesucht, bestellt, gelesen und zitiert werden.

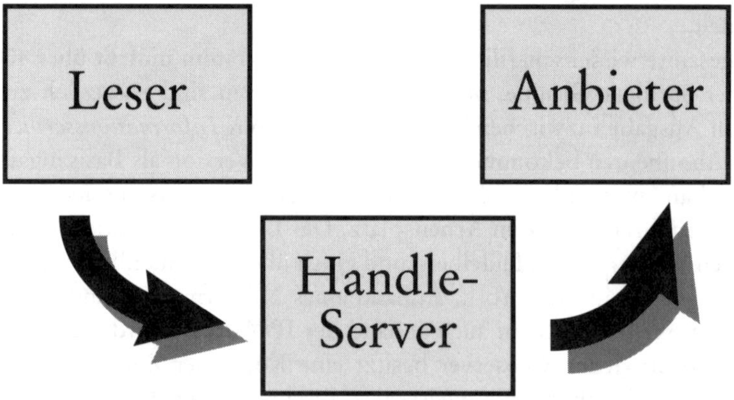

Umleitung von DOI-Anfragen über den Handle-Server

Als leicht auch für Online-Dienstleistungen anwendbares Abrechnungsverfahren ist das ‚Abonnement' weit verbreitet. Aber auch spezielle Lizenzen für bestimmte Nutzergruppen und Konsortien finden Anwendung. Besondere Abrechnungsverfahren wie Micro-Payment, die auf der Zeitdauer des Zugriffs oder auf die Informationsmenge bezogen werden, werden derzeit nur in geschlossenen Diensten oder nicht flächendeckend eingesetzt. Der Springer-Verlag ist mit einigen Angeboten im Dienst ‚*Global-Learning*' der Deutschen Telekom vertreten. Auch eine Teilnahme und Demonstration des *E-Cash*-Prototypen der Deutschen Bank diente der Vorbereitung neuer Dienstleistungen des Verlages.

Zukünftige Entwicklungen sind die Aufnahme von bisher unter den Begriff ‚Buch' fallenden Publikationen. Es werden multimediale Bücher entwickelt, und Loseblattsammlungen werden zu Expertensystemen, die mittels interaktiver Entscheidungsbäumen Betriebe leiten helfen. Die Vermarktung wird dabei sicherlich nicht nur das Abonnementsverfahren der Zeitschriften übernehmen. Mit der Einführung des DOI-Systems können Inhalte von Online-Services leicht mit anderen Online-Services im Internet verbunden werden. Ändern wird sich der Erwerb der Information, insbesondere wenn die Verlinkung zur Verrechtung wird, indem qualifizierte Beziehungen zwischen komplementären Informationsangeboten einschließlich der Abrechnungsmöglichkeiten geschaffen werden. Je mehr miteinander intelligent verbundene Information zur Verfügung steht, desto mehr divergiert die elektronische Publikation von ihrem gedruckten Äquivalent. Wie mag wohl die wissenschaftliche Publikation in fünf oder zehn Jahren aussehen?

Die Geldbörse für E-Cash

Adressen:
Webserver des Springer-Verlags: www.springer.de
Medoc-Server des Springer-Verlages: medoc.springer.de
LINK Informationsservice, Heidelberg: link.springer.de
LINK Informationsservice, New York: link.springer-ny.com
Forschungsprojekte des Springer-Verlages: www.springer.de/projekte
Webserver von Global-Info: www.global-info.org

VOLKER THURNER

Dienstleistungen des traditionellen Buchhandels

I. Einleitung

Der Zugang zum Internet ist mittlerweile, zumindest in der wissenschaftlichen Welt, zu einer Selbstverständlichkeit geworden. Beim Anbieten von Inhalten ergriff der traditionelle Buchhandel im Vergleich zu anderen Branchen sehr früh die Initiative und stellte beispielsweise Katalogdaten online zur Verfügung.

Zugute kam hier, daß der komplette Publikationsprozeß schon seit Mitte der 80er Jahre aus Gründen der Wirtschaftlichkeit datenbankgestützt abgewickelt wurde: Aus der Datenbank wurden direkt Belichtungsdateien generiert und dadurch aufwendiger und fehlerträchtiger Neusatz vermieden. Dadurch war es kein Problem, durch einfache Schnittstellendefinition auch eine Onlineversion der gedruckten Kataloge zu produzieren und den Prototyp eines Online-Bookshops in Angriff zu nehmen .

Neben den traditionellen Sortimenten etablierten sich inzwischen auch eine ganze Anzahl von „Online"-Buchhandlungen. Bemerkenswert ist, daß es den klassischen Versandbuchhandlungen in dieser Anfangsphase weit weniger gut gelang, im Onlinesektor Fuß zu fassen als den klassischen Sortimenten.

Erfahrung im Direktvertrieb, die vorhandene Infrastruktur und die bestehenden Kundenkontakte versetzen den Buchhandel in die Lage, bei der Beschreitung neuer Distributionswege für elektronische Informationen Akzente zu setzen.

II. Datenkonvertierung

Die Konvertierung von Daten aus externen Datenbanken in einheitliche Datenstrukturen ist für den Buchhandel seit vielen Jahren alltägliche Praxis. Aus unterschiedlichsten Quellen mit uneinheitlichen Schnittstellen wird eine einheitliche Datenstruktur erzeugt, da außer VLB, Books in Print, Bookbank, DNB, Bookfind, BNF, BNB, RNB auch jeder Verlag, der in der Lage ist, Daten strukturiert zur Verfügung zu stellen, ein eigenes Format benutzt. Und leider konnten sich auch die bibliothekarischen Austauschformate nicht in der Buchhandelsbranche durchsetzen.

Flexibel anpassbare Konvertierungssoftware ist umso notwendiger, als frühe Bestrebungen des betriebswirtschaftlichen Ausschusses des Börsenvereins des Deutschen Buchhandels, eine Standardisierung bibliographischer Daten anzustreben, weitestgehend nur im Austausch von Bestelldaten zwischen Buchhandel und Zwischenbuchhändler griffen.

Diese Situation beeinflußt nicht nur den buchhandelsinternen Geschäftsverkehr, sondern hat auch Auswirkungen auf die Nutzer dieser CD-ROM-Datenbankprodukte in Bibliotheken. Beispielsweise wird eine Ende der 80er Jahre von Lehmanns entwickelte Software, mit der lieferantenunabhängig Bestelldaten aus ca. 20 unterschiedlichen Datenbanken (einschließlich einiger Online-Verbundkataloge) konvertiert und generiert werden können, immer noch von über 100 Bibliotheken eingesetzt, darunter auch einigen Universitätsbibliotheken – trotz mittlerweile sehr leistungsfähiger integrierter Erwerbungsmodule bei Bibliotheks-Verbundsystemen.

Zur Zeit wird bei Lehmanns versucht, den bibliographischen Angaben eines Dokuments Kurzbeschreibungen, Inhaltsangaben oder Leseproben möglichst auch dann automatisch zuzuordnen, wenn die Konvertierung von Printvorlagen erfolgen muß.

III. Kataloge/Bestellsysteme

Leistungsfähige Recherche-Software ist die Grundlage für ein erfolgreiches Online-Angebot. Mittlerweile gibt es einige sehr gute Beispiele (http://www.buchkatalog.de, http://www.buchhandel.de), die auch von Buchhandlungen direkt via Link genutzt werden können, ohne sich selber um Datenbankaktualisierungen oder Verwaltung von Warenkörben kümmern zu müssen.

Dieses Verfahren hat aber für den Buchhändler den entscheidenden Nachteil, nicht selber inhaltlich Einfluß auf die angebotene Datenbank nehmen zu können, sei es mit der zusätzlichen Integration von Abbildungen, Inhaltsangaben, Rezensionen, Leseproben, Klappentexten oder gar des vollständigen elektronischen Dokuments. Eigene redaktionelle Aufnahmen sind – wenn überhaupt – nur sehr umständlich integrierbar.

Gerade das Angebot zusätzlicher Informationen, die über die rein bibliographischen Angaben hinausgehen, wird für die weitergehende Vermarktung von Online-Produkten, neben dem eigentlichen „wo finde ich was“, unverzichtbare Voraussetzung für eine Kaufentscheidung sein und über kurz oder lang, neben der Güte und dem Umfang der zugrundeliegenden

Datenbank, vor allem im wissenschaftlichen Bereich ein Hauptnutzungskriterium werden.

Hier waren wir den großen amerikanischen Bookshops merkwürdigerweise voraus, da diese allenfalls Titel aus der Bestsellerliste zusätzlich inhaltlich erschlossen haben.

Der Problematik des Nachweises von Bestelldaten in den jeweiligen lokalen Systemen -bei elektronischen Bestellungen fehlt im Regelfall eine Bestellunterlage, außer der Nutzer behilft sich mit Bildschirmausdrucken oder ähnlichem – wird beim Lehmanns Online Bookshop insofern Rechnung getragen, als automatisch eine Rückübermittlung der Bestelldaten per eMail in einem strukturierten Format erfolgt. Als möglichst einfaches Format wird das Austauschformat UK-Marc benutzt, welches auch bei den Whitaker-Bookbank-Produkten Verwendung findet und sicherlich ohne größeren Aufwand in kundenseitige Bestellsysteme implementiert werden kann.

Zusätzlich zur Online-Recherche über das World-Wide Web bietet Lehmanns eine Datenbankschnittstelle per eMail an, wobei wahlweise die Titeldaten auch im strukturierten Format geliefert werden können:

search@lehmanns.de – bibliographische Angaben und alle Zusatzinformationen (außer Bildern)

msearch@lehmanns.de – bibliographische Angaben im UK-Marc Format.

Als Ergänzung zur Monographiendatenbank liegt auf dem Lehmanns-Server auch eine kostenlose Testversion der Medline auf, mit eingeschränktem Zeitraum, aber vollem Funktionsumfang der SilverPlatter Retrieval Software.

IV. Datenlieferungen für unternehmensinterne Netze

Immer mehr Firmen und Institutionen bauen unternehmensinterne Intra- oder Extranets auf. Neben dem Kantinenplan und der Telefonliste ist eine der möglichen Anwendungen mit nahezu garantiert hoher Akzeptanz eine Literaturdatenbank mit einer auf das Unternehmensprofil zugeschnittenen fachlichen Ausrichtung. Dies entspricht den „klassischen" Neuerscheinungsdiensten, allerdings mit entscheidenden Vorteilen:

- Die Informationen stehen nach dem Einspielen in die Datenbank allen angeschlossenen MitarbeiterInnen sofort zur Verfügung – umständliches Kopieren und Verteiler entfallen
- Umfangreiche, beschreibende Texte können geliefert werden, in der Printversion undenkbar, wodurch im Idealfall der für alle am Distributionspro-

zess Beteiligten zeit-und kostenintensive Ansichtsversand reduziert werden kann

- Die Fachgruppenzuordnung kann bei feinerer Gliederung wesentlich besser gesteuert werden, da zum eigentlichen Dokument lediglich Zuordnungsschlüssel geliefert werden.
- Titelmeldungen einzelner Verlage, die für eigene redaktionelle Aufnahmen klassifiziert werden, fließen in den Neuerscheinungsdienst mit ein
- Echte Einsparungen an Papier, da -wenn überhaupt- nur noch die tatsächlich gewünschten Titel ausgedruckt werden müssen

Die Firmen oder Institutionen sind für die Retrieval-Software selbst verantwortlich, auf welcher Plattform die Daten angeboten werden, ist dadurch weitgehend unwesentlich. Eine Minimallösung sind statische HTML-Seiten, die auch direkt von Lehmanns geliefert werden können. Normalerweise werden die Daten nach vom Kunden vorgegebenen Kriterien aufbereitet und zugestellt, dort in eine Datenbank eingelesen und – mit Bestell- oder Ausleihfunktionen versehen – den Mitarbeitern angeboten. Auch und gerade hier gilt, daß nur mit möglichst umfangreicher zusätzlicher Information der größtmögliche Nutzen erzielt wird. Lehmanns erprobt dieses Verfahren derzeit mit dem Fachinformationszentrum der Siemens AG, monatlich werden ca. 2-3 000 Titelsätze generiert und per WWW-Download ausgetauscht.

V. Anbieten von eigenen Inhalten

Im Zeitalter der Online-Publikation fällt natürlich ein gravierender Nachteil des verbreitenden Buchhandels besonders ins Gewicht: Er verfügt über keine oder wenig verwertbare Originaldokumente und ist deshalb für den Vertrieb auf die Produktion der Verlage angewiesen. Nun zeichnen sich elektronische Publikationen unter anderem dadurch aus, daß diese wesentlich kostengünstiger hergestellt werden können als Printprodukte. Nachfrageabhängige Auflagen können ohne Schwierigkeiten zu nahezu identischen Kosten produziert werden. Ein Beispiel: die Nachpressung der sehr erfolgreichen deutschen debian-Linux-Distribution, einer Doppel-CD mit Installationsanleitung, kostete bei Stückzahlen jeweils zwischen 500 und 1000 praktisch genau so viel wie die für die Kalkulation des Verkaufspreises maßgebende erste Auflage. Der Kostenvorteil bei wesentlich höheren Startauflagen ist innerhalb der Gesamtkalkulation so minimal, daß dieses bei der Errechnung des Verkaufspreises nicht nennenswert ins Gewicht fallen würde.

Diese Kalkulation gilt natürlich immer nur unter der Voraussetzung, daß die

Autoren entweder die benötigte Software selber produzieren oder aber Standardsoftware einsetzen (HTML, Acrobat). Beim Einsatz von Standardprodukten fällt außerdem ins Gewicht, daß Publikationen gleichzeitig sowohl Online, als auch Offline (auf Datenträger oder „Printing-on-Demand"-Produkt) angeboten werden können. In solchen Fällen genügt es den Autoren häufig, sich praktisch ausschließlich mit einem Distributor auseinanderzusetzen, der die übrigbleibenden „verlegerischen" Aufgaben übernimmt und auch direkt den Verkauf an den Endkunden steuert.

So minimieren sich natürlich die Fixkosten, da eine Buchhandlung weder über Lektorat noch Herstellung oder (Wiederverkäufer-) Vertrieb verfügt und letztendlich auch keine separate Auslieferung unterhalten muß, zumal dann, wenn der potentielle Markt durch ein eigenes Filialnetz mit angeschlossenem Online-Bookshop zu einem erheblichen Teil abgedeckt werden kann.

Einige Produkte sind für diesen verkürzten Publikationsprozeß prädestiniert: neben Tagungsbänden, die zu den reinen Beiträgen in dieser Publikationsform auch durch die Ergebnisse der Diskussion aufgewertet werden können (Lehmanns wird voraussichlich ein solches eMail-basiertes Verfahren anläßlich der Frühjahrstagung der DPG erproben) sind sicherlich auch Dissertationen in dieser Form denkbar, sofern die rechtlichen Voraussetzungen dafür gegeben sind.

VI. Archivplatz für Autoren und Verlage

Voraussetzung für die klassische Buchhandlung ist ein möglichst geeignetes Ladenlokal, Voraussetzung für den Online-Vertrieb sind leistungsfähige Server in einer möglichst schnellen Umgebung. Was nützt schon die schönste Anwendung, wenn die 64-Kbit Anbindung bereits beim 3. Besucher hoffnungslos verstopft ist. Das Vorhalten von Serverkapazitäten und Bandbreite ermöglicht Autoren und Verlagen ohne eigene Netz-Infrastruktur kostengünstig die Nutzung sowohl von Archivplatz als auch Softwareschnittstellen bis hin zur Datenbanknutzung. Eine gleichzeitige Integration in die Online-Datenbank versteht sich von selbst.

VII. Neue Partnerschaften

Internet-Technologie ermöglicht Kooperationen mit anderen, nicht unbedingt buchhandelstypischen Partnern, die früher kaum zustande gekommen wären. In erster Linie sind hier Kooperationen mit den Online-Services der Printmedien zu nennen. Werden die klassischen „Lesershops" noch in Eigenregie betrieben, wird dies im Online-Bereich schon viel aufwendiger. Datenbankpflege und Fakturierung gehören normalerweise nicht zum Kerngeschäft einer Zeitung oder Zeitschrift. Eine ideale Aufgabe für eine Buchhandlung, die den Inhalt „Buchladen" im Online-Angebot beispielsweise einer Tageszeitung zuliefert – möglichst im Layout des jeweiligen Dienstes. Besonders attraktiv für den Nutzer der Literaturdatenbank ist es, zusätzliche Links auf rezensierte Titel zu finden.

Lehmanns unterhält u.a. Kooperationen mit:

http://www.berlinonline.de – Online Service von Berliner Zeitung, Tip, Berliner Kurier

http://www.tagesspiegel.de – Online Service des Berliner Tagesspiegel

http://www.goon.de – Online Service des Axel Springer Verlags

http://www.med-online.de – Informationsdienst für Mediziner, Apotheker und Veterinärmediziner

http://www. dv-markt.de – Zeitschriftenabstracts, Stellenmarkt, Infos für die DV-Welt

VIII. Abrechnungsverfahren und Inkasso

Der verbreitende Buchhandel verfügt über langjährige Erfahrung mit Abrechnungsverfahren und Zahlungssystemen und bietet daher gute Voraussetzungen für den Einsatz und das Erproben von geeigneten Zahlungsmodellen für die Abrechnung elektronischer Informationen.

Elektronische Zahlsysteme werden im On-und Offline-Bereich schon seit vielen Jahren erfolgreich eingesetzt, aber immer mit der Maßgabe, daß bei der Lieferung eine persönliche Identifizierung durchgeführt wird (gültige Postadresse, Auslieferungsnachweis).

Weder kommt über die bisher praktizierten Verfahren eine im Zweifelsfall rechtsgültige Bestellung zustande, noch ist das bisher für den Online-Buchhandel ein großes Problem.

Gleichwohl besteht ein großer Bedarf an einem für Kunden und Händler sicheren Verfahren des Austauschs von Informationen, welches über eine bloße Verschlüsselung der Daten (SSL) hinausgehen muß und sowohl für „große" als auch „kleine" Beträge wirtschaftlich betrieben werden kann.

Spätestens der Wegfall einer körperlichen Lieferung bei elektronischen Produkten verlangt nach einer Regelung zum Authentifizieren sowohl von Besteller- als auch Anbieterseite. Ob dies über gängige Passwortmechanismen zufriedenstellend gelöst werden kann, sei dahingestellt.

Ist die Bestellung erstmal erfolgt, hat der Kunde mittlerweile bei zahlreichen Online-Bookshops die Möglichkeit, online den Status des Auftrags zu verfolgen, bis hin zum Tracking der Sendung, nachdem diese bereits die Buchhandlung verlassen hat.

IX. Ausblick

Der wissenschaftliche Sortimentsbuchhandel geht, glaubt man den allgemeinen Trendmeldungen, schwer(er)en Zeiten entgegen. Solange dem Kunden Waren im klassischen Sinn angeboten werden sollen, gibt es wenig Alternativen zum Vertrieb über die Sortimente.

Aber spätestens bei der Lieferung rein elektronischer Produkte müssen die Distributionswege überdacht und neu defniert werden.

Im Rahmen von Global Info – Globale Elektronische und Multimediale Informationssysteme für Naturwissenschaft und Technik – einem Förderprojekt des bmb+f, beteiligt sich Lehmanns, übrigens als einzige Buchhandlung, an den beiden Schwerpunktbereichen „Metadaten“ und „Wirtschaftlichkeitsmodelle“ und versucht, Möglichkeiten sinnvoller Beteiligung auszuloten. Ein Ziel dieses Förderprogramms ist, wissenschaftliche Information direkt online am Arbeitsplatz des Endnutzers zur Verfügung zu stellen.

Die spannende Frage bleibt, ob und wie es dem wissenschaftlichen Sortimentsbuchhandel gelingen wird, auch in der „schönen neuen elektronischen Welt“ einen sinnvollen Beitrag zu leisten.

NEUE DIENSTLEISTUNGEN DER BIBLIOTHEKEN

MARIA ŚLIWIŃSKA

New Services at Polish and East European Libraries

Many new services in Eastern European libraries are currently based on electronic resources. But this is not exclusively true, as I believe that traditional, paper-based information sources will continue to exist and will continue to be used for a very long time, along with the new digital ones.

What are the differences between our services and those in the West? Briefly speaking, we are following your lead, but we are still a long way from achieving the same kind of integration as has been worked on in the West. Our libraries have been forced to work – at least for the last fifty years – in an inefficient political and economic climate. Libraries and information centres depend on sufficient resources to meet the requirements of the Information Age. The problems concerning of resources are emphasized – using only Polish statistics as an example – by the fact that the number of viable libraries is actually decreasing, as you can see in table 1.

In general, significant progress can be observed in the rate of technological implementation. As illustrated in table 2, there is an amazing growth in library automation and technical development within our libraries. Now let us ask, from the librarians' point of view: „What new services can we point out at our libraries?"

Traditional Services / Much Improved

Let me start by describing some very well known traditional services, which have nevertheless been significantly improved. We still collect printed books that are requested by our readers. It is new that – after the 1989 revolution – there are no longer restrictions to obtain such titles like „Open Society" by Carl Popper, or „1984" by George Orwell. Any book published clandestinely abroad or known as an underground „samizdat" title (that used to be published in the 70's and 80's in the country) can also be purchased. Our only restrictions are financial and space. But there is not a single library in the world capable of buying every published title. Our collections development and book selection is only restricted by budgets and handling capabilities, nothing else.

Vendors and Agents

We subscribe to a variety of journals according to readers' demands (and, again, our financial possibilities). But serials acquisition we have now started to purchase through foreign, long well-known in the West, intermediating vendors like Swets, EBSCO, or Langer und Springer, in addition to domestic vendors (who have significantly changed their level of service.) Today, journals are delivered to our readers more rapidly than before and the runs are rather complete. Vendors are selected because of the price they offer as well as for their value-added services, which are increasingly important.

What are these value added services? There can be:

- **electronic copies** of journals to which we subscribe. (These are offered by Swets, Lange und Springer, and EBSCO; but also by smaller publishers like The Institute of Physics Publishing.)
- **document delivery services**. (These are, for the time being, not heavily used in our countries, primarily because of the price. To our way of thinking, we still feel more secure with the accession of full titles, „just in case," rather than relying exclusively on providing access to individual paper „just in time". But, clearly, JIT services are thought to be increasingly attractive and are seriously considered by our universities.)
  In Poland, the Committee of Scientific Research (KBN) is where financial budgetary decisions are made. The KBN has prepared a report, sponsored by the EC, „Background Study for the Planned Governmental Program: Development of the Document Delivery Systems for Science and Education". This has determined some funding directions that affect our libraries.
- **Databases** are available at our libraries mainly on CD-ROMs. CD-ROM networks are becoming increasingly popular. The availability of CD-ROM networks will allow our users to reach databases from their own work-stations.

Less popular in our countries are on-line services. (The reason for this is probably attributable to price, to still not entirely reliable network connectivity, and to problems using foreign databases efficiently and economically from a distance.) Only MEDLINE has been used regularly and for many years. It has recently been offered to our countries free of charge. This is not only greatly appreciated, but allows us to channel the saved subscription fees into other important purchasing needs for our libraries. Libraries are providing access to some popular databases like First Search from OCLC. This service was tested among Polish libraries last year. (But because of the significant amount of money necessary to subscribe to this service at the national level, funds were not approved by the KBN.)

There are also trials for using some important databases like INSPEC on a national level, and to take advantage of the reduced price than can be obtained by any individual library.

Our users are also interested in the American JSTOR project, which was recently offered to a limited number of our libraries.

Some libraries like The Estonian National Library are not able to deliver all the required specialised services to their clients, so those libraries have opted to lease library space to western organisations like CESIN (the Consortium for International Earth Science Information Network) who provide access to databases, instead.

Catalog and Classification Systems

Very important services are based on library catalogues, where users can find information about what is available in the library. Traditional card catalogues still predominate, although several libraries are in the process of installing electronic card catalog systems. It was the custom in Polish libraries – as in Germany – to use our own classification systems, based on philosophical knowledge classification schema. This is the reason that there is no single classification system as there is in American or English libraries, where typically, the Dewey or the Library of Congress classifications were used. UDC classification was the system most popular in our countries. The bigger research libraries often used and developed their own classification schemes. In the era of computerised catalogues this is a real disaster. But progress can be seen.

Just a few years ago, (from 1992) The Mellon Foundation awarded important grants to over one hundred libraries in Hungary, the Czech and Slovak Republics, and Poland. With these grants, libraries began purchasing and installing integrated library software. Last year two Baltic countries (Latvia and

Estonia) were also awarded grants by the Mellon Foundation. Lithuania, who didn't succeed in qualifying for a Mellon grant, decided this year to invest on it's own account. Governmental resources have been budgeted for the modernization of sixteen Lithuanian libraries.

This brings us to a sort of parity with the West. CEE libraries are dealing with the same automation systems that are common in the West: Aleph, VTLS, Innopac, Tinlib, Horizon, Voyager. And we have the same problems with system vendors as Western libraries do. Libraries that have purchased integrated automated systems primarily decided to adopt and customize the Library of Congress Subject Headings (sometimes through the French RAMEAU-Poland facility). A user can now have the same retrieval structure at all libraries in the country. Unfortunately there are still not enough records in our catalogues to make a serious critical mass. Individual libraries try to improve the situation in various ways.

The National Library in Prague scanned millions of catalogue cards, and is currently busy creating proper records from them. Polish libraries started by creating Authority Files. And those who purchased VTLS have started to cooperate in the cataloging effort, gradually joining other libraries with different systems (Horizon, Innopac). This is not easy because of differences in format and inconsistent interfaces, to say nothing of simply erradicating input and typing mistakes. Buying systems that are oriented for the American market also takes some customisation. But the cataloging situation is improving. A central union catalogue for all of Poland is being planned. We hope that–thanks to these kinds of efforts – our readers will receive the same excellent quality catalogue services, locally, in the near future, that is available internationally.

Bibliographies

Prepared bibliographies are also a service provided by our libraries. Some of these are already accessible on Internet. Just at my library at Nicholas Copernicus University, we exclusively prepare a few important bibliographies such as the international „Polish-German Cultural Relations“ bibliography or the bibliography of „The History of Pomeranian and Baltic Countries.“

Exhibits

Another field of new services is in promoting exhibits and educational displays. Our libraries have traditionally taken this to be a task of some importance, and have consistently mounted numerous and interesting exhibits. In the past, such exhibits had to be approved by a censor. In the new and open climate, we can organise any exhibition we find interesting for our users. The only justification is one of merit, not politics. Some exhibits are obtained from other countries or libraries in the region, and beyond, and we often send ours in exchange.

Additionally, there are exhibits of books to accompany lectures or meetings organised at our libraries by publishing houses. These are primarily aimed at book promotion, but can be interesting in their own right. Some years ago, it was difficult to just buy a book. Now, when restrictions about purchasing no longer exist, even a good book needs promotion.

Market-related

After our political changes and the introduction of a free-market economy, new special services are required. One of the most important, these days, is business information. Dedicated business resources are developing slowly. We still can't even dream about the kinds of services I saw at the new business branch of the New York Public Library, where local business people can use hundreds of computers to search for information, have access to dozens of seminar rooms in which to organise small meetings, or can consult qualified library staff and specialists. Again, slow progress is visible in our region. Libraries are starting to use all the available means of delivering information to business patrons.

In Poland the most advanced business center is in the Public Library in Szczecin, where local business is very active and interested in international cooperation with Germany, England, and other countries. In such an environment, unique information is required, and punctuality and reliability in research is demanded of the library. Unfortunately, relatively few businessmen yet recognize the potential value libraries have for their success. But we know that such specialized services are gradually becoming more and more important. After the first years of being preoccupied with the startup phase of a business, business executives are beginning to realize that it is time to develop it and make it more competitive. To reach this higher level of development, not only information, but also techniques of obtaining and managing such information, are required. This can most easily be found at libraries, since the professional „information broker“ is not yet a possible career in most of our countries.

Patent information is connected with, and is helpful for the business information centres. In Poland, patent information is treated as a special service provided by the Polish Patent Office, rather than integrated within normal library networks. Recently, however, in a joint project involving the Polish Patent Office and some libraries, Regional Patent Centres have been formed. Such centres collect patent information (Polish data in traditional, printed form; and foreign data on CD-ROMs). These regional centres also collect and make available a wide variety of standards, which are one of the most popular source of requests from users.

Environment

Another specialised service can be identified in „ecological information.“ This is particularly important for countries in which heavy industry has strongly polluted the environment, as is often the case in CEE countries. The primary source for such services is The Regional Environmental Centre (REC) which is located near Budapest, Hungary. Co-operation on an international level is proceeding well, thanks to the formation of grassroots organizations like „The International Organisation for Information Specialists“, which came into existence in 1993. One of the first results of an international collaboration of IOIS „chapters“ (or beginning chapters, since some countries are still experiencing difficulty legalizing and establishing organizations similar to „non-profit“ organizations in the West) was the publication of an EcoDirectory, providing information about Environmental collections and libraries with significant environmental collections in seven CEE countries. This directory was published in traditional (printed) form, but also exists in an electronic version. An electronic IOIS discussion list was created to help solve problems in which easy communications could provide some solutions, as well as to facilitate an active flow of information. The REC is updating and expanding the digital version of the EcoDirectory, a task that seems well worth the effort. IOIS chapters were formed from a co-operation with Western experts, an US-AID grant, and the involvement of the World Wildlife Fund-US.

European Documentation Centres

In several selected CEE libraries exit, what is called „European Documentation Centres.“ These Centres collect important material about the EU: European Union legal acts, proceedings, etc. which are very important to us at a time when our countries are preparing for integration within the European Union. More and more depend on access to the electronic discussion list

„Euro-doc", which helps them to find specific documents or information for their clients.

Network Access

Only relatively few libraries in our region have been able to organise Internet access for their patrons with public-access Internet connections as a special service. Among these is my library at UMK. This network cluster is, in fact, one of the biggest in the country (with 12 work-stations). While they are primarily there for access to Internet information resources, the workstations are also equipped with Microsoft Office, giving users easy access to word processing or spread-sheet functions.

This is not a perfect solution, because there are always long queues of students waiting for available computers. If I were to compare our situation with the availability, per capita, of similar public-access computers in England we would compare very badly, indeed. But this is merely a financial problem. Our libraries do not have sufficient funds to buy more computers for students. But we are, instead, planning to provide a lot of plug-in capabilities in the Library extension building, to let users use their own lap-tops. If our Internet connectivity costs became prohibitive, we plan to change the small computer cluster into a pay-for-use „cyber-café".

Printing

The Library print-shop is another new service available. Our print shop was made possible by a TEMPUS grant, with which we were able to purchase two laser printers necessary to make on site printing services available to our users. We also purchased a scanner with the Library's own funds, to augment the flexibility of the service.

At the Pharmacological Library in Cluj-Napoca, in Romania, Sally Wood-Lamont proved that individual student use could justify a self-sustaining printing facility. It has now been functioning for several months as an entirely new service for users.

Training and Education

Since electronic information requires specific new skills, some patrons (especially those more comfortable with traditional research methods) feel understandably lost. For this reason, they tend to use the available electronic resources ineffectively or not at all. To remedy this situation libraries are giving educational courses and user-directed training. There are individual classes on how to best utilize CD-ROMs, how to search patents on-line, or even how to search online library catalogues efficiently.

Libraries also support and convene conferences. At one such, organised by my Library in 1993 on the topic of regional business, we invited not only business leaders, but also professors from the University. The topics of presentation ranged from providing advice on how to prepare a business plan to explaining why European Documentation Centres were important.

The worldwide web

Another new service is found in the almost geometric growth of www home pages that have been created and mounted by individual libraries. Such Internet www sites are visited by many scholars and researchers from all over the world.

Sometimes the work is entirely oriented to scholarly pursuits; others for more private matters. A person from my Library has a particularly unique name. Thanks to our home page she was „found" by her long-lost family which had emigrated to the United Kingdom during the WWII. This is, perhaps, not an anticipated benefit of this new service but it is a useful one and points to both the community-building aspect of Internet communication and the fact that we don't actually know how, and in what ways, the services we are developing today will prove helpful to people within our communities tomorrow.

I hope that in this rapid survey, I have presented a useful picture of the new services in which our libraries are engaged, as well as existing ones that have been significantly improved because of the greater degree of autonomy we experience, the local and international cooperation from which we benefit, and the extraordinary dedication of individuals who are able to see the potential of technology and education.

Economic Model

I will conclude by observing that the majority of library services is still free in our countries. In a free-market economy, our libraries have just started charging fees for some of them, as have our peer institutions in the West. In general, however, I hope we will not go too far down this road. For the patrons of our CEE libraries especially, the open and free access to information is what they most need, and greatly deserve. It would be a shame if the progress of technology and access to information became restricted again, this time for economic reasons that are part of the social, managerial, and political revolution we are undergoing.

Table 1

Type of library	1980	1991	1993	1995
– scientific libraries	1,329	1,235	1,285	1,274
– public libraries	9,315	10,269	9,605	9,505
– special libraries	3,751	1,925	1,591	1,426
– professional literature	3,736	864	667	546
• leisure reading materials	146	170	113	84
• professional/leisure				
• prison libraries		154	154	154
– scientific information centres	1,723	522	412	312
– school and pedagogical libraries	1985		1991/1992	
	19,868		20,879	

Table 2
Electronic publications development

World		Poland	
„STAIRS“ First full text database	← 1968	1976 →	Lenin‘s text Possible to search because of politial reason only
Internet	← 1971	1990 →	First Polish Internet host
DIALOG	← 1972	1992 →	Experimental „Dialog“
LEXIS	← 1973	1992 →	Polish LEX
CD-ROM	← 1985	1994 →	First Polish CD-ROM
WWW	← 1992	1993 →	First Polish home page of Institute of Physics, Warsaw University
Encyclopaedia multimedia	← 1994	1995 →	First Polish multimedia encyclopaedia

BRUCE ROYAN

New Services for the End-User: the Scottish SCRAN Project

With the rise of the Internet as one of the dominant means of information gathering in the late '90s, Libraries, Museums and other cultural institutions need to develop networked services aimed at the End-user if they are to retain their relevance in the new millennium.

The replacement of the online intermediary by the end-user is part of a trend that has produced supermarket shopping, hole-in-the-wall banking, and student-centred learning; the intention of each is a felicitous combination of increased throughput, consumer empowerment and lower unit costs.

The design of any end-user information service has to take into account what the end-user wants from their information: they want it easy, they want it one-stop and they want it now.

Easy. A supermarket that needed a User Manual would soon go out of business. The availability of information service functions must be obvious, and their use must be intuitive, otherwise they will not be used at all.

One-Stop. Similarly, the end-user is not particularly concerned at the accidents of fate that led to the information they seek residing in public library 'a' rather than university library 'b' or perhaps museum 'c ' or archive 'd'. Ideally, information services must be able to support searching between institutions and access domains.

Now. Finally, our end-user is generally seeking information per se, not a physical location where such information may reside. The market is increasingly for services providing on-demand access to digitised images and machine-readable text.

Enter SCRAN

One such service is the Scottish Cultural Resources Access Network. SCRAN is building an end-user multimedia resource base of library, archive and museum material, for the teaching and celebration of human history and material culture in Scotland. Although founded by major Scottish cultural institutions, their representation on the SCRAN Board is balanced by an equal number of representatives from the education and training sectors, in an effort to ensure that the development of SCRAN is user-needs-driven, and not provider-led.

SCRAN has funding until 2001 of some 15 million pounds sterling, half of it from the UK Millennium Commission and half from Contributors, largely in the form of intellectual property rights. In essence, SCRAN is in a position to fund the digitisation and captioning of images and other multimedia assets, in exchange for a non-exclusive licence to make them available for educational use. In this way, SCRAN expects to build a resource base of 1.5 million text records and 100,000 multimedia resources.

SCRAN and Metadata

SCRAN is providing access to the resources of libraries, archives, museums, art galleries, archaeological corpora etc, each with their own vocabularies and cataloguing conventions. It would be fatuous to try to change these domain standards, but in order to support end user cross-domain access, we have adopted the Dublin Core set of metadata elements, to provide a unified interface to all the different sorts of objects SCRAN is concerned with. SCRAN is therefore acting as a metadata repository, holding pointers to its own digitised resources of built heritage and museum objects in the material world, to detailed, domain-specific records in other databases, to appropriate web pages, and to other subject gateways.

This metadata is held in what are known as SCRAN Basic Records. SCRAN Full Datasets consist of a SCRAN Basic Record (perhaps enriched with further indexing), plus a multimedia resource (flat or 3D image, movie or sound clip, animation, PDF, Virtual Reality object or whatever), plus up to 3 paragraphs of Caption material. Captions give a brief introduction to a topic, a description of the object represented in the multimedia, and some background information if necessary; all written to be understood by the intelligent, non-specialist, reader.

SCRAN on the Web

All SCRAN material is held in a searchable database format, and the results are converted into HTML on-the-fly, so that every SCRAN resource is in essence available on the World Wide Web. It is recognised that unrestricted WWW access effectively releases material into the Public Domain, but this is acceptable because supporting unstructured private study is considered part of SCRAN's educational remit. The IPR of the original rights holders is protected since only thumbnail versions of multimedia material are made available in this way.

End-users in Educational institutions in membership of SCRAN have, in addition, the capability of downloading larger, higher definition images suitable for use in the current generation of multimedia systems. In fact, SCRAN insist that all scanning must be done at a much higher definition still (equivalent to 16 times the size of a current generation screen). This protects SCRAN's investment, since it will be possible to upgrade the specification of educational images in future, without the need to re-scan. It also creates for the original rights-holder a high-quality resource which can be exploited commercially if desired.

What sort of end-user?

As already discussed, SCRAN has a strong educational mission. We are targeting end-users in Primary, Secondary, Further and Higher Education, as well as Lifelong Learners, and so our delivery points include not only educational institutions, but also Libraries, Museums, Community Centres, Tourist Information Centres and the home.

Since its launch in July 1996, the SCRAN Website has registered 100,000 hits from all over the world, and there is a tremendous interest in things Scottish from the Scottish Diaspora: there are up to 60 million people world wide who claim some form of link with Scotland. SCRAN can be seen to have a role in promoting a world-wide awareness of Scottish landscapes and heritage. There must be a point at which educational end-usage would be better described as virtual tourism: but from a SCRAN point of view this does not matter.

Libraries and Museums in the Information Society

As natural delivery points for end-user services such as SCRAN, Libraries and Museums may in future come to be regarded less as storehouses of particular collections of recorded knowledge and material culture, than as gateways to networks of such resources world-wide.

The end-user is being given the capability to assemble for themselves collections of such resources, tailored for their current need into a Virtual Library, a Virtual Museum.

The question to be asked is, if the Information Society is going to be built on virtual collections, will there be a future role for the real information professional? And of course, the answer is that none of this will be possible without the acquisition, conservation, description, organisation and presentation skills of the information professional. It may be true that End-Users will be the Main Players in the Information Society. But it will be information professionals that direct the play, fabricate the scenery – and lift the curtain!

GERT STAAL

The Internet Radically Impacts End-User Expectations of Secondary and Primary Information Sources

Consequences and Lessons to be Learned

The author has identified friction between user expectations and the librarian's perspective, as well as friction between user expectations and market realities to be some of the underlying causes for the relative poor penetration of electronic information on the desktop. Today the author will bring forward some ideas that are central to our company, and the way forward we see in unlocking scientific information resources on the Internet.

The User Expectation
Based on his or her experiences with Internet usage, the end user will have certain expectations when accessing primary and secondary scientific information resources. Let me add here by saying that I think there is no one typical user of Internet resources, but that each user will share, at least to some degree, the following requirements about information:

- information should be current
- information should be 'free', i.e.: if not 'free' in the sense of not-gratis, then at least freely accessible without transactional charges and/or password protection
- information should be accurate/reliable
- information should be integrated: the end user is not really interested in single information provider's offerings, but in a combination of all possible resources.

Of course these expectations are fuelled by the current functionalities, or the conceived/extrapolated functionalities of Internet in the future, based on what is known today.

Why the User Perspective?
Users will, in our opinion, increasingly dominate the discussion on the requirements of information services. There are several very good reasons for

that. In the first place, very obvious but forgotten mostly, because end users are the sole aim why information resources are there: essentially primary and secondary information is put on the Web for the end user, who uses the Web for a score of other purposes too!

Secondly, the average end user has used the Internet for exploring information resources for a longer time than publishers have put their resources there, and with a much wider scope. This gives end users a vastly better position to comment on how information should be represented. Yet much of the discussions, even today, seem to focus on new functionalities of software packages, rather than address underlying end user and librarian's behaviour.

End User Expectations and Market Realities

The end user will typically surf sites for practical information, and will view the Internet as an integrated 'source of knowledge'. His/her preference, for scientific materials, would be to access a single system, and hope to find all their resources indexed there, in one fell swoop. Now that is a panacea that is still around the corner. I'll explain why.

First of all, many print publishers have vested their money in developing one site for their electronic materials only, thereby making one of the greatest end-user centred functionalities, namely integration with other materials through hyperlinking, difficult on a large scale using traditional means.

Furthermore, there is no interoperability between the secondary and primary information business model. Typically these come from different sources altogether. Even if that is not the case, then mostly the combined secondary and primary resources offered by one publisher are normally just a subset of the total offerings in a given field.

Thirdly, the issue of scaleability is not addressed. Even though prices of hardware (in particular disk space and memory) are dropping fast, it is inconceivable that there will be a new Electronic Library of Alexandria soon, one that contains all and will contain all for centuries to come. Sheer growth of the body of scientific literature alone would prevent that. In stead of building a library of Alexandria, perhaps we should concentrate on building its 'wings'. A system that is truly scaleable therefore should be able to 'point' both to local information as well as remote holdings.

However, there may be a desire to maintain some diversity in terms of information systems used, also from a user perspective.

The Librarian's Perspective

Of course, the librarian has recognised all of this, but there are more things to information than the user perspective. A librarian is better trained and equipped to judge the value of competing products. It is here that the disparity begins: the end users endorses a product by either using it or leaving it alone, but the librarian still has a final say in most transactions, whether advisory, endorsing, purchasing or otherwise. At least he or she will normally pay for services and be responsible for licensing in an academic environment, and to a large extent in the corporate environment. Therefore, the librarian is faced with a task that is sometimes at odds with user's interests, namely:

- to purchase (users want it all, librarian has a limited budget)
- to manage access rights to the user community (user wants full and unlimited access, librarian has to be a gatekeeper of access rights to respect license agreements). This surfaces e.g. in the licensing and purchase of electronic journals, as well as in the purchase and offering of online ordering to document delivery/ILL systems
- maintaining/safeguarding the system (user wants 24-hour access to a free system, librarian has to keep the system in the air financially and technically).

Balancing
In order to develop a successful product, it is absolutely vital to keep in mind that it will be necessary to meet both users' demands and librarians' needs, even though that may imply that almost contradictory demands will have to be married: electronic content access control is to be matched with openness/public availability of information, systems access control with interoperability of systems.

Many Internet primary/secondary sources have been moderately successful, in an overwhelming number of cases they at least were performing well below expectations. It is now time that we start, in a generic fashion, analysing factors that play a role in their success or failure.

The Internet as a delivery medium of full text information has not particularly been hassle-free so far. In fact, one could almost say it has a reputation for not being so:

Some factors are generic:
- there is the general issue of network (i.e. technical) speed: every user knows that in Europe the Internet has a main cardiac arrest after 2pm, especially when accessing northern American sites. The hunger for bandwidth is so great, that the growth of new bandwidth cannot keep up with the growth in demand. Unless some serious alternative and parallel networks scale up soon, the Internet will remain a questionable and somewhat unreliable delivery mechanism. The need for bandwidth is most obvious in a full-text envi-

ronment. A typical scientific article in PDF format will vary between 0.5 and 1 MB. Now that in itself is not a large file, but it is when faced with a community of 20,000 students for a single university, not a small portion of which may be online simultaneously.

- furthermore, there is the issue of pre-print: not so much vanity in the name of science has driven many authors to sending their articles to pre-print servers, but the need to increase the publication speed of scientific work, relating to outside pressures on people. This seems to be particularly true in quickly developing areas of science: high-energy physics, astronomy, etc. Many services in this area, however, are still quite under-developed even if the potential is there. More: end users are aware of this unleashed potential which is proven by the mere fact that these start-up services exist parallel to publication programmes.
- as with publishers (see above) whether primary or secondary, have not been very successful in marketing format parallel with content. Many have tried-and erred, some have set up services the end users may not be waiting for.

Some factors are user-related:

- users have not been accustomed to purchasing information online. They haven't been used to paying for information whatsoever. Therefore the economic models that were applied in some instances have failed.
- users have found that there is simply not enough critical mass to go on: approximately 2 to 3 percent of current scientific information is now produced in a reproducible, archivable electronic format.
- the complexity of the offerings: novice users find it extremely difficult to navigate to the right information, given their relative innocence in certain subject areas even in the printed environment

Some factors are librarian-related:

- librarians usually disliked being tied to individual publisher's systems, and usually have had a favour for integrating access through third-party aggregators like e.g. Swets or EBSCO, but could only find part of the information really needed there
- there is the issue of evolving standards: XML versus HTML?, DOI or SICI? – battles that will last for some time. Battles also, that have not been fought yet. New campaigns are on the horizon.
- Librarians have not liked the economic models that were applied in some instances, bypassing the librarian completely, which has not stimulated acceptance.
- Librarians have been cautious about direct and electronic access to ILL &

document delivery services to certain groups of users, since no good management system existed to support it.
- librarians have had concerns about archiving materials, related to capacity, and to the stability of formats and platforms, as well as copyright

Partly due to a combination of causes mentioned above, varying from site to site, users have hardly any fulltext access (if available at all), whereas users may be exploiting Internet for other purposes, as I refer to the use of Internet as a source of practical information, for email purposes, for ftp, shopping etc.

So we are faced with a paradoxical situation. Librarians and end users recognise that the introduction of real-life up-to-date, full content of scientific information on the Web is a milestone. Yet this information is to date only delivered in exceptional situations in the desired form.

The historical background should be taken into account. We all know that electronic access to full text promises the kind of paradigm shift we should compare to the invention of print. For instance, we all know that the copyright problems we now face equal the historical copyright problems that surfaced when the printing press was introduced. Drawing historical parallels, now that we are at it, reveals to me that electronic publishing is probably in its first stages of its evolution.

There is no binding factor, so it seems. No connection yet between user's needs and what they are been served. No proper connections are yet made in many of the economic models, the business models, and the technology platforms, although this will change over time.

Centuries of experience in print only has a limited value in the electronic age. SilverPlatter has been in electronic publishing probably longer than most publishers have been, and we think we have some insight into how and what a user's needs are, and at least we have a view on what these models and platforms are. Although the issues are different for secondary and primary information in many respects, we learned that what the market is waiting for are knowledgebases containing both. Not just one central monolithic repository that unites materials from all kinds of sources, in all sorts of formats, but diversified, de-centralised repositories. It is the links that matter, the integration that counts. With SilverLinker we will build a platform , that will balance the needs of the end-user and the librarian alike, a step on what we think is the right evolutionary path.

ELEKTRONISCHES URHEBERRECHT – NÄCHSTE SCHRITTE

JENS GASTER

Richtlinienvorschlag zum Urheberrecht in der Informationsgesellschaft*

Einführung in das Thema

Der Vorschlag für eine Richtlinie zur Harmonisierung bestimmter Aspekte des Urheberrechts und der verwandten Schutzrechte in der Informationsgesellschaft (DOK. KOM (97) 628 endg. vom 10.12.1997) ist die siebte Initiative der Europäischen Kommission zur Angleichung der einzelstaatlichen Bestimmungen auf dem Gebiet des Urheberrechts und der Leistungsschutzrechte[1].

Seit 1991 hat die Europäische Union fünf sog. vertikale Richtlinien erlassen, die sich entweder mit einer spezifischen Kategorie von urheberrechtlich geschützten Werken (Computerprogrammen, Datenbanken), einem speziellen Teilaspekt (Schutzdauer, Satellitenrundfunk und Kabelweiterverbreitung) oder den Rechten einer bestimmten Gruppe von Berechtigten (Leistungsschutzrechte) beschäftigten. Auch die gegenwärtig noch nicht erlassene Richtlinie zur Harmonisierung des Folgerechts verfolgt diesen traditionellen Ansatz.

Der nunmehrige Vorschlag hat demgegenüber eine horizontale Zielrichtung. Er soll auf der Grundlage eines seit 1994 durchgeführten umfassenden Konsultationsverfahrens[2] – zu dem sich mehr als 350 paneuropäische und internationale Verbände äußerten – Kernfragen des Urheberrechts und der verwandten

* Dr. Jens Gaster ist Hauptverwaltungsrat im Urheberrechtsreferat der Generaldirektion Binnenmarkt und Finanzdienstleistungen der Europäischen Kommission in Brüssel. Die in der nachfolgenden Einführung in das Thema geäußerten Ansichten sind allein solche des Verfassers. Der weitere Text ist ein Auszug aus der Begründung des Richtlinienvorschlags.

[1] Zu den vorherigen Initiativen näher *Gaster*, The Harmonisation of Copyright and Related Rights, in: Zerdick et al. (Hrsg.), Exploring the Limits – Europe's Changing Communication Environment, ECC Report 1997, Berlin 1997, 204 ff. Eine ausführliche erläuterte Version dieses Richtlinienvorschlags findet sich unter http://europa.eu.int/comm/dg15/de/intprop/intprop/1100.htm

[2] Dazu *Gaster*, Urheberrecht und verwandte Schutzrechte in der Informationsgesellschaft, ZUM 1995, 740 ff;

Schutzrechte insbesondere im Lichte der aufkommenden Informationsgesellschaft einer EG-weiten Harmonisierung zuführen.

Die angestrebte Angleichung der einschlägigen einzelstaatlichen Bestimmungen der 15 EG-Mitgliedstaaten wird insbesondere Wettbewerbsverzerrungen und Beeinträchtigungen der Dienstleistungsfreiheit zwischen den einzelnen Mitgliedstaaten beseitigen helfen. Insoweit ist sie für das ordnungsgemäße Funktionieren des europäischen Binnenmarkts im Zeitalter der Informationsautobahnen unverzichtbar.

Die künftige Richtlinie soll darüber hinaus aber auch internationale Verpflichtungen der Europäischen Gemeinschaft umsetzen. Die Gemeinschaft und ihre Mitgliedstaaten haben bekanntlich am 20.12.1996 in Genf die beiden neuen WIPO-Verträge über Urheberrecht sowie über Darbietungen und Tonträger unterzeichnet[3]. Vor der angestrebten Ratifikation der Verträge – ein entsprechender Vorschlag für einen Ratsbeschluß ist seit dem 24. 4. 1998 anhängig – muß Europa jedoch zunächst seine „Hausaufgaben" machen. Zu diesem Zweck ist derzeit (Herbst 1998) das Europäische Parlament aufgerufen, die künftige Richtlinie in erster Lesung zu beraten.

Die nachfolgenden Ausführungen sind ein Auszug aus der Begründung des Richtlinienvorschlags. Sie legen die Hintergründe und den Inhalt der vorgeschlagenen Regelung dar.

Die Begründung des Richtlinienvorschlags: Einleitung

Mit dieser Richtlinie soll ein harmonisierter, adäquater Rechtsrahmen für Urheberrechte und verwandte Schutzrechte in der Informationsgesellschaft geschaffen werden. Sie soll den bestehenden Rechtsrahmen ergänzen und anpassen, um ein reibungsloses Funktionieren des Binnenmarkts zu gewährleisten und ein günstiges Umfeld zu schaffen, das Kreativität und Innovation innerhalb der Gemeinschaft schützt und fördert.

Angesichts der entscheidenden Bedeutung von schöpferischen Inhalten und Innovationen für die weitere Entwicklung der Informationsgesellschaft hat die Kommission den Schutz des geistigen Eigentums ausdrücklich als einen der Schlüsselfaktoren bezeichnet. Mit den Herausforderungen, die die neuen Technologien an das Urheberrecht und die verwandten Schutzrechte stellen, setzte sich dann das Grünbuch über Urheberrecht und verwandte Schutzrechte in der Informationsgesellschaft vom 19. Juli 1995 auseinander. Nach der

[3] Zum Inhalt der Verträge v. *Lewinski / Gaster,* Die Diplomatische Konferenz der WIPO 1996 zum Urheberrecht und zu verwandten Schutzrechten, ZUM 1997, 607ff; *Reinbothe / Martin-Prat / v. Lewinski,* The New WIPO Treaties; A First Résumé, EIPR 1997, 171 ff.

Veröffentlichung des Grünbuchs erhielt die Kommission Eingaben durch mehr als 350 schriftliche Stellungnahmen, sowie im Rahmen einer Anhörung in Brüssel am 8. und 9. Januar 1996 und bei zahlreichen bilateralen Kontakten mit allen Beteiligten. Den Abschluß dieses Konsultationsprozesses bildete eine von der Kommission vom 2. bis 4. Juni 1996 in Florenz veranstaltete Konferenz.

Die Konsultation bestätigte, daß der bestehende Rechtsrahmen der Gemeinschaft für das Urheberrecht und die verwandten Schutzrechte, auch wenn er nicht explizit auf die Informationsgesellschaft zugeschnitten ist, für dieses neue technologische Umfeld von entscheidender Bedeutung sein wird. Dieser Rechtsrahmen muß jedoch angepaßt werden. Alle Kategorien von Rechtsinhabern und die Rechteverwerter vertraten den Standpunkt, daß geschütztes Material auf eine neuartige Weise genutzt wird, die von der jeweiligen Zustimmung nicht gedeckt oder in den einschlägigen Rechtsvorschriften nicht vorgesehen ist. Schließlich wollen Nutzer und Investoren wissen, welche urheberrechtlichen Vorschriften sie zu befolgen haben werden. Alle Betroffenen wiesen nachdrücklich darauf hin, daß das Urheberrecht und die verwandten Schutzrechte im Rahmen des Binnenmarkts weiter angeglichen und den neuen Herausforderungen durch Digitalisierung und Multimedia angepaßt werden müssen. Das Europäische Parlament und die Mehrheit der Mitgliedstaaten teilen diese Ansicht und haben die Kommission aufgefordert, Harmonisierungsmaßnahmen vorzulegen, um ein kohärentes, Kreativität und Investitionen förderndes Umfeld im Rahmen des Binnenmarkts zu schaffen. In ihrer Mitteilung von 1996 faßt die Kommission die Ergebnisse des Konsultationsprozesses zusammen und erläutert die hinter ihrem politischen Konzept stehenden Erwägungen vor allem in bezug auf die Prioritäten und die Wahl der Herangehensweise.

Die Kommission muß in zwei Bereichen tätig werden. Erforderlich ist zum einen eine Harmonisierung des Rechtsschutzes in der Form, daß das Urheberrecht und die verwandten Schutzrechte den neuen Chancen und Risiken angepaßt werden, um gleiche Bedingungen für einen Urheberrechtsschutz über nationale Grenzen hinweg sicherzustellen, damit der Binnenmarkt für neue Produkte und Dienstleistungen mit urheberrechtlichem Gehalt Wirklichkeit wird. Zum anderen müssen auf technologischer Ebene adäquate Systeme für die elektronische Verwaltung der Rechte und deren Schutz entwickelt werden. In der Mitteilung werden vier Bereiche genannt, die umgehend gesetzgeberische Maßnahmen erfordern, um bestehende oder potentielle Handelsschranken zwischen den Mitgliedstaaten zu beseitigen: das Vervielfältigungsrecht, das Recht der öffentlichen Wiedergabe, Maßnahmen gegen die Umgehung oder den Mißbrauch elektronischer Verwaltungs- und Schutzsysteme sowie das Verbreitungsrecht einschließlich des Erschöpfungsgrundsatzes. Im Arbeitsprogramm der Kommission für 1997 sowie in ihrem „Dynamischen Aktionsplan zur Informationsgesellschaft" wurde die vorliegende Initiative zur Harmonisierung bestimmter Aspekte des Urheberrechts und der verwandten Schutzrechte in der Informationsgesellschaft angekündigt. Die Bedeutung der Vorlage gesetzgeberischer Maßnahmen im Bereich des geistigen Eigentums wurde auch in der Mitteilung der Kommission über eine „Europäische Initiative für den elektronischen Geschäftsverkehr" hervorgehoben.

Ausgangspunkt des Vorschlags ist zwar der binnenmarktorientierte Konsultationsprozeß, doch steht er in seiner jetzigen Form in engem Zusammenhang mit internationalen Entwicklungen, auf die er sich sogar zum Teil stützt, da die Märkte für die Verwertung von Werken und sonstigen Schutzgegenständen in immer stärkerer Wechselbeziehung zueinander stehen.

Dies trifft vor allem auf das digitale Umfeld der Informationsgesellschaft zu, die keine nationalen oder regionalen Grenzen kennt. Entsprechende Schutzstandards wurden auf internationaler Ebene bereits in Form zweier neuer Verträge der WIPO angenommen, des „WIPO-Urheberrechtsvertrags" (WCT) und des „WIPO-Vertrags über Darbietungen und Tonträger" (WPPT), die den Schutz der Urheber bzw. den Schutz der ausübenden Künstler und Tonträgerhersteller zum Gegenstand haben. Mit diesen Verträgen wird der internationale Schutz des Urheberrechts und der verwandten Schutzrechte auf den heutigen Stand gebracht, einschließlich durch Maßnahmen, die sich auf die sogenannte digitale Agenda beziehen. Gleichzeitig werden die Möglichkeiten zur weltweiten Bekämpfung der Piraterie verbessert. Mit der Richtlinie wird ein Großteil dieser neuen internationalen Verpflichtungen umgesetzt werden.

Die wirtschaftliche, soziale und kulturelle Dimension des Marktes für Urheberrecht und verwandte Schutzrechte

I. der Markt für urheberrechtlich geschützte Waren und Dienstleistungen

Der Markt für urheberrechtlich geschützte Waren und Dienstleistungen umfaßt eine breite Palette von Produkten und Dienstleistungen, die Schutzgegenstände zum Inhalt haben und die von herkömmlichen Erzeugnissen wie Druckerzeugnissen, Filmen, Tonträgern, graphischen und plastischen Kunstwerken, elektronischen Produkten (insbesondere Computerprogrammen) bis hin zu Satelliten- und Kabelsendungen, CD- und Videoverleih, Theater- und Konzertaufführungen, Literatur und Musik, Kunstausstellungen und -auktionen reichen. Die davon betroffenen Rechtsinhaber umfassen Urheber, ausübende Künstler, Tonträgerhersteller, Filmhersteller und Sendeunternehmen.

Umsatz und Wertschöpfung in den durch Urheberrecht und den verwandten Schutzrechten geschützten Bereichen haben in den letzten Jahren erheblich zugenommen, und zwar oft in größerem Umfang als die Wirtschaft insgesamt.

Gefördert wurde das Wachstum der letzten Zeit durch die weitere Verbreitung der Digitaltechnik und durch die Entstehung neuer Verbreitungsarten (z.B. Kabel, Satellit und digitale Übertragung). Diese technologischen Entwicklungen haben zu neuen und leistungsfähigeren Produkten und Dienstleistungen geführt, die als geistiges Eigentum geschützt sind oder geistiges Eigentum enthalten (z.B. VHS, CD-Audio, CD-ROM und CD-I). Die Entwicklung hin zur Konvergenz von audio-visuellem Sektor und den Sektoren Telekommunikation und Informationstechnologie wird dieses Wachstumspotential noch verstärken. Digitalisierte Inhalte jeder Art – seien es Ton, Daten, Bilder, Text oder eine Kombination davon (in Form von Multimedia) – werden über eine Vielzahl von Verbreitungskanälen (Satellit, Kabel, Telefon oder in materieller Form als CD oder CD-ROM) zur Verwertung durch Fernsehen, Computer oder sonstige elektronische Vorrichtungen bereitgestellt.

1. Der Offline-Markt

In Europa und andernorts entfällt auf Offline-Anwendungen (CD-Audio, VHS, CD-ROM, CD-I usw.) nach wie vor der größte Anteil an diesem neuen Markt des geistigen Eigentums, da die Netze noch nicht in der Lage sind, große Datenmengen in angemessener Qualität und Geschwindigkeit zu übertragen. Diese Offline-Produkte dienen in erster Linie Freizeitaktivitäten, Informations- und Bildungszwecken, Finanztransaktionen und Kommunikationszwecken. Marktanalysen zufolge werden die Verbraucher in Europa zunehmend Inhalte nachfragen, die besser auf die kulturelle und sprachliche Vielfalt Europas zugeschnitten sind. Die europäischen Mediengruppen sind bereit, diese Herausforderung anzunehmen. Die traditionellen Verlagshäuser und audiovisuellen Unternehmen werden zunehmend im Bereich des elektronischen Publizierens tätig, dessen Anteil am Verlagsmarkt Schätzungen zufolge bis zum Jahr 2000 5-15% mit einem Wert von 8,8-12,4 Mrd. ECU ausmachen wird. Diese Entwicklungen werden auch den KMU zugute kommen, die im Gegensatz zum US-amerikanischen Markt auf dem europäischen Multimediamarkt bereits in beträchtlichem Umfang vertreten sind.

Noch schneller als bei Online-Einrichtungen entwickeln sich die Kapazitäten der Offline-Träger. Eine DVD kann z.B. je nach Beschaffenheit etwa zehnmal soviel Daten wie eine CD in perfekter Qualität speichern. Die elektronische Unterhaltungsindustrie schätzt, daß bis zum Jahr 2000 25 Mio. DVD-Laufwerke verkauft werden, was den Anbietern von Inhalten erheblichen Raum für die Entwicklung neuer Märkte für Filme und Musik oder Multimedia bietet. Diese neuen Produkte enthalten darüber hinaus interaktive Elemente wie mehrsprachige Dialoge und Untertitel, die für europäische Verbraucher besonders interessant sind. Dank der neuesten Entwicklungen werden die Nutzer nun in der Lage sein, ihre eigene Audio-CD in perfekter Qualität zu bespielen oder Text, Ton oder Filme beliebig oft auf eine unbespielte CD zu kopieren. Hierdurch erhält die Vervielfältigung zum privaten Gebrauch, die derzeit in den meisten Mitgliedstaaten zugelassen ist, eine völlig neue Dimension.

Der digitale Rundfunk, mit dessen Einführung in einigen Mitgliedstaaten bereits 1996 begonnen wurde, wird den Markt für Urheberrecht und verwandte Schutzrechte weiter vergrößern. Er bietet die Möglichkeiten, das Haupthindernis der Analogtechnik, nämlich die Knappheit der Übertragungswege, zu überwinden. Das Ergebnis wird eine sehr viel größere Programmauswahl sein mit häufig sehr spezifischen Angeboten.

2. Der Online-Markt

Online-Anwendungen über Internet oder andere Netzwerke werden nach und nach dem breiten Publikum geöffnet, um die wachsende Nachfrage nach Diensten „auf Abruf“ zu befriedigen. Eine Reihe solcher Dienste „auf Abruf“ werden bereits seit 1995/1996 auf dem europäischen Markt, insbesondere im Vereinigten Königreich, in Frankreich und Deutschland, angeboten, allerdings erst noch als Prototyp oder im Versuchsstadium. Interaktive Dienste auf Abruf zeichnen sich dadurch aus, daß ein in digitaler Form gespeichertes Werk oder ein sonstiger Schutzgegenstand Dritten in der Weise dauerhaft zugänglich gemacht wird, daß Nutzer aus einer Datenbank die von ihnen gewünschten Musikstücke oder Filme anfordern können, die dann über das Internet oder andere Hochgeschwindigkeitsnetze als digitale Signale auf ihren Computer übertragen werden, mit dem diese Signale je nach Nutzungserlaubnis wahrnehmbar gemacht oder abgespeichert werden können. Dienste auf Abruf und bis zu einem gewissen Grad auch Mehrkanal-Rundfunk können Verbraucher veranlassen, auf den Kauf oder die Miete materieller Kopien von z.B. Videos, Büchern, wie z.B. Enzyklopädien, Musikaufnahmen oder einer Kombination dieser Produkte zu verzichten. Angebot und Verbrauch werden so vielfach auf die Wünsche der Verbraucher zugeschnitten sein, einschließlich hinsichtlich der Wahl der Sprache für einen Film oder Hintergrundinformationen zu einem Film, einem Musikstück oder einem Buch.

Angesichts der erheblichen technischen und finanziellen Investitionen, die erforderlich sind, um geschütztes Material (Text, Video, Ton, Produktkombinationen usw.) in guter Qualität interaktiv über elektronische Datenbanken online abrufen zu können, gehen die Meinungen, wann diese Dienste wirklich den Markt durchdringen werden, auseinander. Schätzungen reichen vom Jahr 2000 bis zum Jahr 2005, obwohl der Musikmarkt bereits erfolgreich damit begonnen hat, Musik in sogenannten elektronischen Kaufhäusern („Electronic Shops") zu verkaufen, wobei die Entwicklung in den USA am weitesten fortgeschritten ist. In Europa startete 1995 im Vereinigten Königreich die erste „digitale Online-Jukebox". Andere Online-Music Shops folgten 1997 in Frankreich. Weitere virtuelle Music Shops werden zur Zeit u.a. in Deutschland und im Vereinigten Königreich aufgebaut.

Diese Entwicklung bedeutet allerdings nicht, daß die Analogtechnik in Kürze verschwinden wird. Alle Marktteilnehmer räumen ein, daß die Analogtechnik noch einige Zeit – Schätzungen zufolge zwischen 5 und 15 Jahren – neben der Digitaltechnik fortbestehen wird. Dies ist u.a. darauf zurückzuführen, daß die Herstellung von digitalen Produkten und Dienstleistungen und die entsprechende Hardware im allgemeinen nach wie vor sehr kapitalintensiv ist.

II. Chancen und Risiken

Mit den neuen Möglichkeiten zur Schaffung und Verwertung geistigen Eigentums über die Landesgrenzen hinaus und sogar weltweit sind potentiell beträchtliche wirtschaftliche, soziale und kulturelle Vorteile verbunden. Sie dürften substantielle Investitionen in Kreativität und Innovation einschließlich der Netzinfrastruktur bewirken, die ihrerseits zu Wachstum und Wettbewerbsfähigkeit der europäischen Industrie und zu höheren Marktanteilen beitragen sollten, und zwar sowohl bei den Inhalten und der Informationstechnologie als auch allgemeiner in weiten Teilen der Industrien und des Kultursektors. Hierdurch werden gleichzeitig neue Beschäftigungsmöglichkeiten entstehen. Das neue Umfeld wird voraussichtlich gemeinschaftsweit zu einem größeren Angebot an geschützten Inhalten beitragen, die von einem dynamischen Markt und effizienten Vertriebskanälen zu erschwinglichen Preisen für professionelle Nutzer oder die breite Öffentlichkeit bereitgestellt werden, sofern ein angemessener Schutz und ausreichend große Märkte gewährleistet werden können. Zu erwarten ist auch ein breiteres Spektrum an spezialisierten kulturellen Inhalten, die die sprachliche und kulturelle Vielfalt Europas besser zum Ausdruck bringen und den Kulturaustausch in Europa fördern.

Das zunehmende Online-Angebot von Werken und sonstigen Schutzgegenständen in digitaler Form schafft jedoch beträchtliche neue Risiken für Pirateriedelikte in großem Umfang, die bereits in der Offline-Umgebung in zahlreichen Mitgliedstaaten für weite Teile der Urheberrechtsindustrie große Probleme bereiten, insbesondere im Bereich der Software, der Musikaufnahmen sowie der audiovisuellen und Videoproduktionen. Diese Situation bedeutet nicht nur einen Schaden für den wirtschaftlichen und kulturellen Wohlstand, sondern auch für das Funktionieren des Binnenmarkts. Die unerlaubte Bereitstellung von Computerprogrammen, Tonträgern, Lichtbildern, Videoclips oder heimlichen Mitschnitten von Livekonzerten auf Websites der neuen Datennetze verschaffen heute schon Millionen von Verbrauchern in der ganzen Welt unrechtmäßig Zugang zu urheberrechtlich geschütztem Material. Häufig kopieren unautorisierte Websites Material von regulären Websites, beispielsweise des Musikmarkts. Einige der Websites werden von Piraten betrieben, die unerlaubt hergestellte Waren wie CDs oder Tonbänder zu gewerblichen Zwecken an gutgläubige Kunden veräußern. Obwohl das geschützte Material in vielen Fällen ohne Entgelt rechtswidrig zugänglich gemacht wird, kann der wirtschaftliche Schaden für Rechtsinhaber und Rechtsverwerter ebenso groß sein wie im Fall der (gewerblich betriebenen) Piraterie. Der Urheberrechtsindustrie entgehen bereits heute durch die unautorisierte Übertragung geschützten Materials über Datennetze erhebliche Einnahmen, und es mehren sich die Bedenken, daß die weitere Zunahme der illegalen Online-Übertragung von geschütztem Material den legalen Online-Verkauf ernsthaft gefährden könnte.

Das neue Umfeld erfordert eine weitergehende Rechtsangleichung

I. Rechtsetzungsbedarf

Es bedarf dringend geeigneter Maßnahmen, um ein günstiges Umfeld zu schaffen, das Kreativität und Investitionen fördert, und zwar sowohl im Hinblick auf die traditionellen Märkte im Bereich des geistigen Eigentums als auch die neu entstehenden. Rechtssicherheit in Form eines transparenten, modernen und effektiven Schutzes des geistigen Eigentums wird hier eine wichtige Rolle spielen. Ohne einen adäquaten, effektiven Urheberrechtsrahmen würde die Schaffung von Inhalten in der neuen Multimedia-Umgebung an Boden verlieren oder durch Piraterie zu Lasten der Urheber, ausübenden Künstler und Hersteller von geschütztem Material ausgebeutet werden. Dies hätte unweigerlich sowohl für die benachbarten Wirtschaftszweige als auch für die Nutzer von geschütztem Material wie Online- und Offline-Diensteanbieter und vor allem für die Verbraucher negative Auswirkungen, da diesen unter Umständen weniger oder geringerwertige Inhalte zur Verfügung stünden.

II. Weitergehende Rechtsangleichung auf Gemeinschaftsebene im Bereich des Urheberrechts und der verwandten Schutzrecht als Gebot des Binnenmarktes

Infolge der neuen Technologien hat sich die Verwertung von literarischen, musikalischen oder audiovisuellen Werken und sonstiger Schutzgegenstände wie Tonträgern oder aufgezeichneten Darbietungen über die Landesgrenzen hinaus bereits deutlich erhöht. Diese Entwicklung soll und wird sich zweifellos verstärken. Die bestehenden Unterschiede im Rechtsschutz zwischen den Mitgliedstaaten werden daher ein größeres Gewicht erhalten. Weitere Divergenzen könnten auftreten, wenn die Mitgliedstaaten die Regelungen ihrer Urheber- und verwandten Schutzrechte einseitig den neuen technologischen Entwicklungen anpaßten. Dies könnte zu Handelsverzerrungen vor allem in der Form führen, daß Online-Dienste nur noch in Mitgliedstaaten mit einem geringeren Rechtsschutz angeboten würden. Besteht in den Mitgliedstaaten kein angemessener, vergleichbarer Rechtsschutz für Urheberrechte und verwandte Schutzrechte oder mangelt es an Rechtssicherheit, so könnten die Rechtsinhaber und die Verwerter der Rechte zögern, die Verwertung ihres Materials online zu erlauben, zumindest in den Mitgliedstaaten ohne oder mit einem weniger wirksamen Rechtsschutz. Dies könnte für eine tragfähige Entwicklung der Informationsgesellschaft in Europa mehrere Stolpersteine im Weg belassen. Um einen echten Binnenmarkt für urheberrechtlich geschützte Waren und Dienstleistungen zu schaffen, ist daher ein stärker harmonisierter Rechtsschutz im Bereich des Urheberrechts und der verwandten Schutzrechte erforderlich.

Ein Binnenmarkt, der sich durch vergleichbare effektive und transparente Schutzbestimmungen über die nationalen Grenzen hinaus auszeichnet, kommt nicht nur den Rechtsinhabern zugute, sondern auch den Nutzern und Investoren (z.B. Diensteanbietern). Er trägt zu angemessenen, vergleichbaren und sicheren Investitionsbedingungen und Rechtssicherheit in allen Mitgliedstaaten bei. Rechtsinhaber und jene, die geschütztes Material verwenden, werden so in die Lage versetzt werden, die grenzüberschreitende Verwertung von urheberrechtlich geschützten Waren und Dienstleistungen weiter voranzutreiben. Dies ist für die Entwicklung der Informationsgesellschaft in Europa und insbesondere für den elektronischen Geschäftsverkehr entscheidend, da die Verfügbarkeit geschützten Materials in den Netzen, wie vorstehend beschrieben (vgl. Kapitel 1, I.), nach wie vor hinter der potentiellen Nachfrage zurückbleibt. Gleiche Bedingungen über nationale Grenzen hinaus werden merklich zur Vielfalt der Inhalte und zur Nutzung von Größenvorteilen bei der Verbreitung der neuen Produkte und Dienstleistungen beitragen, die für die Realisierung der Informationsgesellschaft unabdingbar sind.

Wie die Kommission in ihrer Mitteilung ausgeführt hat, muß der Rechtsschutz auf Gemeinschaftsebene in folgenden Bereichen wegen ihrer Bedeutung für den Binnenmarkt umgehend gesetzlich geregelt werden:

- Vervielfältigungsrecht
- Recht der öffentlichen Wiedergabe
- technologische Maßnahmen und Informationen für die Wahrnehmung der Rechte

– Verbreitungsrecht bezüglich materieller Vervielfältigungsstücke einschließlich seiner Erschöpfung.

Die Mitteilung befaßte sich auch mit anderen Themen (in bezug auf digitale Rundfunkübertragungen, anwendbares Recht, Wahrnehmung der Rechte und den Schutz der Urheberpersönlichkeitsrechte). Diese Themen, die keinesfalls weniger wichtig für die Verwertung von Urheberrechten in der Informationsgesellschaft sind als die vorgenannten vorrangigen Themen, erfordern weitere Überlegung oder Maßnahmen, bevor politische Entscheidungen getroffen werden können. Bezüglich einiger dieser Themen bedarf es weiterer Untersuchungen der Marktentwicklungen, bevor eine politische Entscheidung über ihre weitere Behandlung getroffen werden kann. Dies trifft insbesondere auf das Thema des Schutzes der Urheberpersönlichkeitsrechte im Zusammenhang mit der Informationsgesellschaft zu, wo eine Initiative für die Harmonisierung vorbereitet werden könnte, sobald dies notwendig erscheint. Andere Themen bedürfen möglicherweise eher der Klärung und Erläuterung (wie z.B. der Bereich des anwendbaren Rechts und der Rechtedurchsetzung). Entsprechende Arbeiten sind schon deutlich fortgeschritten.

Ziel dieses Vorschlags ist es, den in Europa traditionell hohen Urheberrechtsschutz aufrechtzuerhalten und gleichzeitig eine gerechte Abwägung zwischen den Interessen und Rechten der verschiedenen Kategorien von Rechtsinhabern sowie zwischen Rechtsinhabern und Nutzern von geschütztem Material sicherzustellen. Der Vorschlag führt nicht zu radikalen Veränderungen des bestehenden rechtlichen Rahmen des Binnenmarkts im Bereich des Urheberrechts und der verwandten Schutzrechte. Geändert hat sich nur die Umgebung, in der Werke und sonstige Schutzgegenstände geschaffen und verwertet werden, nicht die dem Urheberrecht zugrundeliegenden Konzepte.

Seit den WIPO-Verhandlungen wird die Haftungsfrage im Bereich des Urheberrechts und der verwandten Schutzrechte, d.h. die Frage, wer für etwaige Verstöße haftet, intensiv erörtert. Dieser Vorschlag enthält zwar eine allgemeine Bestimmung über die Durchsetzung der Rechte des geistigen Eigentums, aber keine eigentliche Regelung der Haftungsfrage. Haftungsvorschriften für Urheberrechtsverletzungen gibt es bereits auf nationaler Ebene. Sie gelten im Prinzip auch für den digitalen Bereich. Dies wird durch die aktuelle Rechtsprechung auf Ebene der Mitgliedstaaten bestätigt. Einige Mitgliedstaaten setzen sich für die Einführung einer sogenannten Selbstkontrolle auf der Basis von Verhaltensregeln ein, um sowohl gegen rechtswidrige, schädliche Inhalte in Netzen als auch gegen Verletzungen des geistigen Eigentums vorzugehen. Diese vom Markt ausgehenden Mechanismen werden von den Beteiligten selbst hervorgebracht.

Wie bereits während der WIPO-Verhandlungen festgestellt wurde, ist die Haftung ein horizontales Thema, das nicht nur für das Urheberrecht und die verwandten Schutzrechte relevant ist, sondern auch für eine Reihe weiterer Rechtsbereiche und Sachverhalte, die vom Markenrecht über irreführende Werbung bis hin zu übler Nachrede und obszönen Inhalten reichen. Es ist daher geboten, die Rechtslage für die einzelnen Beteiligten (vor allem Zugangsanbieter, Diensteanbieter usw.) auf der Grundlage einer horizontalen, eigenständigen Regelung im Rahmen des Binnenmarkt-Rechts zu klären. Im Rechtsetzungsprogramm der Kommission für 1998 werden bereits Vorschläge für die Schaffung eines Rechtsrahmens für den elektronischen Geschäftsverkehr und für andere elektronische Dienste angekündigt, die verschiedene rechtliche Aspekte in bezug auf die Dienste in der Informationsgesellschaft, einschließlich des elektronischen Geschäftsverkehrs, harmonisieren werden. In diesem Zusammenhang ist eine Richtlinie, die unter anderem die Fragen der Haftung klären soll, für die ersten Monate des Jahres 1998 geplant. Die Kommission hat bereits mit entsprechenden Vorarbeiten begonnen, die unter anderem eine Studie umfassen. Im Mittelpunkt der Arbeiten steht die Frage, welche Regelungen für eine Anwendung auf Gemeinschaftsebene angemessen sind. Ziel ist es, die verschiedenen Aufgaben und Tätigkeiten unterschiedlicher Internet-Akteure zu definieren und ihre Haftung, insbesondere für fremde Inhalte, zu klären. Diese Initiative sollte, soweit möglich, innerhalb eines ähnlichen Zeitrahmens wie diese Richtlinie in Kraft treten.

Um eine Regelung zu finden, die den Interessen aller Beteiligten gerecht wird, ist nicht nur der horizontale Charakter der Haftungsfrage angemessen zu berücksichtigen, sondern auch das Erfordernis eines Gleichgewichts zwischen den Rechten und Interessen der Beteiligten, die Rechtsanschauungen und Rechtstraditionen der Mitgliedstaaten und nicht zuletzt auch die Besonderheiten, die Rechtsverletzungen im Bereich des Urheberrechts und der verwandten Schutzrechte gegenüber anderen Bereichen gegebenenfalls aufweisen.

Zwar haben sich infolge der zunehmenden Verbreitung der Digitaltechnik die Möglichkeiten zur Verwertung von Werken und sonstigen Schutzgegenständen mittels Waren und Dienstleistungen, die über die Landesgrenzen hinaus gehandelt werden, erhöht, doch hat sich an der innewohnenden Territorialitätsbezogenheit der Urheber- und der verwandten Schutzrechte, so wie sie in den internationalen Übereinkommen geregelt ist, nichts geändert. Die Rechte werden für ein bestimmtes Land nach den dort geltenden Vorschriften gewährt. Als allgemeine Regel gilt, daß für Verwertungshandlungen, einschließlich der Rechtsverletzungen, die nationale Rechtsordnung maßgebend ist, auf deren Grundlage das betreffende Recht gewährt wurde und deren Schutz in Anspruch genommen wird. Dies gilt auch für grenzübergreifende Verwertungshandlungen mit der Folge, daß das Recht mehrerer Länder gleichzeitig anwendbar sein kann.

Dieses Problem wurde im Rahmen der Konsultationen zum Grünbuch erörtert. Wie in der Mitteilung vom 20. November 1996 erläutert wird, wurde eine gesetzliche Regelung auf Gemeinschaftsebene zum jetzigen Zeitpunkt nicht als zweckmäßig angesehen. Es wurde mehrheitlich der Wunsch nach Beibehaltung der bestehenden Regelungen geäußert. Eine Rechtsangleichung dahingehend, daß als Ursprungsland einer digitalen Übertragung das Land gilt, in dem die Übertragung stattfindet, und daß dessen Recht allein Anwendung finden soll, wurde nachdrücklich abgelehnt. Begründet wurde diese Ablehnung zum einen damit, daß digitale Übertragungen technisch so beschaffen sind, daß es problematisch ist, einen einzigen Ort zu bestimmen, von dem die Übertragung ausgeht. Dies unterscheidet sie vom grenzübergreifenden Satellitenrundfunk, wo man sich auf Gemeinschaftsebene für diese Lösung entschieden hat. Zum anderen birgt die Anwendung des „Ursprungslandprinzips“ die Gefahr, daß Rechtsinhaber keinen angemessenen Schutz beanspruchen können, vor allem bei Übertragungen aus Drittländern. Dies gilt auch innerhalb der Gemeinschaft, solange die einschlägigen Gesetze bezüglich der Rechte und ihrer Verwertung nicht fast vollständig harmonisiert sind (z.B. Bestimmung des originären Rechtsinhabers, Rechtsübertragung, Schutzumfang einschließlich der Schranken und Ausnahmen des Rechts). Auch könnte auf Gemeinschaftsebene die Anwendung des Ursprungslandprinzips zu einer Verlagerung der angebotenen Dienste in das Land mit dem niedrigsten Schutzniveau für Urheberrecht und verwandte Schutzrechte führen. Dies wiederum hätte Wettbewerbsverzerrungen im Binnenmarkt zur Folge und würde den entsprechenden Regelungen des geistigen Eigentums in anderen Ländern durch die Verringerung des tatsächlichen Werts der gewährten Rechte einen schweren Schaden zufügen. Dies könnte starke negative Auswirkungen auf das Funktionieren des Binnenmarkts wie auch auf Kreativität, Wachstum und Wettbewerb haben. In der Mitteilung zum Urheberrecht vom November1996 wurde diesem Problem ein eigener Abschnitt gewidmet.

III. Notwendigkeit der Erfüllung internationaler Verpflichtungen

Binnenmarkterwägungen waren Ausgangspunkt dieses Vorschlags und bilden nach wie vor seine Grundlage. Die Europäische Gemeinschaft kann es sich jedoch nicht leisten, sich nur auf intern ausgerichtete Initiativen zu beschränken. Die Märkte für die Verwertung geschützten Materials sind heute mehr denn je eng miteinander verzahnt. Dies gilt auch für einen großen Markt wie den Binnenmarkt im Verhältnis zu Drittländern. Je internationaler Kommunikation wird und je mehr Sprachbarrieren überwunden werden, um so mehr werden

Werke und sonstige Schutzgegenstände über Printmedien, Rundfunk oder weltweite Online-Daten-netze verbreitet. Vor allem die verstärkte Verwertung des geistigen Eigentums im Online-Bereich, kennt keine nationalen oder regionalen Grenzen. International vereinbarte Mindestschutzstandards sind daher heute wichtiger denn je.

Der internationale Schutz des Urheberrechts und der verwandten Schutzrechte ist Gegenstand der drei bedeutendsten multilateralen Übereinkommen: der Berner Übereinkunft zum Schutz von Werken der Literatur und Kunst (Pariser Fassung von 1971), des Rom-Abkommens über den Schutz der ausübenden Künstler, der Hersteller von Tonträgern und der Sendeunternehmen (1961) und des Übereinkommens über handelsbezogene Aspekte der Rechte des geistigen Eigentums (TRIPs, 1995). Die Diplomatische Konferenz der WIPO vom Dezember 1996 führte zur Annahme zweier neuer Verträge im Bereich des geistigen Eigentums: des WIPO-Urheberrechtsvertrags und des WIPO-Vertrags über Darbietungen und Tonträger. Die beiden Verträge, die von über 100 Ländern angenommen wurden, markieren einen wichtigen Schritt nach vorn auf dem Weg zu einem internationalen Schutz des Urheberrechts und der verwandten Schutzrechte und verbessern ganz wesentlich die Möglichkeiten zur Bekämpfung der Piraterie. Sie enthalten darüber hinaus eine Reihe von Vorschriften, die die Grundlage für einheitliche internationale Bedingungen im Bereich des Urheberrechts und der verwandten Schutzrechte im Digitalzeitalter bilden. Die Europäische Gemeinschaft kann selbst Vertragspartei werden. Jetzt kommt es darauf an, daß diese beiden neuen Verträge so schnell wie möglich in Kraft treten. Die Gemeinschaft und die meisten Mitgliedstaaten haben die Verträge bereits unterzeichnet, und die Verhandlungen zur Ratifizierung der Verträge durch die Gemeinschaft und die Mitgliedstaaten sind inzwischen im Gange.

Die vier vorrangigen Regelungsbereiche, die Gegenstand dieses Richtlinienvorschlags sind, entsprechen bzw. sind sogar weitgehend identisch mit den Kernbestimmungen der neuen internationalen Verpflichtungen, wie sie in den beiden neuen WIPO-Verträgen festgelegt sind. Die Umsetzung all jener neuen internationalen Verpflichtungen, die sich auf Gemeinschaftsebene mit Hilfe des vorliegenden Richtlinienvorschlags zufriedenstellender verwirklichen lassen dürfte, ist somit als weiterer, wenn nicht gar hauptsächlicher Grund für diesen Vorschlag hinzugekommen. Die Verpflichtungen aus den neuen WIPO-Verträgen werden mit dieser Richtlinie unter Berücksichtigung des gemeinschaftsrechtlichen Besitzstands und der Anforderungen des Binnenmarkts umgesetzt und in das Gemeinschaftsrecht integriert.

Die Harmonisierungsbereiche im Einzelnen

I. Vervielfältigungsrecht

1. Bisherige Rechtslage

Das Vervielfältigungsrecht gilt seit jeher als Grundpfeiler des Urheberrechts. Es findet sich in praktisch allen einzelstaatlichen Gesetzen und internationalen Übereinkommen und wurde auf Gemeinschaftsebene, insbesondere für Computerprogramme, Datenbanken und verwandte Schutzrechte, teilweise harmonisiert.

In allen Mitgliedstaaten ist ein ausschließliches Vervielfältigungsrecht vorgesehen. Die einzelstaatlichen Urheberrechtsgesetze sind allerdings, was den Umfang dieses Rechts betrifft, extrem unterschiedlich. Es herrscht insbesondere im Hinblick auf das neue elektronische Umfeld beträchtliche Unsicherheit darüber, welche Vervielfältigungshandlungen im einzelnen dem Schutzrecht unterworfen sind. Die meisten Gesetze enthalten eine weit gefaßte Definition der geschützten Vervielfältigungshandlungen und erfassen damit auch Handlungen wie die Digitalisierung eines Werks oder Handlungen wie das Herauf- oder Herunterladen eines Werks von oder in den Arbeitsspeicher eines Computers. Andere Gesetze enthalten zwar auch eine weit gefaßte Definition, setzen den Schwerpunkt jedoch noch immer auf die materielle Vervielfältigung, was zu einer gewissen Rechtsunsicherheit in bezug auf die Einbeziehung elektronischer Vervielfältigungshandlungen allgemein führt. Darüber hinaus ist noch weitgehend ungeklärt, wie vorübergehende Vervielfältigungshandlungen zu behandeln sind, so daß in bezug auf die Verwertung von Schutzgegenständen im elektronischen Umfeld erhebliche Rechtsunsicherheit besteht.

Der Umfang des Vervielfältigungsrechts wird auch durch die Schranken und Ausnahmen, mit denen dieses Recht versehen ist, bestimmt. Diese Ausnahmen und Schranken sind in den Rechtsvorschriften der Mitgliedstaaten in vielen Fällen unterschiedlich ausgestaltet. Einige Mitgliedstaaten (Vereinigtes Königreich und Irland) sehen in ihrer Gesetzgebung beispielsweise eine allgemeine Ausnahme („fair dealing") für Forschungszwecke, für private Studien, Rezensionen und für die aktuelle Berichterstattung vor. Ähnliche Ausnahmen gibt es auch in anderen Mitgliedstaaten, sind dort aber enger gefaßt (z.B. Schweden, Belgien, Deutschland und Griechenland). Ausnahmen für Bildungs- und wissenschaftliche Zwecke bilden eine andere wichtige Kategorie, die in den Rechtsvorschriften der meisten Mitgliedstaaten enthalten ist, in ihrem Anwendungsbereich allerdings stark variiert. In einigen Mitgliedstaaten ist das Vervielfältigen ganzer Werke zu Bildungszwecken gestattet, während in anderen Ländern nur bestimmte Arten von Werken oder Teile davon als Anschauungsmaterial für den Schulunterricht und für Prüfungszwecke vervielfältigt werden dürfen. Noch uneinheitlicher stellt sich die Lage bei Ausnahmen zugunsten von der Öffentlichkeit zugänglichen Einrichtungen wie Bibliotheken und Archiven dar, da es in diesem Bereich keine international vertraglichen Mindestvorschriften gibt. In bestimmten Mitgliedstaaten wie Deutschland, Belgien und Frankreich gibt es zwar keine Sonderausnahmen für Bibliotheken, doch können diese Einrichtungen die allgemeinen Ausnahmen zugunsten des privaten Gebrauchs oder der Nutzung zu Bildungszwecken in Anspruch nehmen. Andere Mitgliedstaaten wie das Vereinigte Königreich, Österreich, Schweden, Finnland, Dänemark, Portugal und Griechenland sehen zugunsten der Nutzung von Schutzgegenständen durch Bibliotheken und Archive besondere Ausnahmen vor, doch bestehen auch hier große Unterschiede, und die Verwendung von digitalisiertem Material wird hiervon nicht unbedingt erfaßt. Was die Verwendung von digitalisiertem Material durch Bibliotheken – sowohl online als auch offline – anbelangt, so bestehen in einer Reihe von Mitgliedstaaten, insbesondere im Vereinigten Königreich, wo die Privilegien der Bibliotheken am weitesten entwickelt sind, bereits Initiativen, um flexiblere vertragliche Lösungen zu finden.

In fast allen Mitgliedstaaten ist die Vervielfältigung von Tonaufnahmen und audiovisuellem Material für den privaten Gebrauch vom ausschließlichen Vervielfältigungsrecht ausgenommen. Diese Ausnahme wird in erster Linie damit begründet, daß sich das Ausschließlichkeitsrecht in diesem Bereich praktisch nicht durchsetzen läßt und daß dies aus Gründen des Schutzes der Privatsphäre auch nicht wünschenswert ist. In Anbetracht der erheblichen wirtschaftlichen Bedeutung der privaten Vervielfältigung von urheberrechtlich geschütztem Material sehen 11 der 15 Mitgliedstaaten keine „freie Werknutzung" vor, sondern eine „gesetzliche Lizenz", d.h. die Rechtsinhaber, deren Ausschließlichkeitsrecht genommen wird, werden mit einem Vergütungsanspruch („Abgabensystem") entschädigt. Diese Systeme sind in Art und Umfang in den Mitgliedstaaten sehr unterschiedlich ausgestaltet.

In den Rechtsvorschriften der Mitgliedstaaten über die Vervielfältigung zum privaten Gebrauch wird in der Regel nicht zwischen Analog- und Digitaltechnik unterschieden. Derzeit sieht nur ein Mitgliedstaat (Dänemark) keine Ausnahme für private Vervielfältigungen vor, wenn es sich bei dem Vervielfältigungsgegenstand um geschütztes Material handelt, das in digitalen Medien verkörpert ist. Dabei kommt es nicht darauf an, ob die Vervielfältigungsvorrichtung digitaler oder analoger Art ist. Die vorliegenden Zahlen deuten darauf hin, daß die analoge private Vervielfältigung neben den neuen Digitaltechniken zumindest für die nächsten fünf bis fünfzehn Jahre ein wichtiger Markt bleiben wird.

Die meisten Mitgliedstaaten haben in den letzten Jahren auch eine Ausnahme vom Vervielfältigungsrecht für photomechanische Vervielfältigungen (Reprographie) in Kombination mit einem Vergütungsanspruch eingeführt. Die Begründung für diese Ausnahme ist ähnlich wie bei der privaten Vervielfältigung von Tonaufnahmen und audiovisuellem Material. Bestehende Abgabensysteme unterscheiden sich nur geringfügig.

Die Rechtsvorschriften fast aller Mitgliedstaaten enthalten diverse andere Ausnahmen und Schranken des Vervielfältigungsrechts sowie des Verbreitungsrechts und des Rechts der öffentlichen Wiedergabe, allerdings in weit begrenzterem Umfang. Hierzu zählen genau definierte, aber stark voneinander abweichende Ausnahmen für Bildungszwecke und/oder wissenschaftliche Zwecke sowie für Bibliotheken und Archive. Daneben gibt es in vielen einzelstaatlichen Rechtsvorschriften eine Fülle anderer Ausnahmen, die zumindest im Hinblick auf das herkömmliche analoge Umfeld wirtschaftlich weniger ins Gewicht fallen. Dabei handelt es sich beispielsweise um Ausnahmen für kurze Auszüge aus der Berichterstattung über Tagesereignisse, Rezensionen, um Ausnahmen zugunsten von behinderten Menschen, für Zwecke der öffentlichen Sicherheit oder für Verwaltungs- oder Gerichtsverfahren.

Auf Gemeinschaftsebene wurde das Vervielfältigungsrecht bereits für zwei Werkgattungen harmonisiert, und zwar für Computerprogramme und für Datenbanken. Diese Richtlinien definieren die Vervielfältigungshandlungen und die zulässigen Ausnahmen vom Vervielfältigungsrecht der betreffenden Urheber. Die Definition der Vervielfältigungshandlungen ist in diesen Richtlinien weit gefaßt und schließt auch vorübergehende Vervielfältigungen ein. Die zulässigen Ausnahmen vom Vervielfältigungsrecht sind erschöpfend aufgeführt. Die Vervielfältigung von Computerprogrammen und elektronischen Datenbanken für private Zwecke ist nicht zulässig. Für Inhaber von verwandten Schutzrechten, d.h. ausübende Künstler, Tonträgerhersteller, Filmhersteller und Sendeunternehmen, wurde das Vervielfältigungsrecht durch die Vermietrechts-Richtlinie harmonisiert. Der Umfang dieses Rechts ist allerdings in dieser Richtlinie nicht genau definiert, und es fehlt an einer harmonisierten Regelung der Ausnahmen.

Auf internationaler Ebene wird das ausschließliche Vervielfältigungsrecht Urhebern, ausübenden Künstlern, Tonträgerherstellern und Sendeunternehmen auf der Grundlage der Berner Übereinkunft, des Rom-Abkommens bzw. des WTO/TRIPs-Übereinkommens gewährt. Angesichts der weit gefaßten Formulierung dieses Rechts in der Berner Übereinkunft wird allgemein davon ausgegangen, daß das den Urhebern in dieser Übereinkunft garantierte Vervielfältigungsrecht alle Vervielfältigungsverfahren erfaßt, und zwar einschließlich elektronischer Verfahren, die für die menschlichen Sinne möglicherweise nicht wahrnehmbar sind. Was als Vervielfältigungshandlung in bezug auf verwandte Schutzrechte anzusehen ist, wird im Rom-Abkommen und im WTO/TRIPs-Übereinkommen allerdings nicht definiert.

Die Frage, ob der Umfang des Vervielfältigungsrechts angepaßt oder präzisiert werden sollte, um elektronische Vervielfältigungen ausdrücklich einzubeziehen, war Gegenstand der Diskussionen im Rahmen der Verhandlungen unter der Schirmherrschaft der WIPO, welche zur Annahme der beiden neuen WIPO-Verträge führten. Was die Definition der Vervielfältigungshandlung anbelangt, insbesondere in bezug auf vorübergehende oder zufällige Vervielfältigungen im elektronischen Umfeld, so wurden neue Bestimmungen für die Rechte der Urheber nicht als notwendig angesehen, da dieses Recht inhaltlich nicht durch den Verweis auf bestimmte Technologien oder Formate beschränkt ist. Die Definition des Artikels 9 Absatz 1 der Berner Übereinkunft wurde auch für das digitale Umfeld als angemessen angesehen und dementsprechend in die Verpflichtungen des WCT aufgenommen (vgl. Artikel 1 Absatz 4 WCT). In einer Erklärung der Diplomatischen Konferenz, auf der die neuen WIPO-Verträge angenommen worden sind, wird zudem präzisiert, daß die bestehenden internationalen Vorschriften ausreichend weit gefaßt sind, um auch Vervielfältigungen im digitalen Umfeld einzuschließen. Die Definition des Vervielfältigungsrechts für ausübende Künstler und Tronträgerhersteller (vgl. Artikel 7 und 11 WPPT) stützt sich ebenfalls auf die weit gefaßte Definition des Artikels 9 Absatz 1 Berner Übereinkunft. Der Wortlaut ist präziser als die entsprechenden Bestimmungen im Rom-Abkommen und im WTO/TRIPs-Übereinkommen.

Auf internationaler Ebene bestehen unterschiedliche Schranken des Vervielfältigungsrechts. Die Berner Übereinkunft enthält diverse verbindliche Ausnahmen (für Tagesneuigkeiten, vermischte Nachrichten und für Zitate) sowie mehrere fakultative Ausnahmen, insbesondere zu Informations- und Bildungszwecken. Diese Ausnahmen gelten für die meisten Rechte und lassen nur die Nutzungsformen zu, die durch den mit der Ausnahme beabsichtigten spezifischen Zweck gerechtfertigt sind und „anständigen Gepflogenheiten“ (fair practice) entsprechen. Artikel 9 Absatz 2 Berner Übereinkunft läßt darüber hinaus Schranken des Vervielfältigungsrechts „in gewissen Sonderfällen“ zu unter der Voraussetzung, daß eine solche Vervielfältigung „weder die normale Auswertung des Werks beeinträchtigt noch die berechtigten Interessen des Urhebers unzumutbar verletzt“. Eine Schranke des Vervielfältigungsrechts ist nur dann gerechtfertigt, wenn alle drei Voraussetzungen kumulativ vorliegen („Drei-Stufen-Test“). Der Umfang des Vervielfältigungsrechts für Urheber einschließlich der Ausnahmen von diesem Recht wurden im WTO/TRIPs-Übereinkommen bestätigt. Darüber hinaus müssen nach diesem Übereinkommen alle Ausnahmen, die für Urheberrechte gelten, dem „Drei-Stufen-Test“ genügen.

Die im Rom-Abkommen und im WTO/TRIPs-Übereinkommen enthaltenen Schranken der verwandten Schutzrechte sind in gewissem Maße umfassender. Einige Ausnahmen vom Vervielfältigungsrecht finden sich in beiden Texten, insbesondere hinsichtlich des privaten Gebrauchs, der Verwendung kurzer Auszüge anläßlich der Berichterstattung über Tagesereignisse, der ephemeren Aufzeichnung durch ein Sendeunternehmen und der ausschließlichen Verwendung zu Zwecken des Unterrichts oder der wissenschaftlichen Forschung. Auch andere Schranken sind zulässig, soweit sie den Schranken entsprechen, die im innerstaatlichen Recht für Urheberrechte gelten. Der für die Schranken geltende „Drei-Stufen-Test“ (Artikel 9 Absatz 2 Berner Übereinkunft, Artikel 13 WTO/TRIPs) wurde für die Inhaber von verwandten Schutzrechten nach dem Rom-Abkommen oder dem WTO/TRIPs-Übereinkommen nicht vorgesehen.

In den beiden neuen WIPO-Verträgen wird davon abgesehen, besondere Schranken und Ausnahmen aufzuführen. Allerdings wird der „Drei-Stufen-Test“ nach Artikel 9 Absatz 2 Berner Übereinkunft und Artikel 13 WTO/TRIPs, auf alle Ausnahmen der durch den Vertrag garantierten Urheberrechte angewandt (Artikel 10 WCT) sowie auf alle Ausnahmen von den Rechten der ausübenden Künstler und Tonträgerhersteller (Artikel 16 WPPT). Diese Bestimmungen sollen nach allgemeiner Auffassung den Vertragsparteien erlauben, die bestehenden Ausnahmen und Schranken auf digitale Technologien anzuwenden und für den digitalen Bereich geeignete neue Ausnahmen und Schranken zu formulieren, sofern diese mit den Vorgaben der Berner Übereinkunft vereinbar sind. Es versteht sich von selbst, daß die sich aus den neuen Verträgen ergebenden Verpflichtungen in jedem Fall einzuhalten sind. Die beiden Verträge enthalten wichtige Klarstellungen und weitere Vorgaben, die von den Vertragsparteien beachtet werden müssen. Für die Definition und Anwendung der Schranken wird vor allem der sogenannte Drei-Stufen-Test ein wichtiger Maßstab sein. Hieraus folgt, daß einige der Schranken, insbesondere auch zum Vervielfältigungsrecht, die auf Gemeinschaftsebene oder auf Ebene der Mitgliedstaaten bestehen, geändert und den neuen WIPO-Verträgen angepaßt werden müssen.

2. Handlungsbedarf

Eine gemeinsame Grundlage sowohl für die Definition der Vervielfältigungshandlung als auch für die Ausnahmen des Vervielfältigungsrechts ist für das reibungslose Funktionieren des Binnenmarkts unabdingbar. Die zunehmend grenzüberschreitende Verwertung von Informations- und Unterhaltungsprodukten und -dienstleistungen einschließlich urheberrechtlich geschützter Werke und sonstiger Schutzgegenstände führt dazu, daß beträchtliche Unterschiede zwischen Ausnahmen und Schranken des ausschließlichen Vervielfältigungsrechts, wie sie derzeit nach den Rechtsvorschriften der Mitgliedstaaten zulässig sind, beseitigt werden müssen, da sie der Erreichung eines Binnenmarkts für diese Produkte und Dienstleistungen entgegenstünden.

Die Gemeinschaft muß auch deshalb tätig werden, um den in den neuen WIPO-Verträgen enthaltenen Verpflichtungen nachzukommen. Wenn auf Gemeinschaftsebene jetzt nichts getan wird, um vorbehaltene Vervielfältigungshandlungen zu definieren und zulässige Ausnahmen anzugleichen, besteht die Gefahr, daß die Mitgliedstaaten im Alleingang unterschiedliche oder sogar abweichende Strategien beim Vervielfältigungsrecht verfolgen, die die Verwirklichung des Binnenmarkts durch die Vertiefung der derzeitigen Disparitäten noch stärker aufs Spiel setzten.

II. Recht der öffentlichen Wiedergabe einschließlich des Rechts des Zugänglichmachens von Werken und sonstigen Schutzgegenständen

1. Bisherige Rechtslage

Der technische Fortschritt hat es möglich gemacht, Werke und sonstige Schutzgegenstände in einer neuen Art und Weise zugänglich zu machen, die sich von den herkömmlichen Verwertungsmethoden erheblich unterscheidet. Dies gilt insbesondere für die Online-Verwertung des geistigen Eigentums über Datennetze, insbesondere „auf Abruf“. Diese „Übertragungen auf Abruf“ zeichnen sich dadurch aus, daß ein in digitaler Form gespeichertes Werk oder ein sonstiger Schutzgegenstand Dritten interaktiv in der Weise zugänglich gemacht wird, daß sie darauf Zugriff haben und die Übertragung zeitlich und örtlich individuell anfordern können. Eine der Kernfragen, die sich in diesem Zusammenhang auf nationaler, regionaler und internationaler Ebene stellt, ist die Frage, ob die bestehenden Vorschriften zum geistigen Eigentum dieser Entwicklung gewachsen sind oder ob sie angepaßt werden müssen.

Wirtschaftlich gesehen ist die interaktive Übertragung auf Abruf eine neue Form der Verwertung des geistigen Eigentums. Rechtlich gesehen besteht im allgemeinen Einvernehmen dahin, daß das Verbreitungsrecht, welches nur für die Verbreitung körperlicher Vervielfältigungsstücke gilt, nicht den Vorgang der Übertragung erfaßt. Auch das Vervielfältigungsrecht erfaßt nicht den Vorgang der Übertragung als solchen, sondern nur die dabei hergestellten Vervielfältigungen. In den Vorschriften der Mitgliedstaaten zum Urheberrecht und zu den verwandten Schutzrechten wird diese Übertragung nicht ausdrücklich durch ein bestimmtes Verwertungsrecht geschützt. Bei der Ausarbeitung und Anpassung der beiden neuen WIPO-Verträge, wo diesem für die künftige Entwicklung der Netzwerkumgebung entscheidenden Faktor auch große Bedeutung beigemessen wurde, waren alle Mitgliedstaaten der Ansicht, daß diese neuen Verwertungsformen durch das Recht der öffentlichen Wiedergabe (oder ein vergleichbares Recht), erfaßt werden sollten. Dieses Recht wird jedoch inhaltlich nicht in allen Mitgliedstaaten in der gleichen Weise verstanden, was auf das nicht ganz einheitliche Konzept dieser „Rechtsfamilien" in bezug auf die in diesem Punkt mehrmals revidierte Berner Übereinkunft sowie das Rom-Abkommen zurückzuführen ist.

Das Recht der öffentlichen Wiedergabe ist in den Mitgliedstaaten in mehrere Rechte mit stark unterschiedlicher Ausprägung untergliedert (Aufführungs- und Vorführungsrecht, Recht der öffentlichen Wiedergabe durch Ton- oder Bildträger, Recht der öffentlichen Wiedergabe durch Drahtfunk, Rundfunk, Recht auf Einspeisung in ein Kabelprogramm usw.). Die bestehenden Vorschriften der Mitgliedstaaten zur öffentlichen Wiedergabe schützen insbesondere nicht immer dieselben Arten von Werken und sonstigen Schutzgegenständen, was zu erheblichen Rechtslücken führen könnte, wenn diese Vorschriften auf die neuen Verwertungsformen „auf Abruf" angewandt würden. So wird zum einen bereits der Begriff „öffentlich" in den Mitgliedstaaten unterschiedlich ausgelegt. Übertragungen „auf Abruf" könnten in vielen Mitgliedstaaten nach dem derzeit geltenden Recht als nicht öffentlich und damit als nicht von diesem Recht erfaßt angesehen werden. Darüber hinaus unterscheiden sich im herkömmlichen, nicht interaktiven Nutzungsumfeld Inhalt und Auslegung der bestehenden Vorschriften über das Recht der öffentlichen Wiedergabe oder die zu dieser Gruppe gehörenden Rechte und deren Abgrenzung untereinander deutlich, was eine beträchtliche Rechtsunsicherheit zur Folge haben könnte. Wesentliche Unterschiede bestehen zwischen den Mitgliedstaaten auch hinsichtlich des Schutzniveaus für Rechtsinhaber (Ausschließlichkeitsrecht oder Vergütungsanspruch) und der Wahrnehmung der betreffenden Rechte.

Erhebliche Divergenzen bestehen zwischen den Mitgliedstaaten darüber hinaus bei den Schranken und Ausnahmen vom Recht der öffentlichen Wiedergabe (oder von einem zu dieser Gruppe gehörenden Recht), die bei einer Reihe von Nutzungsformen (insbesondere für Bildungs- und Forschungszwecke, für Informationszwecke, für bibliothekarische und archivarische Zwecke) denen entsprechen, die auch für das Vervielfältigungsrecht gelten (siehe Kapitel 3, I, a). Einige Mitgliedstaaten sehen jedoch für bibliothekarische und archivarische Zwecke keinerlei Ausnahmen vom Recht der öffentlichen Wiedergabe vor (z.B. Österreich, Belgien, Frankreich, Spanien und Luxemburg). Völlig unklar ist auch, welche der bestehenden Schranken auf die neue digitale Umgebung (insbesondere auf die Online-Verwertung geschützten Materials „auf Abruf") anwendbar sind. Da sich die Ausnahmeregelung für bibliothekarische Zwecke in den meisten Fällen auf bestimmte Formen der Vervielfältigung und der körperlichen Verbreitung geschützten Materials beschränkt, dürfte die Online-Übermittlung geschützten Materials an Nutzer in anderen Orten in vielen Mitgliedstaaten generell nicht vom ausschließlichen Recht der öffentlichen Wiedergabe freigestellt sein (Italien, Schweden, Dänemark, Griechenland, Portugal, Österreich, Belgien, Finnland, Frankreich, Luxemburg und Spanien). In anderen Mitgliedstaaten ist die Rechtslage weniger eindeutig (Deutschland, Niederlande, Vereinigtes Königreich und Irland).

Angesichts der erheblichen wirtschaftlichen Bedeutung, die der Nutzung digitalisierter Werke durch Bibliotheken und ähnliche Einrichtungen und deren Nutzer zukommt, wurden diverse „Bibliotheken-Initiativen“ in die Wege geleitet, um neue Lösungen auf der Grundlage vertraglicher Lizenzen zu finden. Angestrebt wird eine angemessene Kontrolle und eine gerechte Vergütung der betreffenden Rechtsinhaber. Gleichzeitig soll den Nutzern von geschütztem Material, z.B. gemeinnützigen Bibliotheken, ermöglicht werden, ihre Informationsdienste noch effizienter und zu erschwinglichen Preisen anzubieten. Die ersten Ergebnisse erscheinen vielversprechend, zumal es möglich zu sein scheint, zu für alle Beteiligten einschließlich für die Bibliotheken zufriedenstellenden Lösungen zu gelangen.

Zwar geht in den meisten Mitgliedstaaten der Trend dahin, das Konzept der öffentlichen Wiedergabe auch auf die Online-Verwertung geschützten Materials anzuwenden, doch wird gleichzeitig die Notwendigkeit gesehen, die geltenden Vorschriften im Hinblick auf die neuen Verwertungsformen zu präzisieren und gegebenenfalls zu ergänzen. Der genaue Schutzumfang dieses Rechts war allerdings vor allem im Rahmen der WIPO-Verhandlungen heftig umstritten. Im Mittelpunkt der Debatte standen die Ausgestaltung des Rechts und die rechtlich zulässigen Ausnahmen. Wie auch beim Vervielfältigungsrecht sehen sich die Mitgliedstaaten veranlaßt, die zulässigen Ausnahmen vom Recht auch im Hinblick auf die neuen internationalen Verpflichtungen zu überprüfen. In einigen Fällen hätten die herkömmlichen Ausnahmen, wenn sie auf Datennetze angewendet würden, tatsächlich erhebliche negative Auswirkungen auf die normale Online-Verwertung geschützten Materials durch die Rechtsinhaber, vor allem wenn die Online-Übertragung zur hauptsächlichen Verwertungsform wird.

Das Gemeinschaftsrecht erfaßt in seiner jetzigen Form zumindest nicht ausdrücklich Übertragungen geschützter Werke oder sonstiger Schutzgegenstände „auf Abruf“. Auch enthält es kein allgemeines Ausschließlichkeitsrecht der öffentlichen Wiedergabe, das sich auf solche neuen Formen der interaktiven elektronischen Übertragung von Werken und sonstigen Schutzgegenständen anwenden ließe. Das Recht der öffentlichen Wiedergabe ist bisher auf Gemeinschaftsebene nur zum Teil harmonisiert. Durch die Datenbank-Richtlinie wird ein allgemeines Recht der öffentlichen Wiedergabe, Vorführung oder Aufführung harmonisiert. Dieses Recht ist allerdings auf eine Werkgattung, nämlich Datenbanken (Artikel 5), beschränkt. Die Kabel-Satelliten-Richtlinie gewährt Urhebern in Artikel 2 das ausschließliche Recht der öffentlichen Wiedergabe von Werken über Satellit sowie das Kabelweiterverbreitungsrecht für die grenzüberschreitende Verwertung von Programmen, die geschützte Werke enthalten (Artikel 8ff.). Die Computerprogramm-Richtlinie schützt in ihrem Artikel 4 hingegen nur „jede Form der öffentlichen Verbreitung" von Computerprogrammen. Die Online-Übertragung von Computerprogrammen über Datennetze wird nicht ausdrücklich erwähnt. Als die Richtlinie erlassen wurde, war es in der Tat noch üblich, Computerprogramme über Disketten zu verbreiten und nicht online. Für die Inhaber bestimmter verwandter Schutzrechte ist in der Vermietrechts-Richtlinie ein Mindestschutz für bestimmte Formen der Rundfunksendung und öffentlichen Wiedergabe besonderer Schutzgegenstände vorgesehen, wie dort genauer geregelt wird.

Auf internationaler Ebene wurden die vereinzelten Bestimmungen zum Recht der öffentlichen Wiedergabe in der Berner Übereinkunft und im Rom-Abkommen bis vor kurzem höchst unterschiedlich ausgelegt, wenn es um die Frage ging, ob die Übertragung „auf Abruf" von Werken oder sonstigen Schutzgegenständen bereits erfaßt ist. Bei den internationalen Verhandlungen über die neuen WIPO-Verträge stellte sich schnell heraus, daß die bestehenden Vorschriften in diesem Bereich in jedem Fall ergänzt werden müssen, um alle Werkgattungen zu erfassen, und angepaßt werden müssen, um diese neue Form der Urheberrechtsverwertung besser in den Schutz der Urheber und Inhaber verwandter Schutzrechte einzubeziehen.

Der neue WIPO-Urheberrechtsvertrag erstreckt daher das herkömmliche ausschließliche Recht des Urhebers bezüglich der nicht interaktiven drahtgebundenen oder drahtlosen öffentlichen Wiedergabe auf alle Werkkategorien (Artikel 8). Er bestimmt darüber hinaus ausdrücklich, daß das Recht der öffentlichen Wiedergabe auch die drahtgebundene oder drahtlose Zugänglichmachung der Werke in der Weise einschließt, daß sie Mitgliedern der Öffentlichkeit an Orten und zu Zeiten ihrer Wahl zugänglich sind. Mit diesem Teil des Rechts wird die neue, interaktive Tätigkeit erfaßt. Der Wortlaut spiegelt den diesbezüglichen Vorschlag wider, den die Europäische Gemeinschaft und ihre Mitgliedstaaten in den Verhandlungen unterbreitet hatten. Um auch den ausübenden Künstlern und Tonträgerherstellern im Hinblick auf die neue interaktive Umgebung ein angemessenes Schutzniveau zu gewährleisten, führte der WIPO-Vertrag über Darbietungen und Tonträger ein gleichwertiges Ausschließlichkeitsrecht „der Zugänglichmachung" für diesen Personenkreis ein (vgl. Artikel 10 und 14 WPPT).

2. Handlungsbedarf

Insgesamt ist festzustellen, daß die bestehende Rechtslage in den Mitgliedstaaten in bezug auf das Recht der öffentlichen Wiedergabe von Werken und sonstigen Schutzgegenständen durch eine beträchtliche Rechtsunsicherheit und durch Unterschiede zwischen den nationalen Regelungen hinsichtlich der Art und der Ausgestaltung des Schutzes gekennzeichnet ist. Dies gilt nicht nur für die herkömmliche öffentliche Wiedergabe geschützter Werke einschließlich der Online-Wiedergabe, soweit hier noch keine Harmonisierung stattgefunden hat, sondern insbesondere auch für den interaktiven Zugang zu Werken und sonstigen Schutzgegenständen „auf Abruf". Da die Verwertung des geistigen Eigentums „auf Abruf" als einer der größten Wachstumsmärkte angesehen wird, nimmt die Gewährleistung eines adäquaten und einheitlichen Schutzes dieser neuen wirtschaftlichen Verwertungsformen eine zentrale Stellung in diesem Vorschlag ein. Da netzvermittelte Übertragungen „auf Abruf" ihrem Wesen nach oftmals grenzübergreifend und in vielen Fällen auf gemeinschaftsweite Märkte angewiesen sind, um wirtschaftlich rentabel zu sein, bedarf es hier klarer, harmonisierter Vorschriften auf Gemeinschaftsebene für alle Rechtsinhaber, die in diesem Richtlinienentwurf erfaßt sind.

Mit der Harmonisierung dieser Vorschriften würden auch die oben beschriebenen neuen internationalen Verpflichtungen aus den WIPO-Verträgen in einer kohärenten Weise umgesetzt.

III. Rechtsschutz für die Integrität technischer Identifizierungs- und Schutzsysteme

1. Bisherige Rechtslage

Mit den neuen Kommunikationstechnologien werden sich insbesondere im Rahmen der netzvermittelten Online-Dienste neue Möglichkeiten für die Verwertung von Werken und sonstigen Schutzgegenständen eröffnen. Diese neuen Technologien werden jedoch ein neues Piraterierisiko mit sich bringen. Zunehmend bedarf es daher wirksamerer Schutzmaßnahmen gegen unerlaubte Verwertungshandlungen und in Verbindung damit einer Identifizierung des über Datennetze verbreiteten geschützten Materials sowie des betreffenden Rechtsinhabers.

Da technische Identifizierungs- und Schutzsysteme je nach Auslegung in der Lage sind, personenbezogene Daten über die individuelle Nutzung von Schutzgegenständen zu verarbeiten und damit die Online-Aktivitäten individueller Verbraucher nachvollziehen können, muß sichergestellt werden, daß das Recht auf Privatsphäre des einzelnen gewahrt ist. Die technischen Funktionen dieser technischen Maßnahmen müssen daher in Übereinstimmung mit der Datenschutz-Richtlinie entsprechende Vorkehrungen zum Schutz der Privatsphäre enthalten.

Der vorliegende Richtlinienvorschlag zielt in erster Linie auf die Anpassung und Harmonisierung der Rechte des geistigen Eigentums ab. Allerdings bietet auch die Technik Lösungsmöglichkeiten in Form technologischer Maßnahmen, die unerlaubte Verwertungshandlungen verhindern helfen, oder in Form elektronischer Informationen, die mit den Werken oder sonstigen Schutzgegenständen verbunden werden können, um die Verwaltung der Rechte zu erleichtern. Die Interessierten Kreise einschließlich der Rechtsinhaber bemühen sich bereits um die Einführung und Einigung auf solche Techniken. Es steht jedoch zu erwarten, daß parallel zu der Entwicklung und Nutzung von Schutz- und Identifizierungssystemen ein Markt für „Piraterie-Vorrichtungen" entstehen wird, die die unerlaubte Umgehung und/oder Entfernung dieser Systeme ermöglichen oder erleichtern. Von den Interessierten Kreisen wurde die Notwendigkeit unterstrichen, dieser Gefahr mit einschlägigen Bestimmungen auf internationaler und nationaler Ebene zu begegnen, die einen schnellen und wirksamen Rechtsschutz von Identifizierungs- und Schutzsystemen ermöglichen.

Die Rechtsvorschriften der Mitgliedstaaten sehen derzeit, wenn überhaupt, nur recht allgemeine Regelungen in diesem Bereich vor. Die Mitgliedstaaten befürworten zwar im allgemeinen die Entwicklung technischer Schutz- und Identifizierungssysteme, sofern eine solche Initiative ausschließlich vom Markt ausgeht, doch wurde mit der rechtlichen Verankerung dieser technologischen Vorrichtungen noch nicht begonnen.

Auf internationaler Ebene wurde das Problem im Rahmen der WIPO-Verhandlungen über bestimmte urheber- und leistungsschutzrechtliche Fragen erörtert. Die beiden neuen WIPO-Verträge enthalten zwei gleichlautende Bestimmungen über „Pflichten in bezug auf technologische Maßnahmen" und „Pflichten in bezug auf die Informationen für die Wahrnehmung der Rechte". Die erste Bestimmung verbietet die Umgehung technologischer Maßnahmen, von denen Urheber und Inhaber von sonstigen Schutzrechten im Zusammenhang mit der Ausübung ihrer Rechte Gebrauch machen, während die zweite Bestimmung die Entfernung oder Änderung elektronischer Informationen untersagt, die zur Wahrnehmung der Rechte mit einem Werk oder einem sonstigen Schutzgegenstand verbunden sind.

2. Handlungsbedarf

Ein uneinheitliches Vorgehen auf Ebene der Mitgliedstaaten in bezug auf die Vorschriften, die technische Schutz- und Identifizierungssysteme, von denen Urheber und Inhaber von verwandten Schutzrechten Gebrauch machen, rechtlich absichern sollen, würde nicht nur den Schutz des Urheberrechts und der verwandten Schutzrechte erschweren, sondern auch das ordnungsgemäße Funktionieren des Binnenmarkts beeinträchtigen. Ein unterschiedliches Schutzniveau könnte die Entwicklung neuer Dienste auf europäischer Ebene behindern und den Wettbewerb erheblich verzerren. Die Einführung eines gleichwertigen Schutzniveaus in allen Mitgliedstaaten scheint daher notwendig. Damit wäre das reibungslose Funktionieren des Binnenmarkts sichergestellt. Gleichzeitig würden gleiche Bedingungen geschaffen, auf deren Grundlage sich die neuen Dienste der Informationsgesellschaft entwickeln könnten.

Eine Angleichung dieser Vorschriften, die fast einstimmig gefordert wurde, würde nicht nur einen einheitlichen Rechtsschutz auf Gemeinschaftsebene bewirken, sondern stünde zudem auf einer kohärenten Grundlage in Form der neuen WIPO-Verträge.

IV. Verbreitungsrecht einschließlich des Erschöpfungsgrundsatzes

1. Bisherige Rechtslage

Das Verbreitungsrecht (das Recht, die Verbreitung körperlicher Vervielfältigungsstücke zu erlauben oder zu verbieten) ist durch die Vermietrechts-Richtlinie bereits für vier Gruppen von Inhabern verwandter Schutzrechte (ausübende Künstler, Sendeunternehmen, Tonträgerhersteller und Filmhersteller) harmonisiert worden. Zwar umfaßt die Harmonisierung des Verbreitungsrechts auf Gemeinschaftsebene auch bestimmte Werkgattungen wie urheberrechtlich geschützte Computerprogramme und Datenbanken, doch wenden die Mitgliedstaaten bei anderen Werken, die nicht von der Computerprogramm-Richtlinie und der Datenbank-Richtlinie erfaßt sind, unterschiedliche Bestimmungen in bezug auf das Verbreitungsrecht an. In einigen Mitgliedstaaten gibt es beispielsweise kein eigenständiges Verbreitungsrecht. Hierzu zählen Länder, deren Vervielfältigungsrecht auch das Recht des Urhebers erfaßt, den Bestimmungszweck der Vervielfältigungsstücke einschließlich ihrer Wiederverwendung oder des Wiederverkaufs zu kontrollieren (z.B. Frankreich, Belgien), sowie Länder, in denen das Verbreitungsrecht unter das Veröffentlichungsrecht fällt (z.B. Niederlande, Irland und die skandinavischen Länder). Eine andere noch größere Gruppe von Mitgliedstaaten sieht nicht für alle Werkgattungen ein eigenes Verbreitungsrecht vor (Deutschland, Österreich, Spanien, Griechenland, Italien, Portugal und Vereinigtes Königreich).

Darüber hinaus gelten in den Mitgliedstaaten auch unterschiedliche Beschränkungen des Verbreitungsrechts, unabhängig davon, ob das Recht selbst ausdrücklich oder nur implizit eingeräumt wird. Die wichtigste Beschränkung ist die Erschöpfung des Verbreitungsrechts nach dem Erstverkauf. Einige nationale Rechtsvorschriften (außer in Belgien, Frankreich, Luxemburg und Portugal) bestimmen ausdrücklich, daß der erste Verkauf eines Vervielfältigungsstücks, der mit Zustimmung des Rechtsinhaber im Inland erfolgt, die Erschöpfung des Verbreitungsrechts in dem betreffenden Land bewirkt (nationale Erschöpfung). Der Rechtsprechung des Europäischen Gerichtshofs zufolge, die den Grundsatz des freien Warenverkehrs in der Gemeinschaft mit dem Schutz der Rechte des geistigen Eigentums zu vereinbaren sucht, erschöpft sich das Verbreitungsrecht mit dem Erstverkauf in der Gemeinschaft, sofern – wie bei der nationalen Erschöpfung – der Verkauf durch den Rechtsinhaber selbst oder mit dessen Zustimmung erfolgt (Erschöpfung in der Gemeinschaft).

Einige Mitgliedstaaten haben den Erschöpfungsgrundsatz nicht auf ein bestimmtes Gebiet beschränkt. Deshalb wenden sie zumindest in einigen Fällen das Prinzip der internationalen Erschöpfung an, so daß der Erstverkauf des Gegenstands durch den Rechtsinhaber oder mit dessen Zustimmung an irgendeinem Ort der Welt die Erschöpfung des Verbreitungsrechts bewirkt. Dies kann für die Funktionsweise des Binnenmarkts und für die Nutzer und Rechtsinhaber innerhalb der Gemeinschaft zu ernsten Konsequenzen führen.

2. Handlungsbedarf

Wie bereits erwähnt, gehen die Mitgliedstaaten bei der Bestimmung der zustimmungsbedürftigen Verbreitungshandlungen von Werken unterschiedlich vor und verfolgen gleichsam in gewisser Weise entgegengesetzte Strategien bei den Ausnahmen vom Verbreitungsrecht, insbesondere was den Erschöpfungsgrundsatz anbelangt.

Nach Artikel 6 Absatz 1 des neuen WIPO-Urheberrechtsvertrags haben die Urheber das ausschließliche Recht, die Verbreitung der Originale und Vervielfältigungsstücke ihrer Werke zu erlauben. In Absatz 2 heißt es weiter, daß der Vertrag nicht die Freiheit der Vertragsparteien berührt zu bestimmen, unter welchen Voraussetzungen sich das Verbreitungsrecht nach dem ersten mit Zustimmung des Urhebers erfolgten Verkauf oder der ersten sonstigen Eigentumsübertragung des Originals oder eines Vervielfältigungsstücks erschöpft. Mit einer Angleichung des Verbreitungsrechts für alle Werkgattungen auf Gemeinschaftsebene würden daher auch die neuen Verpflichtungen nach Artikel 6 Absatz 1 WIPO-Urheberrechtsvertrag umgesetzt.

Das reibungslose Funktionieren des Binnenmarkts kann nicht gewährleistet werden, wenn die Mitgliedstaaten unterschiedliche Bestimmungen in bezug auf die Erschöpfung der Rechte des geistigen Eigentums anwenden. Dies kann zu Handelsbeschränkungen und Wettbewerbsverzerrungen führen. Wenn beispielsweise Mitgliedstaat A eine Regelung einführt, derzufolge die Einfuhr einer Ware, die ein geschütztes Werk enthält, rechtmäßig ist, wenn diese Ware zuvor in einem Drittland von dem Rechtsinhaber selbst oder mit seiner Zustimmung in Verkehr gebracht worden ist, dann erhält der Rechtsinhaber in dem Einfuhrmitgliedstaat keine Vergütung aufgrund des mit dieser Ware verbundenen Rechts. Wenn allerdings im gleichen Fall Mitgliedstaat B nicht nach dem Grundsatz der internationalen Erschöpfung verfährt, so kann der Rechtsinhaber sein Ausschließlichkeitsrecht im Gebiet von B geltend machen und damit den Parallelimport der betreffenden Ware verhindern. Die unterschiedliche Anwendung des Erschöpfungsgrundsatzes in den Mitgliedstaaten führt daher zu einer erneuten Aufteilung des Binnenmarkts in getrennte nationale Märkte und Gebiete. Aufgrund der Beseitigung der Grenzkontrollen innerhalb der Gemeinschaft würde die rechtmäßige Beschränkung des innergemeinschaftlichen Warenhandels außerdem auch auf praktische Schwierigkeiten stoßen. Insbesondere würden bei diesen Waren Handelsverzerrungen auftreten, und es käme zu einer Verlagerung der Versorgungskanäle.

Alle Mitgliedstaaten müssen daher den Erschöpfungsgrundsatz in einer kohärenten Weise anwenden. Die bestehenden sekundärrechtlichen Gemeinschaftsvorschriften geben in den betreffenden Bereichen der Gemeinschaftserschöpfung den Vorzug vor der internationalen Erschöpfung. Im Bereich des geistigen Eigentums sind die Richtlinien über Computerprogramme, Datenbanken und Halbleitertopographien in diesem Punkt wegweisend. Wie die Vermietrechts-Richtlinie für Inhaber verwandter Schutzrechte sind sie dahingehend auszulegen, daß sie eine internationale Erschöpfung des Verbreitungsrechts nicht zulassen. Es ist daher nur folgerichtig, das geltende Gemeinschaftsrecht auf dieser Basis zu ergänzen.

Aufgrund der erheblichen Diskrepanzen in der Gesetzgebung und Rechtsanwendung der Mitgliedstaaten sowie der Pflichten aus den WIPO-Verträgen sind gesetzgeberische Maßnahmen auf Gemeinschaftsebene erforderlich, um eine umfassende Harmonisierung des Verbreitungsrechts für alle Urheber und Inhaber verwandter Schutzrechte zu bewirken. Gleichzeitig ermöglicht dieser Richtlinienvorschlag die Möglichkeit, kohärente Rahmenbedingungen für die elektronische und körperliche Verbreitung von geschütztem Material zu schaffen und diese Verbreitungsformen klar voneinander abzugrenzen.

Rechtlicher Rahmen

I. Geeignete Rechtsform

Aus Gründen der Verhältnismäßigkeit ist die Kommission der Ansicht, daß die Richtlinie für diesen Regelungsbereich die geeignete Rechtsform ist. Mit einer Richtlinie können die oben erörterten Binnenmarktziele verwirklicht werden, ohne daß den Mitgliedstaaten bei der Wahl ihrer Mittel zur Erreichung dieser Ziele jegliches Ermessen entzogen würde.

II. Geeignete Rechtsgrundlage

In ihrer Mitteilung „Initiativen zum Grünbuch über Urheberrecht und verwandte Schutzrechte in der Informationsgesellschaft (KOM(96) 568 endg.) kündigte die Kommission ihre Absicht an, eine Reihe von Harmonisierungsmaßnahmen im Bereich des Urheberrechts und der verwandten Schutzrechte vorzuschlagen, um den bestehenden Rechtsrahmen, wo dies für das ordnungsgemäße Funktionieren des Binnenmarkts und die Schaffung günstiger rechtlicher Rahmenbedingungen für die Entwicklung der Informationsgesellschaft in Europa notwendig ist, anzupassen und zu ergänzen. Nach Prüfung der Stellungnahmen zum Urheberrechts-Grünbuch von 1995 und ihrer Mitteilung von 1996 schlägt die Kommission Artikel 57 Absatz 2, Artikel 66 und Artikel 100a EG-Vertrag als Rechtsgrundlage für den vorliegenden Vorschlag vor.

Gewisse Divergenzen zwischen den Mitgliedstaaten hinsichtlich des rechtlichen Schutzes von Werken und sonstigen Schutzgegenständen können die Niederlassungs- und Dienstleistungsfreiheit innerhalb der Gemeinschaft insofern erheblich behindern, als die gesetzlichen urheber- und leistungsschutzrechtlichen Bestimmungen in einem Mitgliedstaat die Herstellung von Waren wie CD-ROMs in anderen Mitgliedstaaten verhindern oder die Erbringung von Dienstleistungen wie Online-Diensten in einem anderen Mitgliedstaat ernstlich behindern werden. Artikel 57 Absatz 2 und Artikel 66 sind daher für diesen Vorschlag geeignete Rechtsgrundlagen.

Die Unterschiede und Rechtsunsicherheit hinsichtlich des Umfangs bestimmter Urheberrechte und verwandter Schutzrechte können sich, was den freien Warenverkehr und Wettbewerbsverzerrungen anbelangt, negativ auf das Funktionieren des Binnenmarkts auswirken. Auch Artikel 100a ist daher eine adäquate Rechtsgrundlage für diesen Vorschlag.

Wie oben ausgeführt, hat das neue technologische Umfeld sowohl aus technischen als auch aus wirtschaftlichen Gründen bereits zu einem Anstieg der grenzüberschreitenden Verwertung von Werken und sonstigen Schutzgegenständen wie Tonträgern oder aufgezeichneten Darbietungen geführt. Diese Entwicklungen werden und sollen weiter voranschreiten. Das reibungslose Funktionieren des Binnenmarkts für Urheberrechte und verwandte Schutzrechte erfordert daher ein stärkeres Maß an harmonisierten Schutz des Urheberrechts und der verwandten Schutzrechte als bisher. Der vorliegende Vorschlag fördert den freien Verkehr von Werken und sonstigen Schutzgegenständen innerhalb der Gemeinschaft und beseitigt in erheblichem Umfang Wettbewerbsverzerrungen sowohl unter den Inhaltsanbietern als auch unter den Nutzern geschützten Materials, indem vergleichbare und transparente Schutzvorschriften für Urheberrecht und verwandte Schutzrechte in den Mitgliedstaaten vorgeschrieben werden. Solche gleichen Bedingungen werden erheblich zur Diversifizierung der Inhalte und zu Größenvorteilen für neue Produkte und Dienste beitragen, die für die Realisierung der Informationsgesellschaft unabdingbar sind.

Sowohl hinsichtlich der Wahl der Rechtsform als auch hinsichtlich der Wahl der Rechtsgrundlage folgt dieser Vorschlag der Vorgehensweise, die bisher für Harmonisierungsmaßnahmen im Bereich des Urheberrechts und der verwandten Schutzrechte verfolgt wurde.

SANDY NORMAN

Electronic Copyright and Libraries

Introduction

Copyright is an extremely emotive issue for us as well as for the right holders because librarians are the ones who have to abide by and work within copyright laws set by national governments. To librarians, the topic of copyright generates a whole range of different emotions from confusion and incomprehension, through to frustration and incredulity!

Copyright compliance has had a major effect on library services. Librarians, especially in the UK, frequently refer to it as a „minefield". I would like to share with you how copyright compliance is taken seriously in libraries. I will describe the effects on library services of increases in protection and the necessity of having appropriate exceptions to these copyrights to enable the smooth running of libraries. This is an opportune time with all the discussions following the recent publication of the EC's draft directive on copyright for the information society. I will talk about this as well. I would also like to take this opportunity to highlight the importance of the library service and the role of the librarian in maintaining the copyright balance. My paper will be received by some as controversial but I hope I will also generate a greater understanding of the concerns about copyright from the library point of view.

The digital revolution has made a great impact on libraries. This has created expectations that we will be able to use the technology to improve services to users and so, potentially, be of benefit to all members of society. Although efforts are being made, this has not yet been resolved to the satisfaction of all parties in the information chain. The promise of the Information Society will not be fulfilled until, and unless, a careful balance is maintained between both economic and public interests. It will not be achieved if the rights to packaged information are in the hands of, and tightly controlled by, those with only the economic incentive to make as much money out of these new opportunities as possible, regardless of society's interests. Without the appropriate safeguards to society, such as statutory exceptions, a greater divide will be created between those who have the ability to find and pay for information – the information rich, and those who do not have these advantages – the information poor, at a time when the opportunity exists to narrow or even close this gap.

Librarians fear that with more and more rights given to creators, publishers and producers, access to all packaged information will be confined to those who can pay for it. Those who cannot afford to pay will be effectively disenfranchised and it would be impossible for librarians to provide equitable access to resources needed for education, creativity and the advancement of knowledge. Librarians advocate international harmonisation of the laws but maintain that exceptions to the exclusive rights should remain to ensure, at least, that permitted uses apply equally to information in electronic form as they do to information in print.

Librarians, responsible professionals

Judging by the copyright laws they adopt, there are very few lawmakers who really appreciate exactly what librarians do, so this is an opportunity to explain. The practical day to day reality of abiding by copyright laws is rarely appreciated. Librarians are responsible members of society. We are not pirates. We respect copyright and take it seriously. We have to, as practically all the material handled in libraries is protected by copyright. We also recognise and respect the need for right holders to obtain a fair return on their investments. Librarians, especially in the UK, familiarise themselves with copyright laws and take reasonable precautions against any inadvertent infringement which may take place on the library premises. This is not an easy role to sustain as we are frequently accused by library users of being obstructive in preventing copyright abuse or misuse, while at the same time we are often accused by right holder representatives of encouraging copyright infringement. Also, it is often stated, especially by publishers, that librarians are always trying to obtain something for nothing: to avoid having to pay for information. When librarians talk about free access to information, this is literally taken to mean information for free, whereas what is meant is that we want access to information which is flowing freely, i.e. unrestricted, packaged information which is purchased by libraries and made available by the quickest possible methods to users. We are not trying to ruin publishers. On the contrary we need them to continue to provide quality products for the information society.

Librarians have idealistic aims but then so do most professions. Our aim is to facilitate access to education and knowledge by collecting and making these collections available to those who need them, whoever and wherever they may be. We preserve collections as part of a nation's heritage. We spread the knowledge of our collections and share our resources both nationally and internationally. We have learned skills in searching and retrieving information from internal and external sources and can greatly assist in the learning process. We turn information into knowledge which can be used for personal, education, research or commercial purposes. Our role is, therefore, to help users to identify, obtain and use the information they need. We are part of the flow of information in the information society. However, if this system is not to break down resulting in a loss to society, this vital role needs to be recognised and backed up by governments when formulating copyright laws.

The digital revolution

Technology is available to improve library services, but more often than not, depending on a nation's laws, full advantage cannot be taken because of copyright considerations. Library and information professionals are committed to make works available for all to access. The 4th Law of Library Science is *Save the time of the reader*[1]. Librarians and their patrons, become frustrated, therefore, if access is hampered. For example, many would like to digitise and network parts of their printed collections in order to offer as wide an access as possible to their readers. There are other obvious advantages to this as well: the information can be safely preserved, and is free from the dangers that exist in its printed form – pages ripped out, defaced, stolen etc. This is not material which is already in digital form so it can be argued that it is not competing with the normal exploitation of the work. Access and use could be restricted to registered users of the library so an element of security is offered. However, obtaining authorisation, if no statutory right exists, is time consuming and may even be impossible: many publishers do not respond promptly to permission requests, if at all; some are difficult to trace; some demand prohibitive fees and/or tight licensing conditions; and some refuse. Added to this is the question of whether the publisher holds the rights or whether it should be the author one has to approach. Multiply all of these requests by the number of authors and publishers and the scale of the problem can be appreciated.

The hopes and expectations of librarians in being able to use the new technologies to enhance their services have clashed with the fears of rights owners about the use of copyright protected material. Rights owners fear that, once their intellectual property is in digital form, it will be appropriated by some of

[1] Ranganathan S. R. Library Manual for Library Authorities, Librarians and Honorary Library Workers. Asia Publishing House, 1962.

the less scrupulous nations, or those with inadequate statutory protection, causing wide-spread piracy. This is an understandable fear, although no research has been undertaken to prove that these fears are valid. Some publishers have reported that putting the full text of their works on the Web has actually increased sales.[2] The library profession maintains that given certain rights and safeguards, piracy will not happen to materials under its care, although they cannot be held liable for all acts of infringement in the library premises. They are not, and should not be expected to be, copyright police.

Right holders believe that „digital is different" as uses of their works can be monitored using digital solutions. It is true that digital technology has the potential to enable rights holders to track and charge for every instance of electronic access. This has had a cautious welcome from the library profession. Although technical controls – electronic copyright management systems – can be valuable in guaranteeing the integrity of a product, we are concerned about the their effects when used to underpin copyright protection especially for text-based scientific and technical information. Such controls, designed to prevent copyright abuse, could also be used to demand a high price for information access. Used in this way, it could mean an abuse of a monopoly besides being dangerous to have total control over any information. Added to this is the threat that, circumventing technical controls put in place for copyright protection, even for copying and using under a statutory exception for lawful users, will be illegal under the new EC draft directive on copyright.

In the view of many right holders *all* access and use of works whether in printed, analogue or digital form should be licensed and paid for. This is a dangerous argument as having such market power gives them the mandate – the green light – to impose monopoly prices and potentially oppressive terms on users, including libraries, academic and research organisations, and to ignore the social consequences that follow from the inability of such organisations to make payments for every access. Where is it written that right holders should be entitled to a *maximum* return on investment? An *equitable* return to encourage the creation of new works is all that should be expected. Statements coming from some publishers which assert that, because all digital copying has the potential to be tracked and controlled, there is now no need to apply any exceptions for uncontrolled copying and use, demonstrate the one-sidedness of their argument. What they appear to have forgotten is the other side to copyright: the needs of society. This cause is taken up by the library profession as there is no other profession which is adequately upholding the consumer interest on copyright.

[2] The Stationery Office in the UK

European Union

The precedents being set by the European Union are a worrying factor for libraries. Over the past few years, librarians in the EEA have had to contend with the various changes to copyright such as the extension of the term of protection; public lending having to be licensed; and a new form of database protection with strict rules on extraction and reutilisation. Now the European Commission has issued another directive which is increasing protection while at the same time severely limiting the scope for member states to provide limitations and exceptions. We are not happy with this. The EU is tipping the balance more and more in favour of owner interests.

It is clear from the EC Follow-Up Green Paper,[3] and the response of the subsequent consultation, that the views of the leisure and entertainment industry prevail in the new directive on copyright in the information society. However, although plugging the gaps to preserve exploitation potential of entertainment and leisure works is important, it is unfortunate that education and research uses may be caught up in this protective net.

One of the fundamental principles of copyright is that it should foster creativity and development of knowledge which in turn benefits society. It is in the public's interest to have access to information in all its formats which is widely accessible and which may be freely communicated. This leads to a better informed and educated society which, in turn, leads to the creation of more intellectual property. No-one would argue that this has changed. We still need exceptions and limitations to fulfil this principle. Exceptions are not provided just to annoy publishers, or because at one time it was not possible to collect payments. At the recent Imprimatur conference in Amsterdam, Mr Bernt Hugenholz described exceptions as being „essential instruments" to copyright law and not as „exceptions to a rule". They should be regarded as fundamental rights.

An exception which allows copying for research actually supports the economic argument that copyright provides incentives to potential creators to create new works, it does not negate it. Although *existing* authors need protection to stimulate the digitisation and dissemination of their works, *potential* creators also need encouragement to carry out research for a work. If there are barriers to access (being refused, or having to pay a high price to access and clear rights to copy), the costs of producing a new work will be higher and this could be a disincentive to create. Scientists and academic researchers especially

[3] Follow-up to the Green Paper on Copyright and Related Rights in the Information Society. CEC COM(96) 568 final.

need easy access to data at prices they can afford. Also, much of the information generated which is likely to be copied and used comes from the academic and scientific communities which is paid for out of public funds. Researchers as well as the public should therefore benefit from their output.

The new right of communication to the public adopted by WIPO in the recent treaties and included in the EC draft directive poses a threat to library services. Of especial concern, are activities such as browsing and viewing from a computer screen which are likely to fall under this right. We do not believe that there should be authorisation to browse or view. The definition of browsing and viewing in this sense is akin to looking among the bookshelves for something which catches the eye and examining it to see whether it is appropriate for a purpose. It is accepted that users can browse and „view" works in printed form so there should be no difference in looking at an electronic version. If browsing and viewing have to be authorised, the public is, once more, at the mercy of right holders who could charge whatever they like. This would mean, in effect, that users would be paying for reading. This is totally unacceptable. It was never intended that copyright protection should extend to reading. Rights holders should not be given the opportunity to control the right to read, view, listen or receive or inappropriately monitor the use of information.

Exceptions need to be fair

There needs to be greater flexibility on copyright, rather than a tightening up, if the ideals of the information society, being promoted by many governments, are to be achieved. It is accepted by all players that harmonising the exceptions will not be easy in the EEA because of the different copyright traditions, legal systems and languages. We accept that traditional exceptions do not translate easily from some laws into the digital environment – but this does not mean that they should be abandoned altogether.

Let us examine the differences: many of the continental civil law countries have exceptions for private copying; whereas the common law countries of the UK and Ireland have what is called *fair dealing;* the UK also has a whole bundle of specific exceptions for other special purposes including regulations for copying by librarians. Whilst not advocating that the UK should adopt private copying or the civil law countries adopt fair dealing etc., in the interests of balance the concepts behind fair dealing, copying by librarians and for education and research must be preserved. They should be rethought and adapted to meet society's needs.

The fair use concept which is used in the USA has been suggested as a desirable solution but this is, I understand, not a term which is recognised or which can be translated easily into some European languages or legal systems. Perhaps the less emotive term „fair practice“ should be considered. The term *fair practice* is already used in the Berne Convention so the concept should be familiar to all[4]. Examples of what is fair could be given and in any dispute a test of fairness could then be judged by a court of law, case by case. It should be fair practice, for example, to copy and use reasonable amounts from certain materials by individuals for their own private study.

Conclusion

With the arrival of the digital revolution, the world's collection of knowledge is potentially available for all to access. To be able to share the worlds vast collection of knowledge with all nations, not just for the developed world would be the fulfilment of a library ideal. We want governments to recognise our important role and to give us special treatment in order to be able to use the new technology lawfully in our services and fulfil this aim.

Most of what librarians (public, school, university, special) do is, and always has been, in the best interests of their users. These users are all members of the public and, provided there are barriers to the information flow, will contribute in different ways to the wealth and culture of a nation. Despite some who forecast that there will be no need for libraries in future, librarians will nevertheless endure and will play an important role in ensuring that there is no stratification in society between those who have the means to obtain access to knowledge and those who have not.

[4] Article 10 for example.

HARALD HEKER

Die Nutzung urheberrechtlich geschützter Werke in digitaler Form

I. Einleitung

Kaum vergleichbar mit etwas je Erlebtem werden wir durch eine rasante Entwicklung der Informations- und Kommunikationstechnologien in ein neues Zeitalter, das sog. „Informationszeitalter", geschleudert. Man spricht bereits von der Information als viertem Produktionsfaktor; neben Arbeit, Kapital und Boden. Kennzeichnend für die neue Zeit ist die globale „Vernetzung", das weltweite Kommunizieren der Menschen mittels untereinander verbundener Computer.

Wenn also schon die Einrichtung digitaler weltumspannender Informations-Superhighways für nicht aufhaltbar und auch für unverzichtbar gehalten wird, so müssen folgerichtig auch die notwendigen „Verkehrsregeln" geschaffen werden, um die auf ihnen fließenden Ströme und Bewegungen zu ordnen. Nur so kann ein Chaos auf diesen neuen internationalen Kommunikationsverbindungen vermieden oder ihr Herabsinken zu bloßen Geisterbahnen, auf denen kein Rechteinhaber sein Geistiges Eigentum der Gefahr eines ungenehmigten Downloadings aussetzen würde, verhindert werden.

Es ist ein wahrer Quantensprung, den die Einführung der digitalen Technologie ausgelöst hat. Sie ermöglicht die Umwandlung von geschützten Werken und Leistungen in ein und dasselbe Datenformat, unabhängig davon, zu welcher der bislang unterscheidbaren Werkarten sie gehören, und unabhängig davon, in welchem der bislang deutlich voneinander abgrenzbaren Speichermedien sie verkörpert sind. Texte, Bilder, Filme und Töne können ebenso in digitaler Form gespeichert werden wie bloße Daten und sonstige Informationen. Ein weiteres Wesensmerkmal dieser Technologie ist, daß sie Landesgrenzen und nationale Gesetze nicht kennt, sondern daß die digitalen Superhighways vielmehr binnen Sekunden Kommunikationsverbindungen über die ganze Welt herstellen (Stichwort: global information infrastructure). Mangels entsprechender nationaler und vor allem internationaler Rechtsvorschriften sind Urheber z. Zt. fast ohne jeden Schutz, und zwar im materiellen wie immateriellen Sinn, angesichts des derzeit kaum zu kontrollierenden Zugriffs Dritter auf elektronische Datenbanken und der damit verbundenen Möglichkeit, urheberrechtlich geschützte Werke ohne Genehmigung der Rechtsinhaber nach Belieben zu nutzen.

II. Rechtsfragen

1. Europäische und amerikanische Initiativen

Zu fragen ist, wie die Politik, insbesondere die Rechtspolitik, auf diese aktuellen Herausforderungen reagiert. Sowohl die Europäische Kommission als auch die amerikanische Regierung sehen in der Informationsgesellschaft das Kernstück eines Entwicklungsmodells für das 21. Jahrhundert, mit der der wirtschaftliche Fortschritt Europas und der USA steht und fällt. Die Clinton/Gore-Regierung hat deshalb vor zwei Jahren ein ehrgeiziges Programm gestartet mit dem Ziel, eine „National Information Infrastructure" zu schaffen. Eine von der US-Regierung eingesetzte Arbeitsgruppe kam zu dem – richtigen – Ergebnis, daß der Erfolg einer „National Information Infrastructure" ganz allein von deren Inhalt abhängt. Deshalb, so die Arbeitsgruppe, kann eine solche Infrastruktur keinen Erfolg haben, wenn ihr Inhalt nicht ausreichend geschützt ist.

Auch in der Europäischen Union sind entsprechende Überlegungen schon weit gediehen. Nach dem „Grünbuch über Urheberrecht und verwandte Schutzrechte in der Informationsgesellschaft" vom 19. Juli 1995 (KOM (95) 382 endg.) hat die Kommission Ende letzten Jahres einen Vorschlag für eine Richtlinie zur Harmonisierung bestimmter Aspekte des „Urheberrechts und der verwandten Schutzrechte in der Informationsgesellschaft" (KOM (97) 628 endg.) präsentiert.

Mit dem Richtlinienvorschlag trägt die Kommission zu einem großen Teil den neuen internationalen Verpflichtungen Rechnung, die sich aus dem Abschluß des WIPO-Urheberrechtsvertrags und des WIPO-Vertrags über Darbietungen und Tonträger aus dem Jahre 1996 ergeben. Darüber hinaus will sie aber auch die Gelegenheit nutzen, bestehende oder potentielle Handelsschranken im Gemeinsamen Markt zu beseitigen, indem sie – auf der Basis des WIPO-Urhebervertrags – Regelungen zum Vervielfältigungsrecht, zum Recht der öffentlichen Wiedergabe und zum Verbreitungsrecht (einschließlich des Erschöpfungsgrundsatzes) sowie Maßnahmen gegen die Umgehung oder den Mißbrauch elektronischer Verwaltungs- oder Schutzsysteme vorschlägt.

Die Verleger danken der Europäischen Kommission ausdrücklich für diese Initiative, die notwendig, wichtig und richtig ist. Dies gilt ganz besonders für die ausdrückliche Bestätigung der Geltung des Vervielfältigungsrechts, des Rechts zur öffentlichen Wiedergabe und des Verbreitungsrechts im digitalen Bereich.

Mit großer Sorge erfüllt uns aber, daß nach den Vorstellungen der Kommission ephemere Vervielfältigungshandlungen sowie Vervielfältigungen zum privaten Gebrauch zulässig sein sollen. Die Regelung bestimmter anderer Vervielfältigungshandlungen, vor allem durch Bibliotheken, soll dagegen den Mitgliedsstaaten überlassen werden. Zwar müssen diese Schranken des Vervielfältigungsrechts dem „Drei-Stufen-Test“ von Art. 9 Abs 2 RBÜ entsprechen, doch kann man sich schon jetzt lebhaft vorstellen, daß die Ansichten über unbestimmte Rechtsbegriffe wie „berechtigte Interessen“, „Unzumutbarkeit“ oder „normale Verwertung“ in den Mitgliedsstaaten höchst unterschiedlich beurteilt werden. Dies gilt ganz besonders im Zusammenhang mit der künftigen Rolle der Bibliotheken in der Informationsgesellschaft. In diesem Zusammenhang hätten wir uns eindeutigere Signale der Europäischen Kommission gewünscht.

a) Rolle der Bibliotheken

Nach Ansicht der Bundesvereinigung Deutscher Bibliotheksverbände (Denkschrift „Bibliotheken in der Informationsgesellschaft“, Deutsches Bibliotheksinstitut, Berlin 1997, S. 22) sollen die bisherigen Ausnahmen vom Vervielfältigungsrecht für den analogen Bereich unterschiedslos auch für das Speichern und Weiterleiten von urheberrechtlich geschützten Texten auf digitalem Wege gelten. So ist der notwendige Ausgleich zwischen Allgemein- und Urheberinteressen nach Meinung der deutschen Bibliotheksverbände mit Zahlung der Vergütung gem. § 53 UrhG an die VG WORT bereits erfolgt. Weitergehende Ansprüche von Urhebern und anderen Rechteinhabern seien unberechtigt.

Der Zynismus – dieses Wort muß hier erlaubt sein – solcher Äußerungen durch Vertreter der öffentlichen Hand ist allerdings kaum zu überbieten, denn auch dort weiß man ja, daß in Deutschland jeder Rechteinhaber jährlich im Durchschnitt ganze DM 371,87 für das Kopieren in öffentlichen Bibliotheken erhält bzw. DM 469,40, wenn es sich um das Kopieren in wissenschaftlichen Bibliotheken handelt (vgl. Geschäftsbericht der VG WORT 1996). Dieses Abspeisungsprinzip wollen die Bibliotheksverbände nunmehr auf elektronische Medien übertragen, denn ihrer Ansicht nach ist es unerheblich, über welche Technik man die gewünschte Information erhält. Damit wird der Zynismus nun endgültig auf die Spitze getrieben und das geistige Eigentum zur schrankenlosen Ausbeutung weltweit freigegeben. Denn geflissentlich wird übersehen, daß die Zurverfügungstellung von online-Informationen durch Bibliotheken in dramatischer Weise in die Primärverwertung der Verleger – also in deren ureigenste Aufgabe – eingreift, die auch künftig noch nach herkömmlicher Weise, aber zunehmend auch auf elektronischem Wege betrieben werden wird.

Um einen angemessenen Interessenausgleich zu erreichen, muß die Lösung in anderer Richtung gesucht werden. Bei der Suche nach einer solchen Lösung muß man sich notwendigerweise an den gesellschaftlichen und wirtschaftlichen Entwicklungen orientieren, die die Einführung der digitalen Technik mit sich bringt und versuchen, die Rolle der Beteiligten an der Informationskette neu zu definieren. Dazu gehören neben Autoren, Verlegern und Buchhändlern selbstverständlich auch die Bibliotheken. Sie alle müssen den rasanten Wechsel, der z. Zt. bei den neuen Medien stattfindet, nachvollziehen und entsprechende Anpassungen an ihr bisheriges Wirken vornehmen.

Auf Grund zuverlässiger Studien besteht – wohl weltweit – die einheitliche Auffassung, daß ohne private Investitionen der Aufbau der Informationsgesellschaft nicht gelingen kann. Private Mittel fließen aber nur dann, wenn die Investoren eine realistische Chance sehen, für ihren Einsatz einst auch honoriert zu werden. Angesichts der oben beschriebenen Möglichkeiten der digitalen Technik ist ein diesen Bereich umfassendes, wirksames internationales und nationales Urheberrecht unabdingbare Voraussetzung für das Entstehen der Informationsgesellschaft.

Dies bedeutet allerdings nicht, daß dadurch die Rolle z. B. der Bibliotheken überflüssig werden soll, im Gegenteil: Die Herausforderungen und Chancen sind auch für sie gewaltig; ebenso wie Autoren, Verlage und Buchhändler müssen sie jedoch vielleicht lieb gewordene Denk- und Arbeitsweisen in Frage stellen. Bibliotheken als Vermittler werden sogar wichtiger denn je sein – als Helfer und Dienstleister der Nutzer bei der Suche und Auswahl von Informationen innerhalb weltweit aktiver elektronischer Netzwerke. Da diese zum großen Teil privatwirtschaftlich betrieben werden, ist allerdings ein gleichzeitiges Agieren von privaten Informationsanbietern und von Bibliotheken, wenn diese den kostenlosen Zugriff auf die in den Datenbanken enthaltenen Informationen anbieten, ausgeschlossen. Andernfalls würde die privatwirtschaftlich organisierte Verwertung untergraben; d. h. zu Ende gedacht: Sie würde bei mangelnder Rentabilität nicht mehr stattfinden können.

Denn im Gegensatz zum Herstellen von Printkopien und deren Versendung durch die Post handelt es sich beim Online-Abruf z. B. von Fachzeitschriftenbeiträgen aus Bibliotheksdatenbanken nicht um die Berührung eines sekundären Rechts von Urhebern und Verlagen, sondern um einen elementaren Eingriff in die Primärverwertung des Verlags. Ein solcher Vorgang würde, wenn er ohne entsprechende Vorgaben des Rechteinhabers erfolgte, binnen kürzester Zeit die Verwertung überhaupt unmöglich machen, wenn öffentlich-rechtliche Einrichtungen – sprich Bibliotheken – mit Hilfe staatlicher Subventionen den Rechteinhabern auf dem Weltmarkt Konkurrenz machen.

Ein solches Szenario würde auch zwangsläufig zu einem wohl allseits unerwünschten Wettbewerb der Bibliotheken untereinander führen. Denn welcher Bibliotheksdirektor, z. B. in Hannover oder in München, sähe es wohl gern, wenn seine örtliche Klientel, für die er in erster Linie Dienstleistungen erbringen soll, ihren Wissensdurst in der Uni-Bibliothek von Buenos Aires stillt, weil man dieselbe Information dort zufälligerweise etwas günstiger erhält.

b) Lösungsansatz

Die Lösung dieser Problematik kann wohl nur in bewährter Weise erfolgen, wonach nämlich die Verlage den Bibliotheken, wie schon bisher, ihre Publikationen bzw. deren Inhalte zum Erwerb anbieten. Die Bibliotheken werden entscheiden – ebenfalls wie schon bisher – ob das angebotene Produkt ihren Erwartungen und Preisvorstellungen entspricht. Hier stehen sicherlich auch die Verlage vor einer großen Herausforderung. Kommt es zum Kauf oder zum Erwerb einer entsprechenden Lizenz durch die Bibliothek, so wird z. B. die elektronische Zeitschrift, wie deren Printversion zuvor, in der Regel nur Universitätsangehörigen – wie auch immer man diesen Kreis definieren wird – zur Verfügung gestellt. Wenn der Unterhaltsträger der Bibliothek eine solche Nutzung subventionieren will, so steht ihm dies – ebenfalls wie schon zuvor – völlig frei. Sollen die Informationen allerdings auch anderen als den eigentlich subventionsberechtigten Nutzern zur Verfügung gestellt werden, so kann dies nur zu den vom jeweiligen Rechteinhaber festgesetzten Bedingungen geschehen.

Dieser Einsicht sollte sich letztendlich keiner der Beteiligten entziehen, wenn er Kreativität, die Schaffung und Verbreitung von Wissen und Informationen nicht nachhaltig gefährdet sehen will. In der Praxis ist man deshalb längst dabei, vielfältigste Formen der Zusammenarbeit zu entwickeln. Zahlreiche Pilotprojekte laufen seit geraumer Zeit oder werden gerade angeschoben, wie z. B. SUBITO, die Bund-Länder-Initiative zur Schaffung eines Dokumentenlieferdienstes der deutschen Bibliotheken. Dort haben die beteiligten Bibliotheken den Verlagen bereits zugesagt, für die Phase II von SUBITO die elektronische Weitergabe von Dokumenten durch Bibliotheken auf individuelle vertragliche Vereinbarungen zu gründen. Es wird nun darum gehen, für solche Vorgänge Rahmenbedingungen zu entwickeln, die es den Bibliotheken ermöglichen, die erforderlichen Rechte ohne unnötigen Verwaltungsaufwand zu erwerben. In der gemeinsamen Entwicklung solcher Projekte – nicht durch eine Verkürzung des Urheberrechts – wird also die Lösung der anstehenden Probleme zu suchen sein. Im Grunde ein gar nicht so neuer Weg.

Lassen Sie mich schließen mit einem Wort von Franz Georg Kaltwasser, dem ehemaligen Direktor der Bayerischen Staatsbibliothek („Ein Spielplatz namens Internet", Börsenblatt 99 vom 12. Dez. 1997, S. 12,19):

„Die neuen Techniken werden nicht nur die bislang gewohnten Tätigkeiten verändern, sie ermöglichen auch ganz neue zweckmäßige Aufgaben... Die Technik ist ein Mittel und nicht der Zweck. Die Aufgabe lautet, Informationen in bestmöglicher Weise zu vermitteln und sich dazu der jeweils dafür geeignetsten Technik zu bedienen und nicht umgekehrt, neueste Technik zu installieren und die sehr differenzierten Informationsprozesse dann technischen „Sachzwängen" unterzuordnen. Wenn es mit Augenmaß geschieht, werden die Bibliotheken in der „neuen Informationsgesellschaft" eine bedeutende Rolle der Vermittlung, aber auch der Bewahrung der Kultur und des Wissens spielen."

„Informationen in bestmöglicher Weise vermitteln" – das verstehe ich so: unter Beachtung auch der Rechte von Autoren und Verlegern!

METADATEN

ROSS BOURNE

The European BIBLINK Project

There can be few European research libraries that have neither participated in DG XIII projects nor been at least tempted by the funding that has been available through the European Commission's Telematics Applications Programme. This is not the time or place to describe the impact which the TAP has made on the ways in which our libraries function, and perhaps that impact will only become apparent to the library historian; but whatever history has to say on the subject I can easily believe that our *modi operandi* have been irretrievably changed by the discipline of having to observe deadlines for deliverables, workpackages, progress reports, management reports, cost statements, peer reviews, and all the other requirements we did not realise we were letting ourselves in for. Again, history will have to judge whether, regardless of any technological innovations, those bureaucratic disciplines have actually improved the services we provide for our users. I should like to think that they have.

BIBLINK stands for „Linking Publishers and National Bibliographic Services“ and the BIBLINK project commenced formally in May 1996. Its origins lie in a DG XIII sponsored „concerted action“, which is Commission language for an activity that encourages particular sectors to discuss issues that might result in an activity such as a project or a feasibility study. CoBRA, or Computerised Bibliographic Record Actions, was – and indeed is – a concerted action bringing together European national libraries for just that purpose; amongst other things, it has initiated projects on record file labelling, character set standardisation and the networking of national name authority files. But the real impetus for BIBLINK is twofold:

- the belief that economies can be made by developing better relationships between publishers and libraries and re-using publishers' bibliographic information in library catalogues and databases;
- the growth of electronic publishing, requiring libraries to exercise bibliographic control over documents that while sharing many of the characteris-

tics of conventional print publications, have some features which are not at present covered in traditional cataloguing codes.

These two factors have resulted in a project whose aim is to produce a prototype system for the exchange of metadata between publishers of electronic documents and national bibliographic agencies. In short, the system should enable a publisher to transmit bibliographic data to a national bibliographic agency or NBA, the NBA to adapt the data to its own requirements and then to return it to the publisher, duly enhanced. The advantage for the NBA will be that it is receiving timely and authoritative bibliographic information in advance of publication; the advantage for the publisher will be that its publications will be recorded in the national bibliography as soon as possible after publication – if not before – thus improving its accessibility, and that any metadata contained in the publication will have been verified by the NBA. In order to reach the stage at which such a system can be designed, however, a great amount of research into different aspects of the area had to be carried out. I will describe that research in a little more detail later on – or rather, I will mention the decisions that were made as a result of that research – but firstly I should say something about the people and the institutions that form the BIBLINK consortium and the parameters of the project itself.

The BIBLINK consortium includes the national libraries of France, the Netherlands, Norway, Spain and the United Kingdom and two academic institutions, the Universitat Oberta de Catalunya in Barcelona and the University of Bath, in the form of UKOLN, the UK Office for Library and Information Networking. The consortium is led by the British Library and the consortium agreement is a legally binding document which empowers the British Library to act on behalf of the partners in dealing with the Commission, especially on financial matters. The experience which the partners bring to the project is considerable, especially those partners which – unlike ourselves at the British Library – actually handle electronic publications. The National Library of Norway, for example, has been collecting electronic documents for some years now, and a visitor to Mo-i-Rana, its northern outpost only just south of the Arctic Circle, cannot but be impressed by the efficiency of an operation which ensures a near-comprehensive coverage of all forms of Norwegian material. The Royal Library in the Netherlands, on the other hand, operates voluntary rather than legal deposit, an outcome of which is that they enjoy much closer relationships with their publishers than any of the rest of us. UKOLN at the University of Bath is unusual within the consortium in that they are not a library *per se*: they are effectively a research centre which under various names has been at the forefront of many bibliographic developments for over 20 years. It is UKOLN which hosts the BIBLINK Web page, which can be visited at the following address, *http://www.ukoln.ac.uk/metadata/BIBLINK/*.

BIBLINK is a three year project, divided into two stages of equal length. Stage 1, the research stage, has just concluded; a revised technical annex for Stage 2, which will see the development of the prototype system, has just been agreed. The project has now just under eighteen months to run. Like all Commission-funded projects, partners receive 50% funding, which means that they must find the other 50% from within their own resources; but during the actual demonstration stage the Commission will reimburse only a third rather than a half. As project leader, the British Library has heavy obligations, but we are fortunate in having yielded day-to-day project management to an outside company, Level-7, and this has enabled us to concentrate better on what we at the British Library want from the project as well as our overall responsibility for ensuring that the project remains on track.

The first stage of the project has been about researching the field and obtaining consensus for its conclusions. I will say something about that research in a moment, but the consensus part of the project has been an important component, because in Stage 2 publishers have been enlisted to enable us to demonstrate that a system of creating, converting, enhancing and retransmitting metadata between the two sectors can work. Each of the partners has discussed the results of our research with publishers in each of our countries, and we are confident that those publishers support our findings.

I want now to summarise just what arose from that research. Stage 1 consisted of eight workpackages, two of which were the obtaining of publisher consensus and general consolidation of the results; the six which comprised the bulk of the research were as follows:

- scoping: what were the limits of the task?
- metadata: what metadata formats existed and which were most appropriate to the project?
- identification: as above, which numbering and other systems existed and which were most appropriate?
- format conversion: which tools were available to handle the metadata?
- transmission: how should the metadata be moved between publishers and NBAs?
- authentication: how could the relationship between the metadata and the item itself be assured?

In the Scoping workpackage the range of electronic publishers and electronic publications to be considered by the project was defined. The scope was narrowed to those publications that would traditionally be included in a national bibliography in whatever electronic medium they are published, although to all intents and purposes those media are CD-ROM and the World Wide Web. A taxonomy of publisher types by country, covering the established and newly emerging sectors, was also produced from which publishing partners would be recruited at a later point of the project; those publisher types are, in BIBLINK parlance, „traditional“ or publishers with a background in conventional print publications; „new“ or publishers without such a background; and „grey“ or publishers such as university departments whose primary concern is not publishing and who are increasingly using the Web to disseminate scholarship.

The study of metadata formats identified formats in use or under development in the library and publishing sectors. A comparative analysis was performed on these and the content of the non-library formats compared with MARC formats. At the same time, a separate report examining three SGML metadata formats (TEI, EAD and CIMI) was commissioned and incorporated in the deliverable. National libraries' requirements in this area were also identified. It was concluded that it might be necessary to consider more than one format to accommodate the diverse body of publishers covered by the scope of the project. Dublin Core, the Book Industry Communication/Pira Simplified SGML for Serials Headers (SSSH) and BIC's forthcoming non-serial Document Type Definition (DTD) were recommended for consideration.

After initial comparison of fourteen identification schemes, seven were identified as possibly being appropriate for BIBLINK, including the emerging Digital Object Identifier (DOI) as well as the established ISBN and ISSN systems. These were analysed according to a set of criteria identified by the partners and refined by the workpackage leader. It was not felt to be appropriate to recommend a single identification scheme as none was used by all, or even a majority, of the possible publisher participants. The report recommended five schemes that would be acceptable to the project: ISSN, ISBN, SICI, DOI and URN.

The report from the Format Conversion workpackage examined the feasibility of producing MARC records from formats previously identified for use by BIBLINK. Working in parallel with the Consensus Building workpackage to define a minimum set of data elements, the report mapped the agreed minimum data set to Dublin Core and suggested modifications that would be required for the creation of a usable MARC record. It also mapped SSSH elements to MARC records at serial issue level only. The BIC non-serial DTD cannot, however, be mapped until its definition is complete. The report concluded that Dublin Core could be used to produce a reasonably comprehensive descriptive MARC record for so-called monographs – of which more later – but that SSSH is not a suitable format for descriptions of serials at issue level; for that purpose, either Dublin Core or the format used in the ISSN database could be used.

The Transmission workpackage examined the technical and operational characteristics of the options for transferring metadata from publishers to national bibliographic agencies at two levels: firstly, the low-level transport layer for which four possible options were identified and fully analysed according to criteria specified in the technical annex and others that were identified as work proceeded; and secondly, a higher packaging level comprising such formats as EDI and the Warwick Framework (which grew out of the Dublin Core), which could allow data of interest to a variety of players to be included in the transmission at different points in time. It was concluded that BIBLINK should use Internet protocols for the transmission of data in conjunction with one of three high level formatting options. The final recommendation for the latter was dependent on the outcome of discussions with publishers.

In the BIBLINK context, authentication has been defined as ensuring a one-to-one relationship between a bibliographic record and the publication to which it refers. Two models were considered, one in which the publication is kept in a controlled environment and one in which it is not. It can be seen to encompass other matters which are live issues in the world of electronic publishing, namely version control, rights management and protection of intellectual property. The report studied other projects that are addressing these issues and examined the techniques in use or under development, but came eventually to the conclusion that the provision of a data element containing a checksum figure that had been generated by the publisher or the NBA would meet BIBLINK's requirements.

I would like to make two general comments on progress to date. Firstly, the question of publisher consensus: BIBLINK partners have been greatly encouraged not only by the interest shown by publishers in the project but also by their promise of active support, to the extent that 23 have agreed to be involved in testing the prototype. Those 23 publishers range from major international publishers to relatively small organisations, they come from all five countries of the consortium and each of the three publisher types referred to earlier are well represented.

Secondly, what has become apparent to me during the course of the project so far is the fact that a librarian's conventional distinctions between monographs and serials is breaking down. What do you call a Web document which is not a serial in the classical sense but which is forever changing? Is there an optimal point in the life of such a document when it is appropriate for a library to acquire or download it, or can one do no more than treat the act of downloading as taking a snapshot? I wonder whether by attempting to use what are basically traditional means to handle electronic documents we are not falling into the same trap as early motor car designers, who did no more than adopt the design of the horse and carriage. Some of these questions will be answered, no doubt by another Commission sponsored project, NEDLIB, which will be looking into the whole life cycle of electronic publications. I look forward to NEDLIB's conclusions.

But back to the present. Very shortly a software house will be selected to create what the consortium is calling the „BIBLINK workspace" or BW. The BW will be a shared, distributed database containing records to which a variety of processes may be carried out within the confines of the workspace, such as creation, modification, conversion, and so forth. BW users may include not only publishers and NBAs but also the various standard numbering agencies to whom one or other of the two other user types may need to apply for the appropriate identification number. The records themselves must contain at least the data agreed to be mandatory within the BIBLINK Minimum Data Set (in other words, some of those elements are optional only because they are not applicable to all publications, such as frequency in the case of serials). That minimum data set, by the way, includes only eleven of the fifteen Dublin Core elements, but adds a further seven, making eighteen in total. What will essentially happen in the BW is that publisher records will enter the system (perhaps in Dublin Core format), be converted through a MARC conversion package such as USEMARCON to one of the national MARC formats, be reviewed by the NBA for authority control and subject indexing term, and then retransmitted to the publisher *via* a reverse conversion process, if that is what the publisher requires. Behind this brief scenario are various options and some questions still waiting to be answered: for example, will the BW interface be Web based or e-mail based? What national MARC formats can be handled, bearing in mind full conversion tables available at present as part of USEMARCON are limited to UKMARC and USMARC? Will NBAs themselves have a role in the allocation of Digital Object Identifiers if the DOI system prevails, as it may well do? Likewise, is the Dublin Core likely to become the standard for Web metadata?

The stage where BIBLINK is at present – or rather at the time of writing, which was just before Christmas – is that user requirements and functional specification documents are being drawn up. After a Call to Tender, the latter will be presented to the software house which has bid successfully to create the BIBLINK Workspace; that software house will have just a few months to produce and test the system, which should be ready for the demonstrator phase due to commence in the autumn. In the meantime, the individual NBAs will need to ensure that their internal systems, which are of course outside the scope of the BW, are able to interact with the BW, since the demonstrator phase will be demonstrating the full chain of events, from publisher to NBA and back. The delivery of a final report will conclude the project in May 1999, and as part of that report NBAs will be required to indicate their individual plans to put the results of BIBLINK into action.

I want to round off this presentation by making one or two observations on the overall thrust of BIBLINK. Firstly, it has been an unwritten guideline that BIBLINK exists in the world that we have, rather than the world where we might like to live. While the Telematics Applications Programme is about innovation, that innovation is not intended to be at the expense of proven systems or technologies. BIBLINK has tried to make use of what is available, but to be innovative in the way in which existing systems and technologies are brought together. Secondly, it has been fortuitous to say the least that two systems designed to improve the accessibility and availability of Web publications have been under development throughout the course of the project, the Dublin Core and the DOI systems. BIBLINK partners have contributed to their development. Thirdly and finally, and this goes back to what I mentioned at the outset of this paper, the two factors which led to the BIBLINK project being proposed to and accepted by the European Commission, there is the matter of the relationship between libraries and publishers. BIBLINK's experience of that relationship is that while publishers – quite justifiably – will only help libraries if they can see advantage for themselves, the complexity and unknown future of electronic publications is such that they are more than willing to exchange experience with us. If therefore we can demonstrate through BIBLINK that solutions to those problems are best achieved through co-operation, then I believe we can be optimistic about our future relationships in other areas of joint concern as well.

The author would like to thank his colleague, Robina Clayphan, for commenting on this paper during its preparation, thereby helping to make it more comprehensible.

List of abbreviations

The following is an almost complete list, omitting only those acronyms and initialisms too well known to spell out, such as CD-ROM.

BIC	Book Industry Communication *(joint UK book trade/library organisation)*
BW	BIBLINK Workspace
CIMI	Computer Interchange of Museum Information *(specialist exchange format)*

CoBRA	Computerised Bibliographic Record Actions *(EC sponsored Concerted Action)*
DOI	Digital Object Identifier *(identification system for electronic documents)*
DTD	Document Type Definition *(SGML application)*
EAD	Encoded Archival Description *(specialist exchange format)*
EDI	Electronic Data Interchange *(generic name for electronic trading standards)*
ISBN	International Standard Book Number
ISSN	International Standard Serial Number
MARC	Machine Readable Cataloguing *(library exchange format)*
NBA	National Bibliographic Agency
NEDLIB	Networked European Deposit Library *(EC sponsored project)*
SGML	Standard Generalised Mark-up Language
SICI	Serial Item and Contribution Identifier *(identification system for serial parts and contents)*
SSSH	Simplified SGML for Serials Headers *(SGML application)*
TAP	Telematics Applications Programme
TEI	Text Encoding Initiative *(SGML application)*
UKOLN	UK Office for Library and Information Networking *(research office housed at the University of Bath)*
URN	Uniform Resource Name
USEMARCON	User-controlled Generic MARC Converter *(EC sponsored project)*

BIBLIOTHEKEN IN DER INFORMATIONSGESELLSCHAFT – NATIONALE INITIATIVEN

TOMAS LIDMAN

National Libraries as a Resource for the Future Provision of Information

Introduction

In this lecture it is my intention to present some thoughts and ideas about the tasks of national libraries in a ten-year perspective. Where will we be in the year 2008? In one way, the perspective is narrowly national, but it is also my ambition to try to be more general in my approach. In her lecture, Margaret Haines attempted to outline an information strategy for the entire British nation. In other words, my ambitions are more modest but not necessarily easier to fulfil.

The national libraries face sweeping changes. The task of collecting, describing, storing and making the national cultural heritage available, as it is expressed in words, ideas and thoughts, is becoming increasingly difficult. After remaining practically unaltered for centuries, that task is now being subjected to dramatic change. New knowledge will be presented for use alongside the old, familiar routines. Books, periodicals, advertisements and other printed materials of a more transient nature come to us in new forms – indeterminate and transitory – and difficult to handle. However, the task of the national libraries will remain the same – to reflect the breadth of societal development in our particular sphere of activity. We will have to deal with all the new material, adapt, make new priorities in our budgets and seek new skills among our colleagues. A real challenge in the true sense of the word. The question is – are we up to it?

I would try to answer that question by presenting you with a scenario. What might our national libraries look like in ten years' time? What are the major issues? And perhaps even more important: what would we like to see, and will we be able to influence developments? Naturally I must confess that my predictions rest largely on my knowledge of conditions close to home, that is to say, in Scandinavia, and I am aware that there will most undoubtedly be differences when making comparisons with the larger countries of Europe in particular. At the latest meeting of IFLA in Copenhagen, the national library section's conference focused on strategies for the future. One interesting lecture on this theme was given by the Director General of the Royal Library in Copenhagen, Erland Kolding Nielsen, who discussed the cultural tasks of national libraries in the future. I warmly recommend you to read his report, which made quite an impression on me.

Scenario – in ten Years' Time

Cooperation at the Nordic level has changed. NORDINFO – the Nordic Council for Scientific Information – the operations of which were previously targeted at libraries, now concentrates on supporting specialized IT-projects. And the organization has also been called in question. On the other hand, constructive regional cooperation between the libraries in the Baltic Sea region flourishes. The national libraries in the Scandinavian countries are cooperating more and more closely and are finding common solutions in various problem areas. The languages unite in the new Europe. The Nordic region, in the sense the term has been used since the Second World War, is becoming less distinct as a political and cultural concept.

The national libraries' task of safeguarding the cultural heritage has been retained and is now being strengthened and developed. Admittedly, material in certain areas has undergone a change of character – electronic periodicals, reports and dissertations are becoming increasingly common, the archives left by authors frequently contain electronic preparatory work. But more than one half of any country's collections are still delivered as hard copy. Primarily doctoral theses, novels, popular periodicals and newspapers. Non-commercial scientific and research literature is often published in electronic form and is retrieved by the national library at regular intervals to be stored in massive databases available to the library's readers. The present divisions into audio and visual materials, publications and archive material have been revised. Illustrations, music and text are intermingled in electronic editions which sometimes more closely resemble the official records of public authorities. And for this reason, constructive cooperative projects have been launched between all those institutions who work to preserve the cultural heritage, the purpose being to facilitate investments and costly maintenance work. There is some concern that the electronically stored material will be destroyed in the long term.

An animated discussion about migration models and selection criteria is under way. Problems with intellectual property rights have been solved, allowing the national library the right to supply Swedish printed materials within its organization irrespective of where they were published – in much the same way as libraries are allowed to use conventional materials. CD-ROM as a storage medium has proved to be only a transitional solution and is in practice already obsolete for the handling of documents.

More and more frequently, the basic content of catalogues is supplied by the publishing houses themselves and arrives in electronic form. The national library processes and refines the data to a level from which various bibliographic products can be generated automatically. It is becoming increasingly common for both illustrations and full text to be linked to bibliographical references. A reader can quite simply switch from the bibliographical description to the main body of the text. We see a development whereby catalogue work will focus more and more on an analysis of the subject and content of the text.

The national libraries' computer system has been developed in such a way as to make the system suitable for a whole range of applications. The database itself contains different types of information that are useful to different sectors of society. Book wholesalers, publishing houses, purchasers of books, advertising agencies, schools, teachers, students, researchers and the general public; all of these groups need to consult this central information bank from time to time. Access to information is still regarded as a public service and is free of charge to the user. The system also provides modules for local applications in other libraries. This has been made possible by the adoption of general standards, which means that most systems can now be constructed on a modular basis. A special department at the national library is responsible for this development.

Focus is on the problem of preservation. The preservation plan lays down what material is to be stored in digital form and how the requisite physical storage facilities should be designed. In addition to concentrating on our historic collections of national and foreign printed materials which are slowly disintegrating, particularly attractive collections of periodicals, posters and manuscripts are being digitized. Since the copyright on most of these documents has long since expired they are now available on the Internet, markedly improving both access to and knowledge about them. The national library now has a leading position with respect to new technical applications in this area.

The increased political interest in information policy and the role of the national library in society which emerged in the early and mid-1990s has continued. The expansion of the university and university college system, the Adult Education Initiative and the decentralization of decision-making processes mean that the national library is seen in a new light. Increasingly, it has come to be regarded as a suitable institution for implementing the Government's plans to pursue a state policy for information provision. The digitization of information resources and the expansion of the digital networks have radically changed the accessibility of information. Where that information is stored is becoming less and less relevant. The national library can no longer concentrate all its attention on the library as a warehouse full of books. To understand the situation correctly it is necessary to take a more serious look at the situation of the individual user and the type of information required, and to use these factors as the point of departure for planning the work of libraries. The national library must test a growing number of government measures in order to promote a positive development in this area. Gradually, the tasks of the national library have moved closer to those of the other institutions whose work involves preserving the national heritage. Thus, new tasks have devolved upon the special department for national coordination and planning which was established at the national library in the year 2001. These new duties involve the allocation of government support.

We are witnessing a surge of interest in our history and our cultural heritage in society at large. As the pace of life accelerates – people change jobs more often, are forced to move from one place to another, must be constantly prepared to learn new things – people's need of basic security also increases. It is an increasingly attractive prospect to exhibit and give people access to the national library's collections, representing as they do a broad panoramic vista of societal evolution spanning several centuries. The national library's „products" will be in demand. Technological advances will make previously inaccessible treasures available to a broad public. In addition, a large number of different public events based on the library's various functions are offered: exhibitions, debates, recitations, seminars, etc. As a result of these endeavours the national library is now well established as a cultural institution and is presented as such when its services are marketed both in Sweden and abroad. The national library is also regarded as an attractive cooperative partner by a number of interest groups. Writers and cultural workers see the institution as a natural place to which they can donate their documents. The role of specialized research library has had to be strengthened as a result of major cut at the universities. Regrettably, security requirements now compel national libraries to restrict direct access to sensitive and valuable material. The security aspect is also one of the main subjects of discussion when premises, exhibitions, seminars, etc are planned.

Summary

1. The national libraries will acquire more clearly defined tasks based on their function as libraries. They will have to develop their national tasks and lead the way when it comes to the general development of libraries. Cooperation between different types of libraries should be facilitated. Free and open access to information, a vital component of any democratic society, must be maintained and developed.
2. The national system for information provision will be developed to form a communal information resource involving interested parties from all sectors of society and with a broad range of applications. Together with those who actually construct the database, the national library will be responsible for ensuring that the information contained in it keeps pace with developments in society, and for monitoring the quality and availability of that material.
3. In a changing world, the national libraries must work to ensure that new texts produced in their respective countries are preserved for posterity regardless of their form and content. The emergence of new technology means that libraries will have to adapt their routines and tasks to these new circumstances.
4. New methods for describing the content of texts and illustrations will lead to changes in routines for cataloguing and classifying material. In cooperation with publishing houses, printing shops and the originators, the national library will be forced to take full advantage of the opportunities for improvement that are offered.
5. The national libraries will have to take measures to improve access to their collections. A carefully prepared strategy for digitization of vital parts of the collections will be required in order to highlight the most important material. The result should be made available via the Internet.
6. The question of preservation will become increasingly important, often in conjunction with strictly observed security considerations. The national preservation plan will lay down the guidelines for this work. The national library should have such competence within its organization to ensure that the plans can be implemented.
7. A growing interest in the cultural tasks of the national libraries and the special departments means that they will become established as well-known national cultural institutions. They will be obliged to pursue carefully considered programme and exhibition activities, show their collections, demonstrate their professional skills and seek to actively influence cultural life. National library officials will take part in the debate on library policy.

8. Work at libraries is by its very nature international. We both import and export knowledge. International cooperation between libraries will increase on all fronts, among other things as a result of the integration of the member countries of the European community. The national library must work to facilitate this development. It must make its mark on the entire Swedish library system, but the library itself will also be required to initiate and manage projects.
9. In the light of cuts at university libraries, the role of the national libraries as important research libraries will be strengthened. The national library will have to take pains to acquire a full and representative selection of foreign material in certain vital core areas.
10. The various administrative and library routines of the national libraries will be fully integrated, providing a more reliable basis for planning, and creating conditions for work of high quality.

CHRISTINE THOMAS

Nationale Initiativen in Deutschland

Bibliothekspolitik als Teil der Informationspolitik

Es ist erklärtes politisches Ziel der Bundesregierung, Deutschland auf dem Weg in die Informationsgesellschaft zu unterstützen. Sie hat im Jahr 1996 den Bericht „*Info 2000 – Deutschlands Weg in die Informationsgesellschaft*" herausgebracht, in dem die aktive Gestaltung des Wandels unserer Gesellschaft zur Informationsgesellschaft gefordert wird. Die Bundesregierung geht diese Herausforderung mit drei Schwerpunktaufgaben an:

Der erste Schwerpunkt betrifft *die Entwicklung der Netzinfrastruktur*. Stichworte sind hier „Deregulierung der Telekommunikationsmärkte" und „Ausbau des Hochgeschwindigkeitsnetzes".

Der zweite Schwerpunkt umfaßt die *rechtlichen Rahmenbedingungen*. Die Bundesregierung hat im Juni 1997 das „Informations- und Kommunikationsdienste-Gesetz" verabschiedet und damit ein rechtliches Gerüst für die Entwicklung neuer Dienstleistungen im Informationsbereich geschaffen.

Den dritten Schwerpunkt bilden die *Nutzungen*. Grundlegender Baustein ist das Programm „Information als Rohstoff für Innovation der Bundesregierung" für die Jahre 1996 bis 2000.

Diese Schwerpunkte werden auch als Säulen der Multimediapolitik der Bundesregierung bezeichnet.

Information als Rohstoff für Innovation

Das zentrale Ziel des Programms „*Information als Rohstoff für Innovation*" ist es, jedem Benutzer in Deutschland an seinem Arbeitsplatz einen schnellen und umfassenden Zugang zu den weltweit vorhandenen elektronischen und multimedialen Informationen zu ermöglichen. Die Realisierung dieses Ziels verlangt einen grundsätzlichen Strukturwandel in der wissenschaftlichen und technischen Informationsinfrastruktur, den alle Beteiligten gemeinsam und in intensiver internationaler Kooperation gestalten müssen.

Die uns im engeren Sinne interessierenden Förderschwerpunkte des Programms sind:

1. *Die Weiterentwicklung der wissenschaftlichen und technischen Informationsinfrastruktur zur „Globalen digitalen Bibliothek“*
   Kern dieses Schwerpunktes bildet die nationale Initiative „Global Info“, auf die ich im folgenden noch zu sprechen komme.
2. *Wissenschaftliche Bibliotheken auf dem Weg zu virtuellen Bibliotheken mit elektronischen Speichern*
   Dieser umfaßt die Maßnahmen in der Bibliothekspolitik, zum Beispiel die Initiative SUBITO.

Weitere Schwerpunkte des Programms sind das elektronische Publizieren, die Zukunftsgestaltung der Fachinformationszentren, die internationale Zusammenarbeit und Fördermaßnahmen zur Nutzung elektronischer Informationen in Aus- und Fortbildung, z.B. im Rahmen der Initiative Schulen ans Netz.

Spannungsfelder der Bibliothekspolitik

Die Bibliothekspolitik der Bundesregierung steht unter der Leitlinie des gesamten Informationsprogramms, nämlich der Unterstützung des Strukturwandels. Ziel ist die Verbesserung der überregionalen Literatur- und Informationsversorgung. Die Bibliotheksförderung muß berücksichtigen, daß sich der Weg der Bibliotheken in die neuen Strukturen in Spannungsfeldern vollzieht. Ich möchte im folgenden auf einige Aspekte eingehen.

Erstes Spannungsfeld: Föderale Bibliotheksstruktur versus bundeseinheitliche Dienstleistung

Wenn ich von wissenschaftlichen Bibliotheken spreche, so meine ich in erster Linie die Hochschulbibliotheken an Universitäten und Fachhochschulen in der Bundesrepublik Deutschland. Sie liegen in der politischen Zuständigkeit der Länder.

Die Verantwortlichkeit der Bundesregierung für wissenschaftliche Bibliotheken leitet sich aus verfassungsmäßigen Gemeinschaftsaufgaben des Bundes und der Länder beim Hochschulbau, der auch Bibliotheksbauten und Ausstattungen umfaßt, bei der gemeinsamen Bildungsplanung und Forschungsförderung sowie bei rechtlichen und internationalen Fragen ab.

Wir sind gegenüber anderen europäischen Ländern im Nachteil, weil systematische Planungen auf nationaler Ebene und die Einführung bundesweiter Dienstleistungen nur in schwierigen Abstimmungsprozessen möglich sind. Bei der Initiative SUBITO haben wir gesehen, daß sich solche Prozesse über Jahre hinziehen können. Wir haben aber den Vorteil, daß wir von unterschiedlichen Entwicklungen, ja sogar Wettbewerb zwischen den einzelnen Ländern profitieren können. Wir können bei der Entwicklung bundesweiter Dienstleistungen von bereits vorhandenen Einzelmodellen und erprobten Lösungen ausgehen und die hier gewonnenen Erfahrungen in den Gestaltungsprozeß einbeziehen. Dies war bei SUBITO bisher durchaus von Vorteil. Damit rückt auch die Frage nach der Balance von Wettbewerb und Kooperation zwischen den Bibliotheken in der Bundesrepublik Deutschland in den Vordergrund.

Zweites Spannungsfeld: Gesellschaftlicher Auftrag versus Dienstleistung für ausgewählte Zielgruppen
Die Bibliotheken in der Bundesrepublik Deutschland werden zu über 90% von der öffentlichen Hand finanziert. Der Staat hat die Verantwortung für die Schaffung einer Infrastruktur, die jedem den Zugriff auf die Informationsangebote ermöglicht. Die Informationsdienstleistungen dürfen auch im elektronischen Zeitalter nicht allein dem Markt überlassen bleiben. Entgelte der Bibliotheken für Dienstleistungen dürfen in diesem Sinne nicht prohibitiv sein.

Andererseits wächst überall der Druck auf die Bibliotheken, sich Einnahmen zu verschaffen. Fachlich spezialisierte Bibliotheken, wie Zentrale Fachbibliotheken, entwickeln spezifische Dienstleistungen, z.B. individuelle Informationsdienste für ausgewählte Zielgruppen. Auch die zunehmende Tendenz der Bibliotheken, Dienstleistungen für Nutzer außerhalb des Campus anzubieten, wird die Frage der Gestaltung von Dienstleistungen, vor allem aber von Entgelten neu stellen. Es geht hier um die Frage, ob staatlich subventionierte Entgelte, kommerzielle Preise oder ein Mixtum compositum die künftige Leitidee bestimmen sollen.

Drittes Spannungsfeld: Benutzerzugriff versus Ausleihe
Online-Kataloge, elektronische Bestellungen und Dokumentlieferdienste sowie der Zugriff auf elektronische Volltexte, die über Internet 24 Std. am Tag zugänglich sind, machen den persönlichen Gang in die Bibliothek in vielen Fällen überflüssig. Eher zögernd akzeptieren Bibliotheken den direkten Benutzerzugriff und bieten entsprechende Möglichkeiten an.

Die wachsenden Möglichkeiten des Online-Zugriffs setzen in den Bibliotheken eine veränderte Organisation und veränderte Dienstleistungen voraus. Alte und neue Angebotsformen schließen sich aber nicht aus: In der Praxis zeigt sich z.B., daß diejenigen Bibliotheken, die gute Online-Serviceleistungen anbieten, zugleich längere Öffnungszeiten haben. Entscheidend ist, daß sich die Bibliothek als modernes Dienstleistungszentrum sieht. Dies setzt ein entsprechendes Dienstleistungsverständnis voraus. Hier besteht großer Reformbedarf, der auch auf einen Bewußtseinswandel und auf Aus- und Fortbildung der Bibliothekare abzielt. Um das Bewußtsein für die Veränderungen im Informationsmarkt zu schärfen, wurde von der Europäischen Kommission das Projekt „New Book Economy" im Rahmen der Gemeinschaftsinitiative ADAPT des Europäischen Strukturfonds gestartet. Das Bundesministerium für Bildung, Wissenschaft, Forschung und Technologie unterstützt das Projekt für den Bibliotheksbereich. In das Projekt sind europaweit alle Bereiche der Buchbranche – Bibliothekswesen, Verlagswesen und Buchhandel – einbezogen.

Viertes Spannungsfeld: Informationsbeschaffung versus Bestandspflege
Anders als in der Vergangenheit, in der das Ansehen der Bibliothek allein durch den Buchbestand geprägt war, wird künftig der Erfolg einer Bibliothek stärker daran gemessen, wie schnell, zielkonform und vollständig sie dem Benutzer die gewünschte Information beschaffen kann – woher auch immer.

Die Bibliotheken stehen vor der schwierigen Aufgabe, ihren Geschäftsablauf und den Bestandsaufbau an die veränderten Bedingungen des Informationsmarktes anzupassen. Eine stärkere Kosten- und Leistungsorientierung ist für sie dabei im Wettbewerb um zufriedene Nutzer und knappe Haushaltsmittel von strategischer wirtschaftlicher Bedeutung.

Die Universitäts- und Landesbibliothek Düsseldorf und die Universitätsbibliothek Magdeburg erproben in dem von uns geförderten Projekt COMBI gemeinsam neue Beschaffungswege für Informationen unter den Gesichtspunkten Kostenorientierung, Wirtschaftlichkeit und Marktorientierung. Anstelle der traditionellen Fernleihe kommen vorzugsweise elektronische Dokumentliefersysteme zum Einsatz, wenn die Quellen vor Ort nicht verfügbar sind.

Nationale Initiativen

Das Bundesministerium für Bildung, Wissenschaft, Forschung und Technologie hat in den letzten Jahren zwei große Initiativen gestartet: Global Info und SUBITO.

Global Info
Global Info ist ein Forum, bei dem insgesamt 52 am Informations- und Publikationsprozeß Beteiligte, Autoren, Leser, Fachgesellschaften, Verbände und Forschungsorganisationen, Fachverlage und Fachbuchhandlungen, Fachinformationseinrichtungen und wissenschaftliche Bibliotheken gemeinsam das An-

gebot und die Nutzung von elektronischen und multimedialen Volltexten gestalten wollen. Das Förderkonzept wurde im April 1997 ausgeschrieben. Hierdurch sollen fachübergreifende, kooperative Initiativen zur Gestaltung eines grundsätzlichen Strukturwandels in der wissenschaftlichen und technischen Informationsinfrastruktur mit folgenden zentralen Programmzielen unterstützt werden:

1. Der effiziente Zugang zur weltweiten Information vom Arbeitsplatzrechner des Benutzers aus.
2. Das Zusammenwirken aller Beteiligten im Rahmen von internationalen Kooperationen.
3. Die Entwicklung der Informationssysteme in möglichst großer wissenschaftlicher und wirtschaftlicher Eigeninitiative und Selbstverwaltung.

Ein Gutachtergremium hat 16 Hochschulen und 13 Fachverlage für zweijährige Vorprojekte ausgewählt, die jeweils mit 100 TDM gefördert werden. Außerdem wurden 7 ausländische Verlage sowie 16 deutsche Bibliotheken und Fachinformationseinrichtungen für eine aktive Mitarbeit gewonnen. In Arbeitsgruppen werden fünf Schwerpunktthemen behandelt: „Ergänzen und Bearbeiten von Inhalten", „Vernetzung von Lehr- und Lernmaterialien", „Formale Beschreibung", „Nutzung von Inhalten" und „Wirtschaftlichkeitsmodelle und Abrechnungsverfahren". In den Arbeitsgruppen werden Pflichtenhefte für Sonderfördermaßnahmen vorbereitet. In den Sonderfördermaßnahmen werden dann die konkreten Projekte durchgeführt, in denen die Modelle für das Angebot und die Nutzung von elektronischen und multimedialen Volltexten, deren Qualitätssicherung und Vernetzung entwickelt und erprobt werden sollen. Die Beteiligten sollen in den Sonderfördermaßnahmen zusammenwirken. Dies erfordert ein Aushandeln oft divergierender Interessen. Global Info soll eine Plattform für den notwendigen Interessenabgleich sein. Auch Bibliotheken können hier gefördert werden. Sie sollten in Global-Info ihre gemeinsamen Interessen einbringen und an dem Know-How- und Technologietransfer teilnehmen.

Subito

Subito ist eine gemeinsame Initiative der Länder und des Bundes. Sie wurde vor mehr als drei Jahren, im Oktober 1994 gestartet. An ihr sind Bibliothekare, politische Vertreter, Wissenschaftler und Vertreter von Verlagen und Fachinformationseinrichtungen beteiligt. Die Geschäftsstelle ist beim Deutschen Bibliotheksinstitut angesiedelt. Aufgabe von SUBITO ist es, die überregionale Literatur- und Informationsversorgung zu beschleunigen. Von Beginn an waren drei Realisierungsschritte geplant:

SUBITO.1 liefert gedruckte wissenschaftliche Aufsätze an den Arbeitsplatz.

SUBITO.2 soll zusätzlich elektronische Dokumente bereitstellen.

SUBITO.3 soll die elektronische Bestellung und Schnell-Lieferung von Büchern ermöglichen.

Der Dienst SUBITO.1 ist realisiert. Seit Oktober 1997 wurde der Pilotbetrieb für den neuen, bundesweiten Dienst der deutschen Bibliotheken aufgenommen. Zeitschriftenartikel können nun vom Benutzer in einem Arbeitsgang und direkt am Arbeitsplatz elektronisch recherchiert und bei einer beliebigen Bibliothek bestellt werden. Die Dokumente werden innerhalb von drei Werktagen als Kopie direkt an den Arbeitsplatz geliefert. Eillieferungen erfolgen innerhalb von 24 Stunden. Die Lieferung kann nach Wahl elektronisch, per Fax oder per Post erfolgen und ist entgeltpflichtig. Lieferbar sind in der Zeitschriftendatenbank nachgewiesene Publikationen. SUBITO.1 ist ein elektronischer Dokumentlieferdienst mit bundesweiter Gültigkeit, garantierten Leistungsmerkmalen und einheitlichen Konditionen. Die technischen Entwicklungen für SUBITO wurden in einem weiteren Gemeinschaftsprojekt DBV-OSI entwickelt, das wir gemeinsam mit der Deutschen Forschungsgemeinschaft gefördert haben und das unter der Federführung Der Deutschen Bibliothek durchgeführt wird.

Zur Zeit beschäftigt sich die Bund-Länder-Initiative parallel mit SUBITO.2 und SUBITO.3. Hierzu sind entsprechende Arbeitsgruppen eingesetzt worden. Im Rahmen von SUBITO.3 soll – analog zu SUBITO.1 – eine Dienstleistung geschaffen werden, die die elektronische Bestellung und die (konventionelle) Lieferung von rückgabepflichtigen Dokumenten (Monographien) zu SUBITO-Konditionen beinhaltet, d.h. direkt vom und an den Endnutzer bei garantierter Bearbeitungszeit. Die Ausarbeitung des Funktionskonzeptes wurde begonnen.

Erheblich komplexer und schwieriger ist die Ausgestaltung der Dienstleistung SUBITO.2, da wir hier auf die elektronischen Publikationen abzielen und uns mit den schwierigen Fragen der vernünftigen Ausgestaltung einer Copyright-Lösung beschäftigen. Die Arbeiten stehen erst am Anfang. Es gibt noch mehr Fragen als Antworten und Lösungsansätze. Die wichtigste Aufgabe besteht darin, daß sich die Bibliotheken über ihre Interessenlage und zukünftige Rolle klar werden und gemeinsame Vorstellungen zu einer Struktur für die Versorgung mit elektronischen Volltexten entwickeln. Hierzu hat eine Arbeitsgruppe in dem Papier „Die virtuelle Fachbibliothek“ bereits Überlegungen geäußert und ein arbeitsteiliges Vorgehen der Bibliotheken vorgeschlagen.

Auch die Deutsche Forschungsgemeinschaft hat zu den Sondersammelgebieten Konzepte für ein verteiltes System entwickelt. Wir sind hier auf dem Weg, die Vorstellungen einander anzunähern und zu gemeinsamen Lösungen zu kommen. Bei der Ausgestaltung der Dienstleistung SUBITO.2 gegenüber dem Benutzer sind wir erst bei dem Problemaufriß. Es wird an Szenarien gearbeitet, in denen die unterschiedlichen Nutzungsmöglichkeiten elektronischer Publikationen und die damit verbundenen unterschiedlichen Probleme, wie die Frage von Copyright und Lizenzen, dargestellt werden.

Vorreiter in diesem Bereich ist ein Pilotprojekt, das vom Bundesministerium für Bildung, Wissenschaft, Forschung und Technologie an den Universitätsbibliotheken Bielefeld und Dortmund unter dem Namen *IBIS* gefördert wird. Für spezifische Fächer werden arbeitsteilig elektronische Dokumente ausgewählt, erschlosssen und bereitgestellt. Dabei werden die elektronischen Quellen entweder selbst vorgehalten und Zugriffsrechte erworben oder es wird die Nutzung vermittelt. Ziel ist, die bibliothekarischen Dienstleistungen in einem integrierten System zusammenzuführen. Von allgemeinem Interesse sind bei diesem Projekt die Erfahrungen,

- mit welchem Aufwand Internetquellen erschlossen werden können,
- welche Werkzeuge dafür eingesetzt werden können,
- wie die Bibliotheken zusammenarbeiten können,
- wie sich die Betriebsabläufe der Bibliothek verändern,
- wie die Benutzer auf das Angebot reagieren
- und wie die Verträge bei urheberrechtlich geschützten Materialien gestaltet werden können.

Der stufenweise Aufbau einer ersten elektronischen Bibliothek begann an der Technischen Universitätsbibliothek Hannover unter dem Projektnamen *TIB-QUICK 2000*.

In der ersten Stufe werden aus technischen und urheberrechtlichen Gründen zunächst die vom Bundesministerium für Bildung, Wissenschaft, Forschung und Technologie geförderten Forschungsberichte aufbereitet und auf dem Server bereitgestellt. Bis Ende 1997 waren es 440 Forschungsberichte. Inzwischen sind Dissertationen und Habilitationen der Universität Hannover hinzugekommen. Zur Zeit wird geprüft, welche weiteren, bereits in elektronischer Form vorliegenden Veröffentlichungen integriert werden können. Das Konzept ist auch offen für elektronische Dokumente anderer Anbieter (Verlage, Wissenschaftliche Fachgesellschaften).

Weitere Initiativen

Neben den nationalen Initiativen gibt es eine Fülle von Initiativen auf lokaler und regionaler Ebene. Durch seine föderale Struktur ist Deutschland besonders reich an lokalen und regionalen Lösungsansätzen und Programmen.

Zugleich haben sich die Wissenschaftlichen Bibliotheken jedoch stets auch als Teil des nationalen und letzlich globalen Informationssystems verstanden. Sie können von der Bundesregierung erwarten, daß sie für die anstehenden Entwicklungsaufgaben den Handlungsrahmen schafft. Die Bundesregierung hat sich dieser Aufgabe gestellt und z.T. zusammen mit der Deutschen Forschungsgemeinschaft Maßnahmen gefördert, von denen ich Ihnen einige vorgestellt habe.

Entwicklung einer nationalen Informationspolitik

Die Sektion „Wissenschaftliche Universalbibliotheken“ des Deutschen Bibliotheksverbandes hat gemeinsam mit den Leitern wissenschaftlicher Rechenzentren in einem Memorandum im Jahr 1994 die Einrichtung eines „Sachverständigenrates für eine nationale Informationspolitik“ gefordert. Bisher ist eine kohärente, abgestimmte politische Strategie für den Umgang mit den neuen Technologien und die Unterstützung des Strukturwandels nicht erfolgt, vielleicht aber auch nicht vonnöten. Ich bin der Auffassung, daß wir mit den nationalen Initiativen „Global Info“ und „SUBITO“ Diskussions- und Arbeitsforen geschaffen haben, in denen die Beteiligten gemeinsam die anstehenden Probleme bearbeiten und zu Entscheidungen kommen können.

Global-Info stellt ein übergreifendes Forum für die Gestaltung der Informationsversorgung dar. Anders als in SUBITO ist mit der Einbeziehung internationaler Verlage und der globalen Ausrichtung der Rahmen hier direkt auf den internationalen Wissenschaftsmarkt ausgerichtet. Mit Global-Info steht den Bibliotheken eine Plattform zur Verfügung, ihre Interessen im Machtspiel der Kräfte auch durchzusetzen. Gleichzeitig können und müssen die Bibliotheken von den dortigen Diskussionen und Entwicklungen profitieren.

Mit SUBITO steht ein geeigneter Rahmen für die weitere Förderung im Bibliotheksbereich zur Verfügung, zugleich eine Plattform für die Zusammenarbeit mit den Ländern. Außerdem haben die SUBITO-Gremien gezeigt, daß sie nicht nur diskutieren, sondern auch eine handfeste Dienstleistung realisieren können. SUBITO.1 ist erst der Anfang. SUBITO.2 und SUBITO.3 werden ebenso weitergeführt werden müssen.

An Grundsatzpapieren zur Informationsgesellschaft scheint es mir nicht zu fehlen. Die Deutsche Forschungsgemeinschaft, der Deutsche Bibliotheksverband, die Länder und die Bundesregierung haben Empfehlungen und Programme vorgelegt. Eines haben wir bei SUBITO gelernt: Fortschritt wird nur durch zähe gemeinsame Arbeit an der Realisierung von konkreten, klar umrissenen Dienstleistungen erzielt.

Die Bundesregierung wird auch künftig den Schwerpunkt ihrer Bibliotheksförderung auf die Entwicklung überregionaler Dienstleistungen für Wissenschaft, Wirtschaft und Gesellschaft legen und dabei die Möglichkeiten der zweckorientierten Zusammenarbeit mit anderen Partnern unterstützen. Für die Bibliotheken ergibt sich dabei die Chance, die Entwicklung der kommenden Jahre mit zu bestimmen und durch nutzergerechte Dienstleistungen auf modernstem technischen Stand eine Schlüsselstellung in der künftigen Informationsgesellschaft zu erringen.

EFFEKTIVE AUS- UND WEITERBILDUNG ALS VORAUSSETZUNG FÜR DIE MEISTERUNG DER NEUEN HERAUSFORDERUNGEN

HANS-GEORG STORK

European Initiatives for the Professional Development of Librarians

1. Introduction

Let us define our terms first: *Professional development* comprises all activities that make an individual fit for doing a certain job, for growing in that job and for keeping up with changes that have an impact on the nature of that job. It may hence enable a person to transcend eventually the job he or she has been trained for and to do quite different jobs with equal and perhaps more satisfaction. It should maintain and possibly expand a person's qualifications. Undoubtedly, over the past couple of decades librarians have not been spared the challenges of the *information age*. On the contrary: they have had to cope with profound changes in their professional environment. The demands on their know-how (or *know-where*?) and services are not likely to decrease in the foreseeable future. Therefore, talking about the *professional development of librarians* is just as timely and appropriate as talking about the development of any other group of professionals that are affected by that silent revolution brought about by the rapidly evolving information and communication technologies.

European initiatives is of course the most distinguishing element of the title of this paper. At first glance one might assume we are refering to what is happening in each of the European countries, to what various national organisations, schools and authorities are doing for their particular constituency to modernise training and (continuing) education in librarianship. However, taking such a broad view would certainly mean going beyond the scope of a short contribution to a conference. Rather, our use of the geographical qualifier refers to activities financially and otherwise supported by the European Commission (EC), the executive branch of the European Union government. Nothing less should be expected from a speaker affiliated to that institution.

Yet, talking about *EC initiatives* related to professional development and vocational training requires some explanation. Is it not up to each Member State of the Union to determine its own ways of dealing with these matters? In Germany, for example, this right is with each of the sixteen *Länder*, who are autonomous in structuring and managing their institutions of education and training at all levels. So why *European* initiatives? Do they not violate the principle of *subsidiarity*[1], proclaimed fundamental in the Maastricht and Amsterdam treaties? Well, the answer is (possibly) *yes and no.* Clearly, initiatives aiming at *imposing* institutional structures or even specific curricula would most likely provoke an outcry of protest. There is not and there must not be a European super-ministry of education. On the other hand, the subsidiarity principle also implies that suitable government action on *lower-level* issues may be called for if and only if that action provides some added value that could not be achieved at a lower level of government. This is in fact the very essence of many European funding programmes, such as the *Framework Programmes for Research and Technological Development.* They are designed to combine forces, to support cross-border initiatives, to reduce disparity, to create conditions favourable for a single European market and to foster a sense of European unity in general.

In that light the European Commission has indeed an obligation for suitable action in the field of education and training. This fact has been recognized at the highest political level and even been codified in the treaties establishing the European Union[2]. It has led to major Europe-wide awareness campaigns, such as the *European Year of Lifelong Learning* in 1996, preceded by the publication of a *White Paper on Education and Training* (in 1995), setting the political agenda.

In this article we shall focus on opportunities for the professional development of librarians, as well as on actual benefits, arising from a number of EC supported activities.

[1] Each level of government should not interfere in dealings of a lower level, in matters that can best be dealt with at that lower level.

[2] Articles 126 and 127 of the Treaty establishing the European Community stipulate respectively that „*the Community shall contribute to the development of quality education by encouraging cooperation between Member States and, if necessary, by supporting and supplementing their action*“ and that „*the Community shall implement a vocational training policy which shall support and supplement the action of the Member States*“.

2. *Opportunities*

2.1 Leonardo and Socrates

The Commission department in charge of matters directly related to *Education, Training and Youth* is Directorate General XXII. Its mission is based on Articles 126, 127 of the Maastricht treaty (cf footnote 2). DG XXII runs several programmes of which LEONARDO and SOCRATES are the ones that mainly interest us here. They are probably also the best known. LEONARDO is directly concerned with vocational training. Adopted for a period of five years (1995-1999) its *key objective is to support the development of policies and innovative action in the Member States, by promoting projects in the context of transnational partnerships which involve different organisations with an interest in training*[3]. Other measures include

- placement and exchange programmes;
- analyses and surveys examining problems and issues concerning vocational training;
- networks and dissemination projects;
- the development of open and distance learning.

Its implementation is mainly through Calls for Proposals (CfPs) which so far have been launched annually. LEONARDO projects should make contributions to achieving at least one of the following subgoals:

- improving vocational training systems and arrangements in the Member States,
- improving vocational training measures, including university/enterprise cooperation, concerning enterprises and workers,
- developing language skills and knowledge, and disseminating innovation in the field of vocational training.

Among the many projects chosen (cf footnote 3 for the URL of the LEONARDO homepage) there are surprisingly few which directly address the training needs of librarians or, for that matter, of information professionals in general[4]. Project DECID (Développer les Eurocompétences pour l'information et documentation), to be undertaken by ECIA (the European Council of Information

[3] http://europa.eu.int/en/comm/dg22/leonardo.html

[4] We must not forget, however, the TELEPHASSA project, funded in part under COMETT, one of the precursor programmes of LEONARDO. TELEPHASSA was a joint venture of three academic libraries (Tilburg, Barcelona Autonoma and Patras) and two private companies. One of its follow-ups is the annual Digital Library Summer School organised by TICER (Tilburg Innovation Centre for Electronic Resources BV, http://cwis.kub.nl/~ticer/).

Associations), is perhaps most noteworthy in that regard among those most recently selected. It does not address the library profession but a related one, and as such it may serve as an example of the kind of opportunities the LEONARDO programme offers. It encourages and supports cooperation between relevant bodies and organisations of the Member States in order to arrive for instance at common terms of reference which would facilitate the mutual recognition of qualifications and increase the mobility of staff.

It must be noted that in its implementation LEONARDO receives specific support from CEDEFOP[5] (the European Centre for the Development of Vocational Training, established in 1975, as an independent European institution).

The second DGXXII programme that provides opportunities especially for students and (academic) teachers is SOCRATES[6]. The main objectives of SOCRATES are:

- to develop the European dimension in education;
- promote improved knowledge of European languages;
- to promote the intercultural dimension of education;
- to enhance the quality of education by means of European cooperation;
- to promote mobility of teaching staff and students;
- to encourage the recognition of diplomas, periods of study and other qualifications;
- to facilitate the development of an open European area for cooperation in education;
- to encourage open and distance education in the European context;
- to foster exchanges of information on educational systems and policy.

It may suffice to mention but one of the many activities supported by the SOCRATES programme: Action Line 1 of its ERASMUS chapter invites applications for *Thematic Network* projects. These projects *aim to define and develop a European dimension within a given academic discipline or other issues of common interest (including administrative issues) through cooperation between university faculties or departments, academic or professional associations*. The *Directory of Thematic Projects 1996/97*[7] lists 28 networks, covering subject areas such as the Humanities, Social Sciences, Science and Technology, Medicine, as well as horizontal themes. Applications may be submitted once per year. According to the programme's documentation a *Thematic Network project might seek to assess the quality of cooperation and curriculum innova-*

[5] http://europa.eu.int/en/comm/dg22/cedefop.html
[6] http://europa.eu.int/en/comm/dg22/socrates.html
[7] http://europa.eu.int/en/comm/dg22/socrates/tnsum/tnpdir.html

tion, promote within an active forum discussions on improvements in teaching methods in specific discipline areas and foster the development of joint European programmes and specialised courses.

Library and Information Science is not one of the currently supported areas, though, but ... there is an opportunity!

2.2 The Telematics Application Programme

Strengthening the European dimension of activities related to the development of human resources through education and training: that is the principal objective of programmes such as LEONARDO and SOCRATES. It is complementing the main objectives of the large multiannual *Framework Programmes* that provide monies to collaborative European RTD (Research and Technology Development) projects. Based on Article 130[8] of the European Union Treaty, they are perceived inter alia as making an important contribution to achieving the long-term goal of a single European market, and to improving the competitiveness of the European industry[9]. They consist of specific subprogrammes that cover basic and applied research in a number of broad areas, such as life sciences, environment, energy and information and communication technologies (ICT).

Advancing the state of the art in any of these areas not only requires dissemination and promotion of results, but also raising awareness and upgrading skills and know-how among the profession. Managing these activities cannot simply be separated from the RTD activities proper. Therefore most RTD subprogrammes and all sectors of subprogrammes include a component called (for instance) „Accompanying Measures“ which caters for these needs.

This holds true in particular for the two sectors of the *Telematics Applications Programme*[10] (one of the three subprogrammes covering the ICT area) that have the most immediate impact on the library and information profession: the *Telematics for Libraries*[11] and the *Information Engineering*[12] sectors.

The Libraries Sector has a fairly long (more than ten years) tradition of supporting the professional development of librarians through the kind of Ac-

8 http://europa.eu.int/abc/obj/treaties/en/entr6d15.htm#141

9 The fourth such programme (1994-1998) is currently being executed and the fifth (1998-2002) is in its final preparatory phase.

10 http://www2.echo.lu/telematics/home.html

11 http://www2.echo.lu/libraries/en/libraries.html

12 http://www2.echo.lu/ie/en/iehome.html

companying Measures just mentioned. It has provided ample opportunity for debate among librarians and other information professionals from all over Europe through workshops and seminars. These are usually held in connection with commissioned studies on specific topics or with collaborative RTD projects that are working toward similar goals. A list of the more recent events[13] *includes the following:*

- From Quantity to Quality, workshop on library statistics (December 1997)
- Metadata Workshop (December 1997)
- Workshop on UNIMARC and related EU Projects (September 1996)
- Workshop on Public Libraries and the Information Society (July 1996)
- EUROPAGATE/SR concertation meeting (February 1996)
- HARMONICA Workshop on Music Information Services (January 1996)
- Deposit Collections of Electronic Publications (December 1995)
- Digital Imaging (November 1994)

Studies are, by the way, a type of Accompanying Measure that allow the Commission services responsible for running RTD funding programmes to investigate in depth particular issues or topics that are relevant for the design and implementation of such programmes.

At least two studies have been commissioned by our Libraries Sector with a view to obtaining reliable data and other information on training for librarianship in the Member States of the European Union. The first of these, finished in 1992[14], examined the curricula of library schools in Europe with regard to their information technology content. Its results, now more than 6 years old, are of course too dated to be of relevance today. At the time they served nevertheless to assess the overall ability of future librarians to cope with technical innovations in their specific domains.

The second study[15], carried out in 1996, took a somewhat more philosophi-

[13] http://www2.echo.lu/libraries/en/support.html; in the early nineties the responsible Commission department even had a special course developed to help librarians acquaint themselves with OSI networking technology. Another activity of the „early days", supporting the professional development of librarians, was the compilation of a *Library Automation Pack* designed to assist librarians in the selection of advanced library automation systems.

[14] *Starre, Jan H.E. van der*: Information technology content of initial professional education and training for librarianship in the European Community. Study prepared for the Commission of the European Community by the International Federation of Library Associations and Institutions. Luxembourg, 1992. (See also: *Starre, Jan H.E. van der:* Library schools and information technology: A European overview. In: Information Processing & Management. Vol.29, No.2, 1993, pp. 241-247)

[15] *Pors, Niels Ole, and Trine Schreiber:* Librarian training in information and communication technologies: A Typology of Needs and Deliverables. Study prepared for the Commission of the European Community by the Danish Royal School of Librarianship. Luxembourg, 1996

cal approach. It focused on continuing education (or the professional development) of practising librarians, in information and communication technologies. Its authors presented a careful analysis of training needs in these areas and of possible (and, above all, efficient) ways and means of delivering the appropriate training. The study and the resulting recommendations were presented to the board of EUCLID, the association of European schools of library and information studies. In the recommendations pointers were set to the LEONARDO and SOCRATES programmes mentioned above.

This second study was also intended to prepare the ground for more widely scoped joint action in the field of training for librarianship, and in fact to entice the library schools in Europe (or at least a representative subset of them) to submit appropriate proposals for such action to one of our Calls. As an aside we note that due to the administrative constraints of our work the only mechanism through which we can fund collaborative efforts of this kind is the Call for Proposal, with its subsequent peer evaluation phase. Unfortunately, this mechanism failed to produce the desired result.

The Library's companion sector in the Telematics Programme, Information Engineering, has been more successful in that regard. Project EUROIEMASTER[16] (Towards the Development of European Education and Training Qualification in Information Engineering) had been proposed to that sector following the Telematics Call in 1995. Although it does not address our particular constituency it is worth mentioning as an example of what may be done under the Telematics Programme to promote the development of a specific group of professionals. The project is being carried out jointly by university departments in Spain, Italy, Ireland and the United Kingdom, and coordinated by an independent consultant. It aims to define (and implement!) a syllabus for postgraduate courses in Information Engineering, to be offered by each of the participating institutions and other interested universities. Accreditation procedures will be the responsibility of the respective institutions. The courses are structured in a modular fashion. They are open to students (who may already be practising information professionals) with different backgrounds. Some of its modules can be delivered via distance education mechanisms, and they can be used by individuals for independent learning or by organisations who wish to upgrade specific know-how and skills of their staff. Apart from these features the project gives rise to closer cooperation among players in the Information Engineering sector (industry, academia, publishers, etc.) on pertinent education and training issues.

[16] http://www2.echo.lu/ie/en/euroiemaster.html

3. Relevant projects supported by the Libraries sector

Having said that our second study of ICT training needs of librarians could not yet be followed up with a fully-fledged collaborative project, it must be added, however, that quite a number of other, more mainstream RTD projects supported by the Libraries Sector have made and are still making significant contributions to the professional development of librarians[17]. Some of them do that implicitly, some have a more or less dominant professional development component, and for at least two professional development is the key issue. I shall cite and discuss but a few examples, taken from the list of both our FP3 and FP4 projects[18] (i.e. projects run under the 3rd and 4th Framework Programmes).

3.1 Hyperlib

HYPERLIB[19] (Hypertext interfaces to library information systems, involving a Belgian university library and a university-affiliated research institute in the UK, funded from 1/1993 to 12/1995) was among the first series of Library projects to be selected after a Call for Proposals (CfP'91). Technically speaking, the project set out to develop and use an SGML document type definition (the *HYPERLIB DTD*) and suitable conversion tools, covering various *library objects*, such as manuals, bibliographies and catalogues. From a user point of view much of the work done under this project provided library staff with more efficient tools for their day-to-day work, e.g. hyperlinked manuals on acquisition and cataloguing. That work included a careful analysis of staff needs, the design of convivial user interfaces and appropriate staff training.

3.2 Bibdel

In January 1994 BIBDEL[20] (Libraries without Walls: the Delivery of Library Services to Distant Users, carried out jointly by three university libraries in the UK, Ireland and Greece respectively, and Commission funded until 9/1995) began to research strategies for remote user access to library catalogues, databases, enquiry services and documents.

By developing three different models of provision through the medium of three universities BIBDEL demonstrated how technology and expertise can be

[17] Allowing a sufficiently generous interpretation of „professional development" we may even go so far as to say that the very existence of a European programme specifically for the technological development of libraries has spawned pertinent activities throughout Europe.

[18] http://www2.echo.lu/libraries/en/projects.html

[19] http://www2.echo.lu/libraries/en/projects/hyperlib.html

[20] http://www2.echo.lu/libraries/en/projects/bibdel.html

transferred between libraries in different countries and adapted to the needs of each. It did not aim to produce a single solution for EU-wide adoption but rather a series of solutions each of which will find application in different geographical areas of different Member States.

BIBDEL's contribution to the development of the profession consisted in two workshops / conferences devoted to the subject matter of the project. The second of these was held only in autumn last year, long after the funding of the project had ended. Speakers at both conferences were from different parts of Europe and so were the participants.

3.3 Educate

Project EDUCATE[21] (End-user courses in information access through communication technology) started at around the same time as BIBDEL and was funded for a period of three years. Its initial target groups have been students of science and engineering who need instruction on how to find and use information sources relevant to their fields. The most visible result of this project is a website[22] that provides precisely this kind of instruction. It includes *net-referenced* textbooks (specially written and/or adapted to meet the requirements of this project) and exercises in information retrieval from e.g. abstracts databases. In a way the EDUCATE product automates a service that is traditionally rendered by many an academic library to its student constituency: teaching them how to find the information they need to pursue their studies.

Obviously, the EDUCATE approach and the actual EDUCATE courses can also be applied to training librarians in the use of networked information resources. And indeed, they have been and will continue to be applied to this end.

University libraries from five EU member states have been involved in EDUCATE. Work continues and is now focusing on including more subject areas (such as chemistry, medicine and also subjects of the humanities) and on enhancing the distance education component, e.g. by providing facilities for discussion, feedback and teacher-student interaction.

3.4 Muriel

MURIEL[23], following a proposal submitted in 1994, was intended to provide students of librarianship and practicing librarians alike with a distance education system. Based on ISDN technology, the project included the adaptation of an authoring tool to the specific needs of the profession, and the creation of ex-

21 http://www2.echo.lu/libraries/en/projects/educate.html
22 http://educate.lib.chalmers.se/
23 http://www2.echo.lu/libraries/en/projects/muriel.html

emplary multimedia courseware on topics such as „the Internet“ and Information Ethics. It ran from 1/95 until 10/97 and involved two library schools, two technology companies, a research library and a national library.

MURIEL is one of the two projects highlighted above as having professional development as their key issue. In fact, the proposal refered to the possibility of defining common European curricula for librarianship training, thereby increasing the mobility of library staff. As the project progressed, however, it became quite clear that this was too ambitious a goal, and the technical component received more attention than the service aspects. It became nevertheless an interesting application of ISDN networking technology, of courseware tools and of *Computer Supported Cooperative Work* (CSCW) concepts to education and training for librarianship. It has been presented and / or demonstrated on several occasions, including ED-MEDIA'96 (Boston), Online Educa '96 (Berlin), MILIA'97 (Cannes) and IFLA'97 (Copenhagen).

3.5 Elvil

A close relative of EDUCATE is project ELVIL[24] (The European Legislative Virtual Library, started in 9/1996 and supposed to run for two years). It is best described by quoting from *http://www.sub.su.se/sam/elvil.htm*, the project's website:

The project consists of three parts:

- *the first part aims at assembling a World Wide Web index on law and politics in Europe in order to gather references to all Internet-accessible computer-based information on European law and politics into one coherent World Wide Web-accessible database;*
- *the second part aims at developing a multimedia educational aid for students of European law and politics, and for teachers and librarians;*
- *the third part aims at constructing a search engine composed of a World Wide Web-interface and software gateways for easy and concurrent access to the national parliamentary databases and to the European parliamentary database.*

ELVIL is based in three universities in Sweden, the United Kingdom and Spain respectively. It receives input from national parliaments and the European Parliament.

3.6 Plail

PLAIL[25] (Public libraries and independent learners, 2/1994 – 2/1996), one of

[24] http://www2.echo.lu/libraries/en/projects/elvil.html
[25] http://www2.echo.lu/libraries/en/projects/plail.html

the early projects under the *Telematics for Libraries* programme had a dual objective: to serve a particular group of users of public libraries, the so called *independent learners*; and secondly, to help enable public library staff to render this kind of service. In doing so PLAIL picked up on recommendations put forward in a study on *Open Distance Learning in Public Libraries*[26], that had been funded by our Sector. And, clearly, PLAIL is one of the projects that have been designed primarily with a view to *training the trainers*, so to speak, the trainers being public librarians in this case. Five key questions, in logical succession, have been underlying this project:

- What are the needs of adult independent learners ?
- What (library) services can meet those needs ?
- To what extent do those services rely on (or could benefit from) information technology?
- What skills are necessary to provide the services ?
- Can those skills be acquired via information technology ?

PLAIL has not only output a number of significant reports based on desk research, providing (partial) answers to these questions, but also multimedia training materials (CD-ROM, Video) to help public library staff to acquire the appropriate skills. It is worth noting that the very composition of the project consortium itself had the effect of transfering know-how from a group of librarians (in the UK) who were already relatively experienced in these matters[27], to colleagues in southern Europe, in particular Portugal, where public libraries have been instituted on a larger scale only fairly recently, and Spain whose public library system does not enjoy a very long tradition either[28]. The involvement of Portugal's Open University turned out to be of great benefit especially in this context.

4. Conclusions and Outlook

In this paper we have argued that it is in the European Commission's remit to give support to activities in the areas of education and training, including vocational training, that would enhance the *European dimension* of these activities. We have given examples of opportunities offered to the library profession at large by Commission programmes such as LEONARDO, SOCRATES, and

[26] http://www.uclan.ac.uk/research/centre/cerlim/reports/odinrep.htm
[27] see for instance: http://www.ncet.org.uk/info-sheets/flexible.html
[28] see also: http://www2.echo.lu/libraries/en/plis/homeplis.html

the specific subprogrammes of the RTD Framework Programmes. We have looked in particular at the Library and Information Engineering sectors of the Telematics Applications Programme that can accommodate pertinent activities in the form of Accompanying Measures. A number of mainstream projects of the Libraries sector are also oriented toward the professional development of librarians.

We contend the time has come for the European library profession (including schools, professional associations and other players) to respond to these opportunities in a proactive way. The intense debate that has been going on within the profession on how to adapt to the exigencies of the emerging *information society* could well be turned into even more effective action for the benefit of practising and future librarians. Combining forces, from the grassroot level upwards, is the clue. Coming back to the title of this paper, it is perhaps fair to give the term *European initiatives* an additional twist: initiatives taken by the European Commission can only be successful if they are met by matching initiatives of those interested in positive change. Examples (other than the above mentioned EUROIEMASTER) exist[29].

The *5th Framework Programme*[30], supposed to become operational by the end of this year, will place an even greater emphasis on the importance of education and (professional) training[31]. Equally important will be the development of the information society. Both will have to be in tune. The need for professional development persists. And so will the opportunities provided by the European Commission for making it happen on a European scale.

29 One of these examples has been set by the Community of European Management Schools (CEMS), an association of 12 universities and Business Schools who, with support from private consultancy enterprises and the Commission's SOCRATES/ERASMUS programme, have successfully implemented a European study programme, leading to an internationally recognised Masters degree (CEMS-Master). (see also: http://www.uni-koeln.de/wiso-fak/dekanat/cems.htm)

30 http://www.cordis.lu/fifth/home.html

31 http://www2.echo.lu/telematics/education/en/resource/publics.html#FifthFWP

BERTRAM GALLUS

Bedürfnisanalyse und vorgeschlagene Maßnahmen für Verlage und Buchhandel – erste Ergebnisse des Projektes „New Book Economy“ in Deutschland

I. Einführung

Elektronische Publikationen, online Dienste, CD-ROM Produkte – all dies sind Produktbereiche, die noch vor 15 Jahren im Buchhandel kaum verbreitet waren. Das Buch stand im Mittelpunkt und mit dem Buch die Kenntnisse und Fertigkeiten, die erforderlich waren, um der Öffentlichkeit den Zugang zu Werken zu ermöglichen. Die Techniken, die hierfür eingesetzt wurden – übrigens aber auch weiter eingesetzt werden – hatten sich über viele Jahrhunderte entwickelt. Die Ausbildung im Buchhandel konnte sich auf gefestigte Inhalte stützen, deren Vermittlung Grundlage für ein Rüstzeug waren, von dem ein Berufsleben lang gezehrt werden konnte.

Lebenslanges Lernen heißt nun aber das Stichwort; mit der Entwicklung elektronischer Publikationen hat sich ein Produktfeld eröffnet, das mit dem traditionell erlernten buchhändlerischen Fachwissen allein nicht mehr bewältigt werden kann. Mit der stetig wachsenden Bedeutung der elektronischen Produkte einher geht daher auch ein wachsender Bedarf an Mitarbeitern mit spezifischen Kenntnissen im Bereich elektronischer Publikationen.

Es liegt daher nahe, daß Ausbildung, aber auch Weiterbildung diesen entstehenden Bedarf berücksichtigen muß. Angesichts der raschen Entwicklung der Technik elektronischer Vermittlungsformen ist aber die Anpassung von Aus- und Weiterbildung ausgesprochen schwierig, da sowohl über den jetzigen Stand der Qualifikationsstrukturen als auch über den Bedarf der nächsten Jahre kaum ausreichende Kenntnisse vorliegen.

II. NBE – Zeitrahmen und Partner

Als Reaktion auf diese Entwicklung und in Hinblick auf den daraus resultierenden Wandel, der tief in diese gewachsene Struktur der bisherigen Wissensvermittlung eingreift, aber auch in Hinblick auf die für die Buchbranche entstehenden Chancen ist das vom Europarat initiierte und aus dem Europäischen Sozialfond – Gemeinschaftsinitiative ADAPT – der Europäischen Union gefördertes Projekt „New Book Economy“ entstanden.

Das Projekt New Book Economy dient der Anpassung der Buchbranche in Deutschland an den durch die sich entwickelnde Informationsgesellschaft und damit auch durch den von electronic publishing verursachten Strukturwandel. Das Projekt wird im Rahmen des operationellen Programms der Bundesrepublik Deutschland zur Gemeinschaftsinitiative ADAPT unter gleichzeitiger Beteiligung von Partnern in Italien und den Niederlanden entwickelt und durchgeführt. Wie in Deutschland arbeiten auch die Partner dort eng mit den jeweiligen Bibliotheksverbänden sowie Verleger- und Buchhändlerverbänden zusammen. Das Projekt wurde vom Europarat initiiert, von ihm wurden die transnationalen Kontakte geknüpft, und er unterstützt auch die Realisierung des Projektes.

Die neuen Informations- und Kommunikationstechnologien tragen dazu bei, die Potentiale von Unternehmen und Beschäftigten der Buch- und Verlagsbranche sowohl national wie auch transnational zu stärken.

Die Buch- und Verlagsbranche wird Teil einer in größeren Dimensionen agierenden Informationsindustrie werden, die durch Synergieeffekte dazu beitragen wird, daß die unveränderlichen Produkteigenschaften des Bildungs- und Kulturguts »Buch« erweitert und durch Multimedia-Eigenschaften ergänzt werden.

Für die Unternehmen der Branche eröffnet sich die Möglichkeit, bisherige Begrenzungen zu überwinden. Dies impliziert, daß sie sich mit neuer Kompetenz neue Märkte erschließen und für den Anwender ein umfassenderes Angebot entstehen wird. Für die Beschäftigten resultiert daraus die Notwendigkeit stärkerer Eigeninitiative und vor allem die Bereitschaft zu Mobilität und Flexibilität.

Die für das Projekt konzipierten Maßnahmen tragen dazu bei, die Unternehmen der Buch- und Verlagsbranche resp. die Beschäftigten dieser Unternehmen am Strukturwandel und damit an der Entwicklung der Informationsgesellschaft und der Informationskultur aktiv zu beteiligen.

Um das Projekt New Book Economy in die Praxis umzusetzen, beinhaltet das Projekt folgende Aktivitäten:

- den Zugang zu neuen Medien anzuregen und zu erleichtern, indem gezielt Qualifizierungsstrategien konzipiert und angeboten werden
- auf der Grundlage von Studien und Analysen Möglichkeiten aufzuzeigen, die digitalen Medien entsprechend dem Bedarf auf den unterschiedlichen europäischen Märkten effektiv zu nutzen und die Auswahl effizienter Trägermedien und Produkte markt- und bedarfsbezogen zu fördern,

- Qualifizierungsmaßnahmen zu entwickeln, zu fördern und durchzuführen, um über die Aus- und Fortbildung von Beschäftigten Unternehmen zu befähigen, elektronische Produkte den Anforderungen des sich formierenden Marktes entsprechend anzubieten,

Die Buch- und Verlagsbranche ist von jeher auch international orientiert. Die elektronischen Medien unterliegen zwar unterschiedlichen nationalen Gegebenheiten, sind aber eine Voraussetzung der nationale Grenzen überschreitenden Informationsgesellschaft.

Wenn die sich durch die neuen Technologien bietenden Vorteile uneingeschränkt durch Unternehmen der Buchbranche genutzt werden sollen, sind Rahmenvoraussetzungen zu schaffen, die die ökonomischen, gesellschaftlichen und kulturellen Aspekte berücksichtigen, insbesondere den Schutz geistiger Eigentumsrechte (Urheberrechtsschutz, Datenschutz) und realistische Nutzerkosten-Abrechnungsverfahren. Auch wenn Verlagsprodukte im Rahmen einer zu schaffenden europäischen Informations-Infrastruktur über Datenbanken, Bildbanken u.ä. verfügbar sein werden, bleiben sie als Kulturgüter privilegierte Medien der Identität; ihre charakteristischen Merkmale müssen auch im Rahmen neuer Multimediaprodukte erhalten bleiben.

Um der Buchbranche zu ermöglichen, auch im neuen Medium ihre hochwertigen Informationsresourcen zu verbreiten, bedarf es der Schaffung von Kapazitäten und eines Know-how Potentials, das vor allem mittels neuer Qualifizierungen zu erreichen ist.

Deshalb zählt die berufliche Qualifizierung und Weiterbildung zu den vorrangigen Aufgaben der sich entwickelnden Informationsgesellschaft, ist die Bereitschaft zu lebenslangem Lernen eine der Grundvoraussetzungen.

Dem Projekt liegt ein integrativer Ansatz zugrunde, der sich sowohl in der Zusammensetzung der Projektpartner als auch in der interdisziplinären Arbeitsweise äußert. In Deutschland ist Projektträger die Internationale Buch Agentur, Berlin, Projektpartner sind für den Buchhandel unter anderem der Verband der Verlage und Buchhandlungen in Nordrhein-Westfalen im Zusammenwirken mit dem Börsenverein des Deutschen Buchhandels, das Deutsche Bibliotheksinstitut und die Bundesvereinigung der Deutschen Bibliotheksverbände.

Die zwei Säulen der Projektarbeit sind Studien und Untersuchungen sowie darauf aufbauend die Entwicklung und Durchführung von konkreten Fortbildungsmaßnahmen und Beratungen.

Für den Bereich Buchhandel und Verlage in Deutschland wurde vor kurzem eine Studie zur Ermittlung des *Qualifikationsbedarfes und der Personalentwicklung bei Verlagen und Buchhandlungen für die Zukunft des elektroni-*

schen Publizierens abgeschlossen, die im folgenden ausführlicher dargestellt werden soll. Eine weitere Studie zur Untersuchung der *Anforderungen professioneller Nutze an elektronische Produkte* wurde gerade begonnen.

Vergangenen Herbst wurde bundesweit eine Reihe von Sensibilisierungsmaßnahmen zum Thema Neue Medien veranstaltet, daran schließt sich nunmehr eine Seminarreihe für Verlagsmitarbeiter und Sortimenter zum Thema Elektronisches Publizieren an. Diese Seminare sind prozeßorientiert aufgebaut und bieten ein Maximum an Handlungshilfen für den beruflichen Alltag.

Weitere konkrete Maßnahmen, wie die Beratung von kleinen und mittleren Unternehmen, die Entwicklung von CBT Kurs Modulen und von nationalen und europäischen Ressource Zentren werden durch Informations- und Präsentationsveranstaltungen im Rahmen von Kongressen, Tagungen und Messen ergänzt.

III. Die Studie zur Ermittlung von Qualifikationsbedarf und Qualifikationsanforderungen im Buchhandel

A. Ziele und Vorgehensweise der Studie

Aus- und Weiterbildung sollen stärker mit den Anforderungen verknüpft werden, die durch die zunehmende Verbreitung und Akzeptanz der elektronischen Medien entstehen. Hierzu sind grundlegende Erkenntnisse über den Qualifikationsstand der in der Branche Beschäftigten sowie über den erforderlichen Qualifikationsbedarf aus der Sicht von Unternehmen und Beschäftigten nötig.

Ziele dieser Studie ist es, Qualifikationsanforderungen, die zur Erstellung und Verbreitung elektronischer Publikationen notwendig sind, zu ermitteln sowie die derzeitige Personalstruktur daraufhin zu prüfen und zukünftigen Personal-, Ausbildungs- und Weiterbildungsbedarf erkennbar werden zu lassen. Sie soll damit dazu beitragen, daß Träger von Weiterbildungsveranstaltungen diese zukünftig noch stärker bedarfsorientiert definieren und durchführen können.

Für die Ermittlung dieser mittelfristigen Anforderungen an die Aus- und Weiterbildung mit Schlußfolgerungen für das Angebot an Aus- und Weiterbildungsmaßnahmen wurden einerseits Trends und Ziele vorhandener Angebote für Aus- und Weiterbildung ermittelt, unter spezieller Berücksichtigung von Veranstaltungen aus dem Bereich des elektronischen Publizierens, andererseits wurden Experten zu den Entwicklungsrichtungen in der Branche befragt.

Für die Bestandsaufnahme der Qualifikationen des Personals sowie des Personalbedarfs in Buchhandlungen und Verlagen wurde eine schriftliche Befragung durchgeführt. Die Erhebungen erfolgten für die neuen und die alten Bundesländer. Erhebungszeitraum der Studie waren die Monate August bis Oktober 1997.

Für die Verlage, die im Mittelpunkt der Darstellung der Studie stehen, wurden repräsentative Stichproben anhand der Mitgliederdatei des Börsenvereins des Deutschen Buchhandels e.V. Adressen gezogen. Darüber hinaus wurde für CD-ROM-produzierende Verlage (Datei „CD-ROM-produzierende Verlage“, 248 Adressen, im folgenden CD-ROM-Verlage) eine Stichprobe erstellt.

Die Umfrage ergab eine Ausschöpfung der Bruttostichprobe von 37 %. Bei der Interpretation der Ergebnisse ist zu beachten, daß es sich bei den an der Befragung beteiligten Verlagen verstärkt um solche Unternehmen handelt, die an den Grundthemen der Studie „Ausbildung“, „Fortbildung“ und „elektronisches Publizieren“ ein besonderes Interesse zeigten.

Die Studie kann in drei wesentliche Blöcke unterteilt werden. Im ersten Block wurde der Stand der Ausbildung, die Berufspraxis sowie die Bedeutung und die Organisation von Fortbildung in den befragten Unternehmen untersucht. Ziel war, zunächst den Ist-Zustand zu ermitteln; dabei spielen die Akzeptanz bisheriger Fortbildungsangebote eine Rolle, aber auch die Ermittlung der Bereitschaft, auf die Herausforderung der neuen Medien durch die verstärkte Wahrnehmung solcher Fortbildungsangebote einzugehen.

Bei der Darstellung der Ergebnisse steht der Bereich der Verlage im Mittelpunkt meiner Ausführungen.

B. Studienergebnisse zur Lage von Aus- und Weiterbildung in Verlagen unter besonderer Berücksichtigung elektronischer Medien

1. Die Ausbildung in den Verlagen

Für den Großteil der Verlage hat die Ausbildung von Mitarbeitern hohen Stellenwert, zunächst erkennbar daran, das die meisten der befragten Verlage Ausbildungsplätze anbieten; dabei ist auffallend, daß gerade die CD-ROM Verlage überdurchschnittlich häufig Ausbildungsplätze anbieten. Aus der Befragung wird ein Wandel in Hinblick auf die Anforderungen an Ausbildungsinhalte deutlich, der dem versierten Umgang mit neuen Medien große Bedeutung zuschreibt.

So halten es 72 % aller Befragungsteilnehmer für „sehr wichtig“ bzw. „wichtig“, daß im Rahmen der Berufsschule PC-Grundkenntnisse in der Textverarbeitung, der Tabellenkalkulation und in der Nutzung von Datenbanken vermittelt werden. 64 % halten die Lehre des Umgangs mit CD-ROM-Produkten bzw. elektronischen Medien und 60 % der Betriebe halten die Schulung des Umgangs mit Software im Bereich des elektronischen Publizieren in der Berufsschule für „sehr wichtig" bzw. „wichtig". Vor allem CD-ROM-Verlage sowie Ausbildungsbetriebe erwarten, daß in der Berufsschule der Umgang mit Software im Bereich des elektronischen Publizierens gelehrt wird.

Wie sehr die Verlage neben der bereits erkannten Bedeutung den Strukturwandel auch als wachsende Herausforderung für die Zukunft ansehen, wird deutlich an der Verschiebung der Bewertung der erforderlichen Fähigkeiten jetziger und zukünftiger Verlagstätigkeit. Werden derzeit als die wichtigsten Fähigkeiten für die Berufspraxis aus der Sicht aller Befragten an vierter Stelle „inhaltliche Kompetenz im Umgang mit PC und elektronischen Medien", „Technische Kompetenz im Umgang mit PC und elektronischen Medien" an siebter Stelle genannt, so wird für die Berufspraxis in drei Jahren bereits an zweiter Stelle „Inhaltliche Kompetenz im Umgang mit PC und elektronischen Medien" genannt, „Technische Kompetenz im Umgang mit PC und elektronischen Medien" und „Elektronisches Publizieren" rangieren an fünfter und sechster Stelle der als am wichtigsten angesehen Fähigkeiten.

Darüber hinaus werden aus Sicht der Befragten vor allem „Elektronisches Publizieren", „Recherchieren und Bibliographieren in Online-Medien", sowie „Redaktion für Offline-/Online Produkte" als an Bedeutung gewinnend angesehen.

2. Weiterbildungsmaßnahmen in den Verlagen

Dieser Einschätzung Folge leistend betreiben 43 % der befragten Verlage organisierte Fortbildung für Mitarbeiter, Führungskräfte und Unternehmensleitung. Ab einem Umsatz von über DM 12,8 Mio. führen sogar über 90 % der befragten Verlage organisierte Fortbildung durch. Mit 81 % werden auch von CD-ROM-Verlagen überdurchschnittlich häufig Fortbildungsangebote wahrgenommen.

25 % aller Befragten äußerten die Absicht, in den nächsten drei Jahren für Fortbildungsmaßnahmen mehr ausgeben als bislang. Besonders hoch ist die Bereitschaft, in die Fortbildung zu investieren in den alten Bundesländern, bei den CD-ROM-Verlagen insgesamt und bei Verlagen mit einem Umsatz von über DM 51,2 Mio.

27 % der befragten Verlage lassen Fortbildungsmaßnahmen extern durchführen, 24 % intern. Bei externen Fortbildungsmaßnahmen bevorzugen die Verlage mehrheitlich Berater aus der Branche, bei internen Maßnahmen wird etwa zu gleichen Teilen mit Trainern aus den Reihen des Unternehmens und mit Trainern aus der Branche gearbeitet. Verlage in der Größenklasse bis zu DM 3,2 Mio. Umsatz nehmen eher externe Fortbildung in Anspruch, ab einem

Umsatz von über DM 12,8 Mio. geben Verlage allerdings der internen Fortbildung einen höheren Stellenwert.

17 % der Befragten lassen anschließend an Fortbildungsmaßnahmen die Umsetzungsmaßnahmen „häufig“ bzw. „sehr häufig“ von Beratern nachwirkend begleiten. Dabei sind es wiederum vor allem die CD-ROM-Verlage, Verlage in höheren Umsatzklassen, Anbieter von elektronischen Produkten und Verlage mit organisierter Fortbildung, die nachwirkende Beratung durchführen.

3. Zusammenfassung zur Aus- und Weiterbildungssituation in den Verlagen

Die ständig wachsenden Anforderungen der Berufspraxis und die hieraus resultierende Notwendigkeit zu kontinuierlicher Aus- und Weiterbildung sind, so lassen die Zahlen erkennen, den Verlagen bewußt und sie betreiben ein in Abhängigkeit von der Größenklasse unterschiedlich intensives Engagement zur Qualifizierung der Mitarbeiter. Auffallend ist, daß Verlage, die sich bereits nachhaltig mit den neuen Medien befassen (CD-ROM Verlage) eine deutlich größere Bereitschaft zu Aus- aber auch Fortbildung haben. Ganz offenbar wird das Fehlen speziell für diesen Bereich geschulter Mitarbeiter in solchen Unternehmen in Hinblick auf die schon größere Bedeutung elektronischer Produkte viel stärker als Mangel erkannt und führt zu entsprechendem Handeln. Damit einher geht auch, daß insbesondere größere Verlage, die auch eher bereit sein werden, eigene, dieses Produktfeld betreuende organisatorische Einheiten aufzubauen, eine starke Tendenz zeigen, Qualifizierungsmaßnahmen zu betreiben.

Für die Beurteilung des Bedarfs an Fortbildungsmaßnahmen sowie für deren Konzeption ist von erheblicher Bedeutung, daß Verlage sowohl externe wie interne, oft von externen Beratern auch nachwirkend begleitete Fortbildungsmaßnahmen durchführen. Auf den erkennbaren Bedarf gerade auch interner Schulungen muß das zu entwickelnde Spektrum an Fortbildungsmaßnahmen in Struktur und Angebotsform eingehen.

C. Studienergebnisse zum Einsatz des PCs als Arbeitsinstrument und beim Aufbau elektronischer Publikationen in den Verlagen

Die Erstellung von elektronischen Publikationen im Verlag ist im wesentlichen von zwei Faktoren abhängig. Zum einen ist dies die Integration des PCs als Arbeitsinstruments; die Verwendung des PCs in der Druckvorstufe ist eine wesentliche Voraussetzung des Umgangs mit digitalen Veröffentlichungsvorhaben. Hierzu gehört auch der Aufbau von Datenbeständen als Zwischenprodukt hin zu Veröffentlichungen sei es in Printform oder als elektronische Publikation. Zum anderen kommt der Kenntnis der Verfahren und Projektschritte zur Verwirklichung elektronischer Publikationen große Bedeutung zu. Ausgehend von der Einführung von PCs in den verschiedenen Bereichen der Unternehmen bis hin zur Schaffung von Produktionsumgebungen in vernetzten Systemen werden Anforderungen an die Ausbildung der Mitarbeiter in den verschiedensten Arbeitsbereichen des Verlages deutlich. Der Aufbau von elektronischen Programmbereichen und das Angebot von Informationen im Internet bauen oft auf solchen Basisstrukturen auf. Neben der Ermittlung des Grades der Durchsetzung mit PCs waren deshalb insbesondere die Ermittlung bestehender CD-ROM Publikationen und ihre wirtschaftliche Bedeutung bezogen auf verschiedene Publikationsfelder (Nachschlagewerke, Anwendersoftware, Lernprogramme, Lexika) Ziel der Befragung, verbunden auch hier mit der Einschätzung der zukünftigen Entwicklung. Auch die wachsende Bedeutung des Internet und die Reaktion der Verlage auf die daraus resultierenden Möglichkeiten wurden abgefragt.

Die Studie ergab, daß 82 % der Befragten in ihren Unternehmen PCs einsetzen. 74 % der Befragten gehen davon aus, daß ihre Mitarbeiter am PC „sehr gut“, bzw. „gut“ geschult sind.

Dennoch sehen 52 % aller Verlage konkreten Schulungsbedarf bei folgenden PC-Anwendungen (Mehrfachnennungen waren möglich):

Elektronisches Publizieren in der Druckvorstufe (24%),
Umgang mit PC-Anwendungen (22 %),
Arbeit mit Redaktionsdatenbanken (19 %),
Umgang mit PCs für Kommunikationsaufgaben (18 %),
Marketing über Online (18 %).

Derzeit haben 55 % aller befragten Verlage Zugang zum Internet, 27% sind bereits selbst mit einer Homepage vertreten. 42 % der Verlage wollen in den nächsten Jahren einen Zugang zum Internet einrichten oder als Anbieter im Internet vertreten sein. Dabei handelt es sich besonders um Verlage mit einem Angebot für wissenschaftliche sowie für spezielle andere Zielgruppen .

Verlagsprodukte oder Dienstleistungen bieten bereits 26 % der Befragungsteilnehmer derzeit bestimmten Zielgruppen über Internet an und weitere 33 % wollen dies zukünftig tun. Bezogen auf CD-ROM-Verlage bieten derzeit 55 % dieser Gruppe Verlagsprodukte für bestimmte Zielgruppen über Internet an.

Korrespondierend mit den Aktivitäten im Internet führen 26 % aller befragten Verlage derzeit elektronische Produkte wie CD-ROM, Disketten in ihrem Programm.

Dabei gibt es einen deutlichen Schwerpunkt in den Bereichen „Ausbildung/Schulbuch" und „Spezielle Zielgruppen".

Bevorzugte Produktbereiche der CD-ROM-Verlage sind vor allem:

Nachschlagewerke für professionelle Anwender (35 %),
Anwendersoftware (29 %),
Lernprogramme (26 %),
Lexika, Wörterbücher (21 %),
Ratgeber/Reiseführer (19 %),

In allen Umsatzklassen ab DM 3,2 Mio. hat der Produktbereich „Nachschlagewerke für professionelle Anwender" den größten Anteil im Verlagsangebot.

Es zeigt sich, daß der Einsatz des PC als Arbeitsinstrument in den Verlagen ausgesprochen weit fortgeschritten ist. Dies ist in erster Linie darauf auch zurückzuführen, daß die Produktionsformen in den Verlagen sich nachhaltig verändert haben und der PC als preisgünstiges und vergleichsweise einfach zu handhabende Instrument im Vorfeld der Druckvorlagenherstellung genutzt wird.

Die Studie zeigt auch eine sehr weit gehende Bereitschaft der Verlage, sofern nicht bereits elektronische Publikationen veröffentlicht werden, dies in naher Zukunft vorzusehen. Fast 40 % der befragten Verlage sind der Auffassung, in den nächsten drei Jahren Elektronische Publikationen zu veröffentlichen; 42 % der Verlage planen einen Internet Auftritt.

Dabei sind die Umsatzerwartungen bei kleineren Unternehmen eher optimistisch, während größere Verlage die Umsatzentwicklung vorsichtiger einschätzen. Dennoch wird aus den Erwartungen deutlich, daß die Verlage mit überdurchschnittlichen Steigerungen im Bereich elektronischer Publikationen rechnen. Aus dieser Annahme ergibt sich auch die grundsätzliche Bereitschaft, in diese Publikationsformen zu investieren und hierfür auch die erforderlichen Qualifizierungsmaßnahmen durchzuführen.

IV. Neue konzipierte Seminare als erste Maßnahme zur Umsetzung der Studienergebnisse

Um den sich aus der Studie ergebenden Qualifizierungsbedarf aufzugreifen wurden Veranstaltungsreihen sowohl für Verlage wie auch für Sortimentsbuchhandlungen konzipiert, die im Laufe des Jahres 1998 angeboten werden. Diese Seminarreihen bauen zum einen auf den Ergebnissen der geschilderten Studie auf, zum anderen auf einer in 1996 vom Börsenverein des Deutschen Buchhandels initiierten und durchgeführten Studie, die das Kaufverhalten und die Erwartungen des Verbrauchers in Hinblick auf den Kauf elektronischer Publikationen zum Gegenstand hatte. Die Ergebnisse dieser Studie haben deutliche Hinweise darauf gegeben, daß der Käufer von elektronischen Medien Erwartungen an den Handel hat, die im wesentlichen deckungsgleich mit den dem Sortimentsbuchhandel zugeschriebenen Kernkompetenzen sind.

Die kompetente fachliche Beratung und die gezielte Vorauswahl von Produkten werden als wesentliche Leistung des Buchhandels beim Verkauf von Büchern angesehen und es zeigt sich, daß in den Fällen, in denen der Sortimentsbuchhandel aktiv elektronische Produkte anbietet, dies vom Käufer angenommen wird. Gelingt es dem Buchhandel diese ihm im Printbereich zugeschriebene Kernkompetenz auch für den Verkauf von Software zu vermitteln wird er als Kaufort für elektronische Produkte immer mehr an Bedeutung gewinnen. Von besonderer Wichtigkeit innerhalb der Ergebnisse dieser Studie ist auch, daß jeder dritte regelmäßige Buchhandelsbesucher gleichzeitig Nutzer eines privaten PCs ist.

Deshalb ist Ziel der Qualifizierungsmaßnahmen für den Bereich Sortimentsbuchhandel, den Buchhandel für den Verkauf elektronischer Produkte weiter zu qualifizieren, um dieses Potential ausschöpfen zu können. Voraussetzung ist aber, die fachliche Kompetenz, die dem Buchhändler für das Printmedium zugeschrieben wird, auch auf das Elektronische Medium zu erweitern.

Für den Bereich der Verlage ist Ziel der Seminarreihe, Fähigkeiten im Aufbau und in der Steuerung von Elektronischen Herstellungsprozessen, aber auch in der Vermarktung dieser Produkte zu vermitteln. Mitarbeiter der Verlage sollen aufbauend auf Kenntnissen bisheriger Verlagsarbeit befähigt werden, entweder neben der Arbeit an Printformen oder zukünftig mit deutlichem oder ausschließlichem Schwerpunkt beim Elektronischen Publizieren Arbeitsfelder wahrzunehmen, die spezielle Kenntnisse erfordern. Dabei sollen neben reiner Wissensvermittlung auch Anleitungen zu projektorientierter Arbeit und der damit verbundenen teambezogenen Zusammenarbeit mit anderen Arbeitsbereichen innerhalb und außerhalb des Verlages gegeben werden.

Um den Praxisbezug herzustellen und um den Teilnehmern der Seminare nicht nur Einzelaspekte dieser umfassenden Materie zu vermitteln, sind die Seminare jeweils in ein für Führungskräfte bestimmtes Überblick verschaffendes Seminar, sowie weitere Vertiefungsseminare für die Mitarbeiter in den Unternehmen aufgegliedert worden.

Die Seminare für Führungskräfte sollen einen entscheidungsunterstützenden Überblick geben. Deshalb sind diese Seminare prozeß- bzw. handlungsorientiert aufgebaut.

Für den Sortimentbuchhandel bedeutet dies, daß das Themenfeld übergreifend anhand der Aufgabenstellung, eine Abteilung Elektronische Medien aufzubauen behandelt wird. Der Teilnehmer wird beginnend bei der Entscheidung, in diesen Markt einzutreten, durch einen zeitlichen Ablauf geführt, in dem verschiedene Arbeitsschritte und Entscheidungen zu vollziehen sind. Am Ende dieses fiktiven Arbeitsplanes werden alle wesentlichen Themen behandelt sein, und der Teilnehmer soll auf Grund des handlungsorientierten Aufbaus gleichzeitig in der Lage sein, diesen Aufbau in Realität in seiner Buchhandlung nachzuvollziehen. Vertiefungsseminare zu einzelnen Themen sollen dann die Mitarbeiter der Buchhandlung befähigen, in ihren jeweiligen Arbeitsbereichen an diesem Aufbau mitzuarbeiten und den Betrieb der Abteilung Elektronische Medien sicherzustellen.

Für den Bereich der Verlage ist das Konzept ähnlich; hier werden den Führungskräften die Kenntnisse um die Integration elektronischer Medien in das Verlagsprogramm anhand des Aufbaus einer projektgesteuerten Produktion einer Elektronischen Veröffentlichung vermittelt. Dabei ist es zunächst gleichgültig, ob die in einzelnen Arbeitsschritten erforderlichen Leistungen im Verlag oder von einem Dienstleister erbracht werden. Wesentlich ist, daß neben der Notwendigkeit des Einsatzes von Projektsteuerungsinstrumenten an Hand des Produktionsprozesses alle für den Verlag wesentlichen Fragen elektronischen Publizierens behandelt werden. Auch bei diesen Seminaren soll der Teilnehmer befähigt werden, durch die im Seminar vermittelte Ablauforientierung anschließend Projekte dieser Art durchführen zu können. Mitarbeiter der Unternehmen sollen in angebotenen Vertiefungsseminaren befähigt werden, einzelne Arbeitsfelder wahrzunehmen.

Die Chancen, die die Herstellung und Verbreitung elektronischer Publikationen für Buchhandlungen und Verlage bietet, können von den Marktteilnehmern nur genutzt werden, wenn die damit einhergehenden Herausforderungen erkannt und rechtzeitig in entsprechenden Handlungsorientierungen umgesetzt werden. Das Bewußtsein hierfür ist in der Branche durchaus vorhanden, so zeigt die im Rahmen des NBE-Projektes durchgeführte Studie. Dieses Bewußtsein in die Nutzung entsprechender Qualifikationsmaßnahmen zu überführen und diese bedarfsgerecht zu konzipieren, ist eine für die Buchbranche zukunftsweisende Aufgabe, an der derzeit mit Nachdruck gearbeitet wird, und die vorgestellte Studie soll diese Arbeit nachhaltig unterstützen, indem Erkenntnisse über den tatsächlichen Bedarf zukünftiger Qualifikationen und Qualifizierungen erhoben werden.

JONATHAN FURNER

Education for the Information Professions: New Developments at the Robert Gordon University

1. Introduction

In these pre-millenial days, any observation to the effect that some aspect of our society is undergoing 'fundamental change' seems hackneyed. When the subject of such an observation is the impact of information or of its attendant technologies, it becomes even more difficult to avoid resorting to cliché. Yet the consequences of the 'information revolution' of the last 50 years continue to ramify, and to provoke pronouncements that make up in dramatic style for what they lack in original content. It is often recorded, for instance, that one such consequence of recent advances in computing and telecommunications technologies is a 'fundamental change' in the nature of professional work in a wide range of employment sectors. Hardly less frequently stated is the standard call-to-arms for those academics responsible for the education of the professionals of the future. The new requirements of employers in the 'emerging markets' should be satisfied by the production of a new breed of graduate! New kinds of knowledge and skill should be the subjects of new kinds of curricula! New curriculum content should be delivered using new teaching techniques! New techniques are the preserve of staff with newly-developed expertise! Fresh? No. Understated? No, again. But: true? Apparently beyond debate.

In this paper, I review the ongoing efforts of the School of Information and Media (SIM) of the Robert Gordon University (RGU) in Aberdeen, Scotland, to respond appropriately and effectively to the demands of students, employers, profession and government. One core element of the School's strategy is the new Postgraduate Diploma / Master of Science degree course in Electronic Information Management (EIM), whose first cohort of ten students matriculated in September 1997, and which is now firmly established alongside the other courses in the School's postgraduate portfolio: the PgDip/MSc in Information and Library Studies, the PgDip/MSc in Information Analysis (which received the Jason Farradane Award from the Institute of Information Scientists in 1994, in honour of its 'outstanding contribution to the development of information science'), and the PgDip/MSc in Publishing Studies. Under development over the two previous years, the EIM course has been marketed as an innovation of unique interest in the United Kingdom, providing successful graduates with a 'skill-set' unattainable elsewhere yet precisely tailored to the demands of the modern job market for information professionals.

In the next section, I place the School's goals in the historical context of published debate about the match between employer demand and graduate supply in the library and information studies/science/service (LIS) sector; in Section 3, I outline the aims and objectives, and the curriculum, of the EIM course; and in Section 4, I draw conclusions that may be of relevance not only to those directly concerned with the design of LIS curricula, but also to those with a wider interest in the quality of output of LIS schools.

2. Contexts

2.1 Employer demand and curriculum content

It is fairly safe to assume that the primary goals of most, if not all the courses (undergraduate and postgraduate) offered by the 16 LIS schools in the UK are vocational in essence [1,2]. One course may vary from another in the degree to which an emphasis is placed on theory rather than practice, but this distinction is between the theory and the practice of information *work*. Educators design curricula with the intention of providing students with the best preparation for employment in the information-related professions; students enrol on these courses in order to gain a qualification that, they trust, will increase their chances of finding professional employment; and employers are expected to respect the validity of that qualification as an indicator of the level of knowledge and skill that the holder is likely to have.

Not surprisingly, much space in the LIS literature is given over to discussion on questions of curriculum content. Given the vocational aim of LIS courses, what sorts of knowledge should be imparted, what sorts of skill developed, in the classes that students take? The short answer, unhelpful as it stands without expansion, is simply to state: 'those very skills that are desired of prospective employees by employers'. In responding thus, one takes a view of educators as reactive beings, in thrall to the requirements of external organisations. Ignoring (for the moment) the wider implications of such a view, we can observe that debate is commonly deflected only to raise the obvious follow-up: What are those qualities that employers look for in applicants for information-related jobs? And then, in circular fashion: What exactly are these jobs (for which, by implication, graduates with LIS qualifications should be more than suitable applicants)?

In published considerations of questions of these types, three related themes recur frequently, typically in concatenated form as a compelling argument for the reform of traditional LIS curricula. These themes are: (i) the impact of *technological advances* on the use of information in everyday life; (ii) the emergence of *alternative markets* for job-seekers with LIS qualifications; and (iii) the value of *generic skills* that may be applied equally effectively whatever the professional function or employment sector of the holder.

2.2 The information revolution

The characteristics of the late-twentieth-century 'information revolution', and the level of its influence on the nature of work in the traditional LIS sector, are well-known. The driving force is *technological*, pushing forward through advances in the fields of computing and telecommunications; the essence of the revolution lies in the *economic* sphere, in the increasing efficiency with which information may be generated, transferred, acquired, collected, stored, located, retrieved, analysed, presented and used in organisations' and individuals' decision-making processes; and many of the consequences are at the *social* level, resulting in change in the typical activity of people not just at work, but in every aspect of their lives.

The most celebrated *technological* advance of the last decade is, of course, the growth of the Internet into the global, publicly-accessible computer network that is today used by millions at work and play. Despite the continuing prevalence (and undoubted accuracy) of the perception that much of the information accessible via the Internet is of limited and ephemeral usefulness, two primary effects of the widespread uptake, unprecedented in scale, of the networking technologies have been (i) to increase public awareness of the existence and range of information stored in digital form and conveniently transferable from remote sources, and (ii) to persuade organisations of the value of the client/server model on which the implementation of internal information systems (intranets) may be so effectively based.

At the *economic* level, a more general effect of the recent technological advances in informatics and telematics has been to heighten organisations' appreciation of the corporate value of their own information stores and assets, of the information-handling skills of their employees, and of those activities by which decision-makers are continuously supplied with access to timely, relevant, accurate, full and easily-digestible information, tailored to the specific needs of the individual. It is now well understood that an organisation which fails to deploy the technology and personnel required for the effective and efficient management of 'the fourth resource' is more than likely to suffer in the competition for profit in the marketplace [3].

The extent of the *social* impact of these changes is demonstrated by the frequency with which the descriptions of jobs and employees' roles in organisations refer to information-based functions and demand information-handling skills of the post-holder. But the impact on people's lives extends beyond the workplace to the home and to leisure time. Social activities of all kinds are becoming more and more dependent on a computerised, networked, information-driven infrastructure; and increasingly, in order to carry out mundane tasks such as shopping for consumer goods, booking a holiday, or even deciding what television programme to watch, it is information-handling skills that are required.

2.3 Emerging markets

Before the mid-1980s, it was certainly the exception rather than the norm for LIS graduates to find employment outside the 'traditional' library sector–this being limited to public libraries, academic libraries, and a few special libraries in commerce, industry, R&D and government. With the publication of influential reports by the Library and Information Services Council [4], the Transbinary Group on Librarianship and Information Studies [5] and Nick Moore [6], the significance of the 'emerging markets' for information professionals and the developing mismatch between employer demand and library-school supply became clear. The size of the traditional sector was in decline; in contrast, the numbers of jobs in *information-related* occupations were rapidly growing; yet the graduates of LIS courses were not meeting the distinctive requirements of employers in these emerging markets, resulting in high levels of graduate unemployment and employer dismay.

The implications of these developments were highlighted by commentators such as Brittain [7,10], Moore [8], Davenport and Cronin [9] and Muddiman et al. [11], to be subsequently restated on numerous occasions in the professional literature, and confirmed to varying degrees by surveys of job availability and employer opinion undertaken in the UK [12], North America [13] and Australia [14]. Explanations tend to run as follows. One effect of the information revolution (as we have seen) has been to increase the relative weight of information-based functions in *all* jobs, not just those traditionally located in the LIS sector. If they are to carry out these functions with an acceptable level of proficiency, the holders of these posts need to be able to call on an appropriate subset of information-handling skills. It is just this subset that, it is assumed, is possessed by the typical graduate of an LIS course. And hence there are very many jobs that may well be classed as falling outside the traditional LIS sector, but for which LIS graduates are (potentially, at least) particularly well-placed to apply.

The key terms here are 'subset' and 'potential'. Clearly, information-handling skills will not be the only ones that are required for effective performance in most of these jobs: in other words, they will form only a subset of the whole skill-set of the ideal post-holder. On the other hand, it is far from clear (so the argument continues) that, in present circumstances, the graduate of a traditional LIS education has more than this inadequate subset at their disposal. The potential nevertheless remains to augment this subset–i.e., for LIS educators to ensure that students are encouraged to develop the complementary skills that will enable them to compete in the emerging markets.

The questions that arise from this kind of debate can be divided into two broad categories. Questions in the first group relate to the way in which the emerging markets are defined. What exactly are these jobs, that are supposedly sufficiently 'information-intensive' to be suitable targets for LIS-graduate job-seekers, but that exist outside the traditional LIS sector? How many of these jobs are there, in comparison with numbers in the traditional sector? In what sorts of organisation are these jobs to be found? What job-titles should job-seekers look out for? What channels should they go through to identify vacancies?

Available evidence appears to suggest: (i) that almost any role whose successful performance is dependent on the effective use and management of information is likely to benefit from the skills of LIS graduates; (ii) that these roles greatly outnumber traditional library-based roles (although to what precise extent is uncertain); (iii) that these roles may be found in sectors as varied as publishing, computing, public relations, health services, marketing, journalism, management consultancy, and financial and legal services; (iv) that, given the wide range of job-titles in current vogue, job-seekers need to be suitably vigilant in order to spot appropriate vacancies; and (v) that traditional sources (such as the UK Library Association's fortnightly *Vacancies Supplement*) tend to provide details only of posts in the traditional sectors.

Questions in the second group relate to the definition of the skill-set that is appropriate for effective performance of non-traditional roles. What exactly are the skills that are required of graduates by employers in the emerging markets? What is the relationship between these skills and those that are imparted in traditional LIS courses?

2.4 Transferable skills

Discussion about 'transferable' skills in the LIS literature is frequently initiated in partial response to questions similar to those posed above. Skills of certain types may be identified as being 'transferable' in the sense of their being largely context-free: they can be appropriately and effectively applied in the performance of a variety of professional functions in a range of employment sectors, and stand in contrast to 'technical', 'specialist' or 'professional' skills that are specific to function and/or sector. A common argument takes as its starting point the assertion that employers see transferable skills as making up a vital part of the set required of the modern, 'hybrid' information professional.

What combination of skills is it, then, that forms the ideal package, portfolio or mix of *core competencies*, as far as employers in the emerging markets are concerned [15-17]? The intention of the educator asking such a question, of course, is that any answer should inform the design of LIS curricula, in order to reverse the tendency characteristic of the mid-1980s, when in many cases information-related jobs would be given to non-LIS graduates with the transferable skills that employers particularly valued. Towards the end of that decade, spurred by the recommendations of the LISC and TGLIS, the UK library schools began the process of curriculum reform that continues today.

Perhaps the most obvious of skills to be identified as transferable are those related to the use of *information technology*. Knowledge and understanding of basic hardware and software (in which category might be included word-processing, spreadsheet, database, desk-top publishing, presentation and Internet applications) is essential for success in an ever-increasing range of occupations. In truth, LIS educators have seldom been slow in taking steps to ensure that all students reach adequate levels of IT skills at the earliest possible stages of their courses, so that these skills may be further developed through practice and application in subsequent modules that do not necessarily have IT has their primary focus. Yet IT skills are not those that are most commonly identified by employers as being of most value in information-related jobs: that distinction is reserved for interpersonal skills.

The catch-all category of *interpersonal* skills might include: communication skills; leadership, teambuilding and motivation skills; negotiating and selling skills; presentation and training skills; and teamwork skills; as well as certain desirable personal attributes, such as: a 'professional' approach; a customer-service orientation; an enthusiastic, positive attitude; numeracy and linguistic ability; confidence and ambition; dedication and focus; flexibility and initiative; and creativity and vision.

Add these two sets of core competencies to solid bodies of knowledge (i) of the fundamental theory of information generation, flow, use and management, (ii) of technical LIS processes such as information seeking, retrieval, evaluation, selection, acquisition, collection, representation (indexing, classification and cataloguing), organisation, analysis, synthesis, presentation, transfer and dissemination, and (iii) of the information sources (printed and electronic) and services (manual and automated) that are available in the sector in which the post-holder will operate, and the result is a vibrant mix of skills that ideally prepares the LIS graduate for a successful career–or so the employers argue. Whether LIS courses are able to attract students of the calibre necessary if they are to emerge as suitably multi-talented, 'renaissance people' is an altogether separate matter.

3. The PgDip / MSc in Electronic Information Management

3.1 Aims and objectives

The aims and objectives of the EIM course are strongly vocationally-oriented, in accordance both with the University's general statement of purpose: ('... to produce versatile and resourceful practitioners who are relevantly qualified for their chosen professions and vocations ...'), and with the historical focus of the UK's 'new universities' (i.e., those ex-polytechnics, colleges and technological institutes granted university status in 1992). The general aim of the course is stated as being 'to prepare students for a professional career in electronic information management and for an effective role within the electronic information industry', and the intended focus is on the development both of traditional, technical skills and of those transferable competencies valued by employers in the emerging markets. More specific aims are specified as follows:

- to establish a specific knowledge base–i.e., to enable each student to acquire a body of knowledge and skills in the field of electronic information management, to the level required (i) for the student to embark on a career in professional practice in any of a variety of contexts within that field, and (ii) for the student to be awarded either the Postgraduate Diploma or the Master of Science degree;
- to develop a wide range of 'enterprise' skills–i.e., to build on the academic attainments of graduate-level entrants, by enabling students to develop: their general intellectual, analytical, creative and imaginative powers; their understanding and judgement; their reasoning and problem-solving skills; their communication, presentational and team-working skills; their time- and task-management skills; their ability to perceive indicative relationships between various strands of study, and to see their place within a wider perspective;
- to encourage independence of thought–i.e., to stimulate an enquiring, analytical and creative approach to professional work in electronic information

management, through the encouragement of independent assessment and critical self-awareness; and

- to generate enthusiasm–i.e., to generate a deep interest in the field of electronic information, and an enthusiasm for the learning process, such that students and graduates are self-motivated to meet the needs of a rapidly-changing professional environment through continuous development of their knowledge of contemporary issues and of their information-management skills.

It is intended that these aims should be achieved through the fulfilment of several objectives, some course-specific, and others more general. The course-specific objectives of the Diploma stage of the course are to enable students to develop:

- a comprehensive understanding of the characteristics of electronic information sources, and of the needs of those sources' users;
- expertise in the commissioning, design, development, delivery, management and use of products, services and systems intended to automate information-handling operations;
- an awareness and personal assessment of current professional practice in the effective management of any process that involves the organisation or communication of information in electronic form;
- the ability to analyse and evaluate the use of alternative procedures, techniques and resources in the application of information technology at any stage of such a process;
- an appreciation of the social, economic and legal implications of such activity, and of the impact of electronic information on all sectors of society; and
- the ability to undertake a critical appraisal of the nature, structure and condition of the electronic information industry and the interaction between the creators, producers, distributors and consumers of electronic information products, services and systems;

The more general objectives are to enable students to develop the abilities:

- to undertake advanced study with an appropriate concern for standards of scholarship;
- to synthesise data acquired from a variety of sources, to conduct rational argument, and to draw appropriate conclusions based on a rigorous and critical approach to the analysis of available data;
- to communicate clearly and effectively, both in oral and written presentations;
- to understand group dynamics, and to work effectively and efficiently as a member of a team;

- to apply, in practice, techniques and procedures that have been learned in a theoretical context or in a different domain;
- to demonstrate an awareness of the position of the objects of study in wider social, economic, legal and technological contexts;
- to undertake continuous self-assessment; and
- to cultivate a deep interest in current issues.

The objectives of the course develop as it progresses from the Postgraduate Diploma stage (Stage 1) to the Master of Science degree stage (Stage 2). As well as providing the fundamental knowledge, skills and stimulation necessary for students to begin practising at professional levels, Stage 1 also provides the appropriate foundation for undertaking independent Master's-level research in Stage 2.

The Master of Science degree stage provides the opportunity for students to use appropriate research methods in carrying out a critical investigation of a specific topic of relevance to the electronic information profession, preferably one that requires a constructive dialogue to be initiated with representatives from commercial organisations, and to present findings in the form of a dissertation. The objectives of the Master of Science degree stage are to enable students to develop the abilities:

- to extend their knowledge base through exploration of specific issues of concern to the electronic information industry;
- to develop expertise in research methods, including techniques of data collection, analysis and interpretation;
- to apply previously-acquired investigative, analytical, critical, creative and research skills to the practical identification of a significant problem, and to the evaluation of alternative solutions;
- to demonstrate intellectual rigour in the synthesis and presentation of information; and
- to develop high levels of self-motivation and independence of thought.

3.2 Curriculum

To ensure that these aims and objectives are met, the EIM course provides a programme of study that covers five core areas in the field: information management, information sources and services; computer systems and telecommunications; databases and information retrieval; and research methods. Each core area is represented in the curriculum by one or more modules as follows:

(a) Information management

Module 1 (double): Information systems management

Coverage: the basic concepts of organisation theory; the key functions and activities of management; the characteristics, use and management of information systems within organisations.

Module 2: Electronic and multimedia publishing

Coverage: the scope, role and impact of electronic and multimedia publishing; technologies for production and delivery; social, economic, legal and political issues.

(b) Information sources and services

Module 3 (double): Information sources and services

Coverage: the meaning of information and the structure of recorded knowledge; the context-specific nature of information need; the characteristics of published sources of information content; the use of information services in enabling information-seekers to satisfy their needs; the process of information access; the social context of information.

(c) Computer systems and telecommunications

Module 4 (half): Basic information technology applications

An introduction to information technology (IT), which provides a basis for the incorporation of further IT-based work in other units. This six-week unit is not assessed.

Module 5: Computer system architecture

Coverage: the role and operation of advanced features of computer systems hardware, and the function and use of systems software.

Module 6: Data communications and networking

Coverage: the fundamentals of telecommunication techniques, including information theory, digital transmission, data communication and data networks.

(d) Databases and information retrieval

Module 7: Database and information systems

Coverage: the fundamentals of database theory; the analysis of data models; the practical use of commercial database products.

Module 8: Computerised information retrieval systems

Coverage: the information retrieval (IR) 'problem'; the elements and functionality of IR systems; the evaluation of IR systems; networking and distributed IR systems.

(e) Research methods

Module 9: Research methodology

Coverage: strategies and techniques for the conduct of applied research; research management skills; the development of a student-specific research proposal.

The teaching in Modules 5 and 6 is delivered by the School of Electronic and Electical Engineering, and in Module 7 by the School of Computer and Mathematical Sciences. In addition to these nine core modules, all students are required to undertake a four-week period of supervised, unpaid work experience (Module 10: Fieldwork placement). Every effort is made to meet the individual wishes of students in regard to both geographical location and the type of organisation in which the placement is undertaken. For the Master of Science degree stage, the student is required to produce a dissertation (as described in the previous section).

4. Conclusions

A tendency to exaggerate the pervasiveness of the effects of the information revolution and the relative significance of transferable skills has recently led some to the conclusion that 'we are all information professionals now'. All jobs, to a greater or lesser degree, involve information-handling activity; information-handling skills are therefore applicable in a very wide range of contexts, and in that sense may themselves be regarded as transferable. Some (employers, prospective students, educators in other disciplines) might make the leap, and ask: Is the level to which students receive education in non-LIS curricula not sufficient for them to undertake the work of an information professional? Are the traditional, technical skills that are the preserve of LIS courses not outmoded in this modern, electronic age of information-for-all [18]?

The answer to both these questions, of course, is a definitive 'no'. In fact, given the volume of information now available and the proliferation of formats, media, systems and services through which it is accessible, a solid education in the theory and practice of information work, founded on the traditional, tripartite structure of sources (bibliography), processes ('cat. and class.') and operations (administration), and maintaining the discipline's distinctive emphasis on the importance of serving the needs of the user, is in fact more essential for the prospective information professional than ever before.

Nick Moore's latest prediction [18,19] is the emergence of four complementary groups of information professionals, each armed with a different skill-set: 'creators', or developers of information products, services and systems, versed in the principles of information technology and information design and in the importance of a user-friendly interface; 'collectors', or gatherers and organisers of both internally- and externally-produced information, skilled in knowledge representation and database design, and highly knowledgeable about the needs of their users, the objectives of their organisations, and the nature of the environments in which those organisations operate; 'communicators', or information retrieval specialists, able to analyse needs, to evaluate potentially-relevant information, and to select that which matches, with efficiency and effectiveness, using specialist subject knowledge, interpersonal and communication skills, and theoretical understanding of information-seeking behaviour; and finally 'consolidators', processing, analysing, interpreting, filtering, synthesising and presenting information, reducing complexity without sacrificing accuracy, 'making sense of the world' for the benefit of busy managers and decision-makers. It is easy to spot the shadows of more traditional figures lurking behind the newly-minted jargon: systems designers, database producers, reference librarians, and research analysts are all there. In today's job descriptions, of course, these same people might be known respectively as webmasters, knowledge managers, online searchers or competitor intelligence executives [20-22].

As the technologies develop and formats and media change, job-titles change accordingly; both the number of opportunities and the degree of respect accorded post-holders by top management increase; but the functions of information-handling remain the same, and it is these functions that are the preserve of qualified graduates in LIS-related disciplines. Rather than concerning ourselves as educators with the identification of new roles or new skills for information professionals, perhaps we should concentrate on graduates' development of new *attitudes*: a new confidence, both in one's ability to apply one's knowledge and skills effectively in different contexts and sectors and in a continuously changing technological environment, and in the fact that the particular combination of technical and transferable skills attainable by LIS graduates is already uniquely marketable and, as the information revolution continues and managers become more appreciative of its implications, ever-increasing in attractiveness to employers. The curriculum of the new postgraduate course in Electronic Information Management is one that provides a particularly thorough grounding in the technical knowledge, managerial expertise and practical, transferable abilities that are essential requirements for the information professional in the digital age, and is thus expected to meet employers' needs for graduates with this special blend of skills precisely and comprehensively.

References

[1] MACDOUGALL, J. and BRITTAIN, J.M. Library and information science education in the United Kingdom. *In*: M.E. WILLIAMS, ed. *Annual review of information science and technology: Volume 28*. Medford, NJ: Learned Information / American Society for Information Science, 1993, pp. 361-390.

[2] ELKIN, J. and WILSON, T., eds. *The education of library and information professionals in the United Kingdom*. London: Mansell, 1997.

[3] BEST, D.P., ed. *The fourth resource: information and its management*. Aldershot: Aslib / Gower, 1996.

[4] LIBRARY AND INFORMATION SERVICES COUNCIL. *Professional education and training for library and information work*. London: Library Association, 1986.

[5] TRANSBINARY GROUP. *Education for librarianship and information science: report of the Transbinary Group on Librarianship and Information Studies*. London: British Library Research & Development Department, June 1986.

[6] MOORE, N. *The library and information workforce: a study of supply and demand*. British Library Research & Development Report, No. 5900. Bath: Parker Moore, 1986.

[7] BRITTAIN, J.M. Information specialists: new directions for education and training. *Journal of Information Science*, 1987, 13 (6), 321-326.

[8] MOORE, N. *The emerging markets for librarians and information workers*. Library and Information Research Report, No. 56. London: British Library Board, 1987.

[9] DAVENPORT, L. and CRONIN, B. Demand and supply in information work. *Education for Information*, 1988, 6 (1), 61-70.

[10] BRITTAIN, J.M., ed. *Curriculum development in information science to meet the needs of the information industries in the 1990s*. Library and Information Research Report, No. 70. London: British Library Board, 1989.

[11] MUDDIMAN, D., MURPHY, M., ROBINSON, L. Information studies: developing the pluralist curriculum. *Personnel Training and Education*, 1990, 7 (3), 43-53.

[12] BRITTAIN, J.M. The emerging market for information professionals in the UK National Health Service. *International Journal of Information Management*, 12 (4), 261-271.

[13] CRONIN, B., STIFFLER, M. and DAY, D. The emergent market for information professionals: educational opportunities and implications. *Library Trends*, 1993, 42 (2), 257-276.

[14] FERGUSON, S. Preparing LIS graduates for the 'emerging market': an Australian educator down under in the UK. *Education for Information*, 1997, 15 (3), 229-233.

[15] BUTTLAR, L., DU MONT, R.R. Assessing library science competencies: soliciting practitioner input for curriculum design. *Journal of Education for Library and Information Science*, 1989, 30 (1), 3-18.

[16] BUTCHER, H. Business information curricula: an employer's list of essential skills and knowledge. *Education for Information*, 7 (4), 335-341.

[17] BUTTLAR, L. and DU MONT, R.R. Library and information science competencies revisited. *Journal of Education for Library and Information Science*, 1996, 37 (1), 44-62.

[18] MOORE, N. Creators, communicators and consolidators: the new information professional. *Managing Information*, June 1996, 3 (6), 24-25.

[19] ABELL, A. New roles? New skills? New people? *Library Association Record*, October 1997, 99 (10), 538-539.

[20] OJALA, M. Core competencies for special library managers of the future. *Special Libraries*, 1993, 84 (4), 230-234.

[21] MENDELSOHN, S. Will a different kind of person be needed to staff the information service of the future? *Information World Review*, March 1996, 112, pp. 28-29.

[22] MARSHALL, J., FISHER, B., MOULTON, L. and PICCOLI, R. *Competencies for special librarians of the 21st century: full report*. Washington, DC: Special Libraries Association, Special Committee on Competencies for Special Librarians, May 1996. Available online at URL: <http://-www.sla.org/professional/competency.html>.

DIE VISION FÜR DIE ZUKUNFT

MARGARET HAINES

The Future of Libraries in the Information Society: The Library and Information Commission's Vision

Aims of the Library and Information Commission

The Library and Information Commission (LIC) is a non-departmental public body which was established in 1995 to be a national focus of expertise on the library and information sector for England and Northern Ireland. It aims:

⇒ to provide a single, coherent and efficient source of advice to Government on all issues in the field;
⇒ to draw Government's attention to emerging issues and to suggest appropriate responses to them;
⇒ to represent UK interests in international policy development in the field; and
⇒ to provide advice on the basis of as full a process of consultation within the library and information (LIS) community and other sectors as possible.

The LIC is also charged with specific tasks including:

⇒ to develop a national research strategy for the LIS sector;
⇒ to manage the UK National Focal Point for the Telematics for Libraries Programme;
⇒ to advise Government on the feasibility of a national information policy; and
⇒ to recommend ways to increase the value for money from publicly funded library and information services through co-ordination and co-operation within the LIS sector.

Structure of the Commission

There are 14 Commissioners including the Chairman, Matthew Evans, who were appointed by the Secretary of State on the basis of their expertise and experience. Individually, they do not represent any constituency or library sector but between them cover a wide range of information related activities such as publishing, library management, library education, local government, corporate information services, etc.

Whilst the LIC's core remit is to provide advice on library and information issues in England and Northern Ireland, its two standing committees – the Research and International Committees, have a UK- wide remit and therefore also include members from Scotland and Wales.

The Research Committee is charged with developing a UK national strategy for research and development in the library and information field and to implement and maintain this strategy in co-ordination with the research programme of the British Library and other relevant bodies.

The International Committee provides advice on issues related to the impact of European Union policies on the UK library sector as well as monitoring and advising on information policy developments elsewhere, particularly in the G8 countries. This Committee also oversees the UK National Focal Point.

A Task Group was recently established to consider cross-sectoral issues in training of library and information workers. This group will focus initially on knowledge management (KM) as this is an issue where the LIS profession can make a significant impact but has as yet not been seen to be a lead player.

In addition to the Committee structure, there is also a small Secretariat led by a Chief Executive which is responsible for ensuring that the LIC acts as an efficient and responsive non-departmental public body; producing all internal policy papers for the Commission and all responses to consultation documents; liaising with Government departments and LIS bodies; and project managing all research for the LIC.

Whilst the LIC receives all its funding from the Department for Culture, Media and Sport, it is there to advise all interested Government departments.

The LIC's Ways of Working

The LIC must work in ways which make best use of its resources and do not unnecessarily duplicate the work of other national agencies. These include:

⇒ Taking a holistic approach

The LIC takes the view that a holistic rather than a sectoral approach is required to ensure the full contribution of the LIS community to society. It therefore focuses on cross-sectoral projects or on projects where the lessons are transferable.

⇒ Focusing work at the national and international level

As a national advisory body, the LIC focuses its attention on national and, as appropriate, UK-wide strategic issues. The LIC may advise on local issues if it can be demonstrated that issues concerned are generalisable.

⇒ Building Partnerships

Alliances with national co-ordinating and professional bodies are important in promoting a UK wide approach to the Information Society. Liaison with European organisations offers the potential for harmonisation of national with European policy developments. Liaison with organisations outside Europe, enables the sharing of experiences and understanding of the global context.

⇒ Proactivity in an advisory role

The LIC reacts to requests from Government for advice but is also proactive in bringing issues to the attention of Government where there will be an impact on the LIS sector or where the LIS sector can make an valuable contribution to the broader debate on Information Society issues.

⇒ Consulting and disseminating results widely

All advice to Government is given on the basis of as wide a process of consultation with the LIS community and the public as possible. Often the time-frame necessitates focused consultation which is why partnerships are so important. Similarly, the LIC's policy is to disseminate information on its activities as widely as possible through conferences and seminars, the Internet, and publications.

⇒ Demonstrating best value

The LIC advises Government on how to achieve best value in the delivery of library and information services to the public and also demonstrates best value in its own operational activities.

The LIC's Vision of the Future of Libraries in an Information Society

The LIC has developed a statement, *2020 Vision*[1] to articulate its vision of the value of library and information services, to set a context for its own action plan and to provide a framework for encouraging Government to demonstrate

[1] *2020 Vision*. London: Library and Information Commission. 1997.

the value of library and information services in economic, education and social policy development.

The following is an abridged version of the Vision statement:

⇒ The LIC believes that the UK will play a leading role in the global information economy through:

connectivity – providing universal access to the products of the human mind;
content – creating a digital library of the UK's intellectual heritage of culture and innovation;
competences – equipping individuals and organisations to play their full role in learning and information society.

⇒ The LIC recognises that library and information services are operating in a rapidly changing external environment where:

- access to information underpins a democratic society;
- information is an international commodity;
- knowledge underpins all successful economic activity;
- industry is increasingly dependent on an informed workforce;
- information must be accessible, organised and managed;
- information skills are fundamental coping skills;
- information needs are increasingly complex;
- technology offers the potential for universal access to information.

⇒ The LIC believes in the added value of library and information services which:

- form a substantial sector of the economy;
- are necessary to the well-being of individuals, communities and society;
- are the memory of society through collecting and preserving knowledge;
- add value by evaluating, making accessible, mediating, packaging and promoting knowledge;
- provide access to opportunities for literacy and lifelong learning, to information and works of creative imagination, and to a socially inclusive cultural and creative environment;
- empower the individual by providing resources, and information for special user groups, and facilitating the development of information skills which are essential for modern-day living;
- embody the value of collective activity, engender a sense of community within places and provide a space where people can feel secure within a shared value system.

⇒ The LIC believes that a holistic rather than sectoral approach is necessary in order to realise fully the potential of library and information services in society.

⇒ The LIC also believes that the added value of library and information services can impact on the external environment in such as way to create a society in 2020 where:

- Governments, companies and individuals will place a top priority on information;
- the UK will be an information/knowledge based society and world leader in connectivity, standards, content development, management and mediation skills;
- industry and commerce will be more knowledge-intensive learning organisations;
- there will be a network of information/knowledge centres which will empower citizens in developing a range of literacies to maximise their potential individually and collectively;
- there will be a digital library collection co-ordinated nationally/internationally embracing the world's creativity in which the UK' s heritage of intellectual property will be globally available in digital form;
- value added content and universal connectivity will ensure that every individual will have unfettered access to global information and knowledge.

⇒ To reach this vision of the UK as an information society in 2020, the LIC will promote and encourage:

- the UK role in the global information economy;
- a coherent approach to information policy at national level;
- initiatives to expand connectivity and content development;
- universal access to information and the skills to allow its proper exploitation;
- the importance of LIS within economic, education and social policy;
- the place of libraries in the future society;
- research to demonstrate the added value of LIS;
- equitable access for those with special needs.

LIC's Achievements To Date

Whilst the purpose of this paper is to share the LIC's vision and plans for the future, it is perhaps useful to reflect on what has already been achieved since the vision statement was produced in 1996:

The LIC's Research Committee has commissioned research on Internet availability in public libraries; digitisation in local authority libraries and archives; library involvement in lifelong learning across sectors.

The LIC's International Committee relaunched the UK National Focal Point for the European Libraries Programme of the EC's DG XIII in 1996 and has provided advice to the EU on copyright, data protection, the role of libraries, etc.

The LIC produced a paper on the feasibility of a national information policy for the UK which included a comprehensive review of information policy developments in other countries commissioned from Nick Moore of the Policy Studies Institute.

The LIC's greatest achievement is the production of a UK-wide strategy to show how public libraries could respond to the challenge of ICT technologies for the benefit of citizens of the UK. *New Library: The People's Network*[2] asserts that while the public library is already one of the most popular, inexpensive and successful of public services reaching 60% of the UK population, much more could be done to maximise the contribution which it should make to communities, especially in the age of the Information Society.

The Report proposes that public libraries need to supplement their existing services and collections with new content and services based on digital and network technologies. This would allow them to enhance their role in: supporting lifelong learning; facilitating citizen access to information; providing services to business; and helping to establish a record of community history and identity.

The Report argues for a managed national network to link together local public library networks and to provide a gateway to other networks. The network would be service managed to guarantee minimum bandwidth and thus predictable, stable and reliable levels of service for users.

The Report also recognises that whilst public library staff are already a highly skilled workforce, a national training strategy will be required to ensure that all 27,000 staff will have the full range of skills necessary for working within this new environment.

The Government response to the Report is expected in April, 1998 but already there have been very encouraging signs in the form of a commitment to use National Lottery money for information technology skills training and for digital content development.

A second major achievement of the LIC is the production of the national re-

[2] *New Library: The People's Network*. London: Library and Information Commission, 1997. (http:www.ukoln.ac.uk/services/lic/newlibrary)

search strategy for the LIS sector. A research mapping exercise was commissioned to determine to what extent past LIS research addressed the priorities of the LIC's Vision and to look at the impact of this research. At the same time, a wide range of LIS and non-LIS organisations were asked to identify the content of a national research strategy. The findings were incorporated into a draft national research strategy called *Prospects: A Strategy for Action*[3] which was widely distributed throughout the UK and Europe. The final version of the Strategy will be released in April 1998.

The Strategy provides a framework for collaboration between agencies to position UK LIS research in a European and global context. Five thematic areas provide a framework within which strategic research needs are identified: connectivity, content, competences and the impact and role of LIS and the economics of LIS delivery. In addition, an action plan is proposed to improve forward planning, funding of research, quality assurance, communication about research and putting research into practice.

To implement the plan, the LIC will work collaboratively with major players in the UK LIS research field particularly with the British Library Research and Innovation Centre and with key international players such as the European Commission's DG XIII.

New Contextual Issues and Opportunities:

In planning its activities for the next four years, the LIC is re-examining its priorities against the background of a new Government policy agenda and changes brought about by the impact of social, economic and technological trends. The areas of change which will have the most impact on the work of the LIC are:

⇒ education and training

The UK Government's anticipated approach to life long learning is likely to specify an overarching framework covering both compulsory and non-compulsory education. It will position the home, community and workplace as key places within which learning takes place and where the principles of the framework are applied. The policy focus is likely to be for a revolution in attitudes in order to increase understanding of, and demand for, lifelong learning. Choices will likely increase for the consumer in terms of learning pathways and qualifications and obtaining credit for learning is likely to be simplified with a new national credit framework.

[3] *Prospects: A Strategy for Action.* London: Library and Information Commission, 1997. (http://www.ukoln.ac.uk/services/lic/research)

A 'University for Industry' is central to this policy as it will provide the underpinning brokerage services and support infrastructure that will enable workers to identify learning pathways and providers appropriate for their needs. A 'National Grid for Learning' is also proposed which will provide a network for schools and will subsequently be opened up to the wider lifelong learning community, connecting public and national libraries, further and higher education institutions and the workplace.

⇒ economic regeneration, regional development and devolution

Successful management of information will continue to be a characteristic of competitive advantage in both the public and private sector. The national and organizational support systems for commerce will change as businesses demand new forms of information and information systems. The impact of the decision to enter/or not to enter the EMU will also be significant in terms of new information needed by businesses and of the changes to financial systems this will require.

At the regional level in the UK, it is likely that Regional Development Agencies will play a role in sponsoring services to support regional enterprise initiatives such as local and regional information and learning networks. This will require new ways of working to construct cost-effective, collaborative networks between libraries, education and training providers and business stakeholders.

The impact of devolution, political re-organisation and constitutional reform within the UK will lead to greater regional diversity, the drive for regional and local autonomy and the creation of devolved structures for social and economic decision making. At the regional and local level, there will be major strategic and implementation demands.

⇒ open government

Changes in society's attitudes to both privacy and freedom of information are also likely to be areas for considerable debate and controversy. Attitudes to the communication rich/communication poor divide; the availability of socially undesirable material; personal privacy and access to government information, will be reflected in legislation and legal judgments.

Proposals to open up government including the recent Freedom of Information White Paper will make public organisations more accountable to people and will increase the extent to which these bodies involve independent individuals in their management. These trends are likely to increase the range and depth of publicly available information which is needed in order that informed decision making can take place.

⇒ European and G8 policy developments

The LIC must be as aware of policy developments within the European Union and the G8 countries as it is of the UK Government agenda. Issues which are particularly important in this regard include:

- technical standards and content policies related to international information networks and digital information provision;
- recent directives on data protection, legal deposit, copyright and intellectual property rights;
- information and communication technology (ICT) related research programmes such as digitisation of multimedia content;
- policies and programmes to enhance the cultural and multimedia sector and to provide access to cultural heritage; etc.

In this regard, the LIC is very interested in contributing to the Green Paper on the Role of Libraries in the Information Society which is being produced by DG XIII in the European Commission and is expected before the summer break. In the website for the Green Paper, it states:

"The purpose of the Paper will be to stimulate discussion toward a coherent approach on how, within the context of an evolving Information Society, libraries can best serve the needs of European citizens by providing mediated access to the growing wealth of digital resources...The Green Paper should invoke responses from member states for future co-ordinated actions at European level aimed at: 1) the actions which can enhance or inhibit access by libraries and 2) suitable infrastructure alliances and learning materials which can assist libraries in meeting user needs."

⇒ social and technological change

The role of the individual within the community may change as social inclusion becomes a higher priority. There is an increasing sector of society that perceives itself as socially excluded or discriminated against including those who are disadvantaged because of disability, language, rural isolation or caring responsibilities. Concerns about the gap between the communication rich and the communication poor is already the subject of public debate.

The emergence of new forms of technology and its applications will have a profound impact upon society. In part, this will be the result of the application of technologies to work systems and processes e.g. the Year 2000 problem but it will also relate to the social and economic impact of technologies on society e.g. applications of digital information and communications services. The integration of ICT skills into the lives of individuals is critical if the benefits of increased economic prosperity and social cohesion are to be realized by the majority of the citizens.

In summary, the LIC recognizes the opportunities and the challenges presented to the LIS sector by new political, societal and technological trends, particularly:

- access to lifelong learning resources and services and to the nation's cultural achievements and heritage;
- linkages between schools, colleges and higher education institutions and the wider learning community;
- mechanisms to improve co-operation and collaboration across library and information sectors through partnerships at local, regional, national and international levels;
- initiatives to recognise and market the pivotal role of public libraries in particular to foster social cohesion; and
- the implementation of *New Library: the People's Network*, the National Grid for Learning, the New Opportunities Fund and the University for Industry.

The LIC will also need to develop partnerships within the LIS sector to:

- ensure that LIS professionals have the necessary skills and continuing development opportunities to manage in new contexts and apply new approaches;
- ensure LIS research programmes address the areas of greatest need in the changing political, economic, social and technological environments and that research results are effectively disseminated to improve LIS impact in these environments;
- ensure that key ICT issues and developments are identified and their implications for the LIS understood.

LIC's Proposed Agenda for Action:

In the next four years, the LIC will develop this national leadership role through work on seven action lines. Specific projects and targets will be set against each action line in annual business plans in addition to targets related to the core functions of the LIC:

- responding to requests for advice from Government on a wide range of issues including the feasibility of national information policy;
- encouraging cross-sectoral co-ordination particularly in the areas of professional development;
- leading the development and implementation of a research strategy for the sector;

- monitoring international library and information policy and research developments; and
- being an effective and efficient non-departmental public body.

Choosing annual targets for these five core areas, particularly in relation to commissioning of research , will be heavily influenced by their relevance to the action lines listed below.

Although the LIC has been pleased to respond to the Government's request for UK wide networking plans in the public library sector, it remains committed to a cross-sectoral rather than a sectoral approach in realising the potential value of library and information services in society.

The seven action lines are:

⇒ Action Line 1: To contribute through Government to the development of a UK national information policy framework.

The Commission has produced for Government a policy paper on the need for a national information policy framework. It will take this forward through closer liaison with key Government officials particularly those in the Departments for Culture, Media and Sport (DCMS), Education and Employment (DfEE), Trade and Industry (DTI) and the Cabinet Office, and will inform this work through policy seminars and papers which look at national and international developments in national information policy. The Commission sees the library network as an integral part of any pro-active national information strategy and itself as the appropriate gateway for the library community to contribute to national information policy.

⇒ Action Line 2: To retain an active leadership role in the implementation of a networked UK public library service.

The LIC will take a leading role in the implementation of the public library network monitoring and reporting on progress, benchmarking against European and other international developments, and encouraging co-operation and participation through awards schemes. The LIC will advise lottery agencies on funding digitisation projects and training for librarians in information communication and technology. It will work closely with local government to maintain momentum and commitment to the network, and co-ordinate rollout of the network National Grid for Learning and relevant initiatives in higher education. The LIC will work with other organisations to promote the importance of information skills training throughout life for the general population and the role of libraries in providing this training.

⇒ Action Line 3: To lead national policy development on the "UK Digital Library".

National policies for digitisation must be cross-sectoral, cross-domain and UK-wide in scope. The LIC will take the lead in promoting national co-ordination of digitisation activities based on the recommendations in its report "*Virtually New: Creating the Digital Collection*"[4]. The Commission will participate in national and international debate on copyright and intellectual property rights as these apply to digital material and advise Government accordingly. It will advise funding bodies such as the lottery agencies on criteria for selecting and prioritising collections for digitisation and work with appropriate bodies in the LIS community on promoting nationally recognised digitisation standards.

⇒ Action Line 4: To ensure that library and information services are central to the Government's plans for a learning society.

The role of library and information services in supporting learning throughout life has already been recognised in Government papers. The LIC anticipates that when the Government's plans for education are rolled out, library and information services will be centre-stage. The LIC will therefore, with DCMS assistance, develop closer relationships with DfEE officials responsible for the National Grid for Learning and the University for Industry as well as their relevant agencies such as the Teacher Training Agency and the British Educational Communication and Technology Agency. The LIC will seek joint planning opportunities with key players in the higher and further education sectors such as the Joint Information Systems Committee of the Higher Education Funding Councils.

⇒ Action Line 5: To develop the role of library and information services in fostering social inclusion.

Library and information services have a pivotal role in fostering social inclusion as they provide the information infrastructure which enables disadvantaged citizens to make informed choices about their lives, exercise their democratic rights and responsibilities, and to interact with other members of the community. The LIC will encourage strategic alliances between library and information services and other community organisations in order to strengthen the role of libraries as hubs in their communities and to overcome the barriers between information rich and information poor .

[4] Virtually New: Creating the Digital Collection. London: Library and Information Commission. 1997. All LIC publications are on its website www.lic.gov.uk

⇒ Action Line 6: To demonstrate the contribution of library and information services to regional and economic development.

The LIC will consider how to promote library and information services in supporting economic activity at local and regional levels and, in particular how they can assist small and medium enterprises in partnership with Training and Enterprise Councils, Chambers of Commerce and other business information providers. The role of library and information services in economic regeneration initiatives and in relation to the proposed Regional Development Agencies (RDAs) will be explored and promoted to Government and to RDAs themselves.

⇒ Action Line 7: To promote the importance of all library and information services to opinion formers outside and within Government.

The LIC will develop strategies to mobilise opinion formers in society who can influence the future development of public library and information services, including the 58% of the population who are library users. Successful initiatives such as the 'Friends of the New York Public Library' scheme will be examined as models. The value and positive impact of library and information services is beginning to be recognised in areas of Government policy such as education and health. The LIC will promote a positive attitude to all types of library and information service throughout Government. It will target departments, particularly DTI, Department for Environment and Transport, and the Treasury, with evidence of the value and impact of all types of library and information services.

⇒ Other Activities

In addition to the activities described under the five action lines, the LIC will continue work on current initiatives of the Commission and its Research and International Committees. This includes implementation of the national research strategy, further development of the LIC role in relation to national information policy, research into knowledge management training for LIS professionals and the expansion of the services provided by the UK National Focal Point under the Fifth Framework of DG XIII.

The LIC's 2020 Vision has captured the imagination and commitment of the LIS sector in the UK. The Vision's core themes of connectivity, content and competences are seen as trademarks of LIC policy development. The Vision has proven to be a sound basis for the LIC's own work programme in its first three years and will continue to underpin the LIC's action agenda for the future.

Autorenverzeichnis

Dr. Friedrich Bode, Referatsleiter, Ministerium für Wissenschaft und Forschung des Landes Nordrhein-Westfalen, Referat – ZA5-, Völklinger Str. 49, 40221 Düsseldorf, E-Mail: za5@www.mwf.nrw.de

Ross Bourne, Project leader, BIBLINK project, The British Library, Boston Spa, Wetherby, West Yorkshire LS 23 7BQ, Vereinigtes Königreich, E-Mail: ross.bourne@bl.uk

W. Keith Dobson OBE, Director of The British Council Germany, Hahnenstr. 6, 50667 Köln, Deutschland, E-Mail: bc.cologne@british-council.sprint.com

Dr. Reinhard Ecker, Leiter, Satz-Rechen-Zentrum Geschäftsstelle Frankfurt a. M., Am Wasserturm 6, 60435 Frankfurt a. M., Deutschland, E-Mail: recker.abc-datenservice@t-online.de

Dr. Jonathan Furner, Lecturer, School of Information and Media, The Robert Gordon University, Hilton Place, Aberdeen AB9 1FP, Vereinigtes Königreich, E-Mail: j.furner@rgu.ac.uk

Bertram Gallus, Geschäftsführer, Carl Heymanns Verlag, Luxemburger Straße 449, 50939 Köln, Deutschland, E-Mail: gallus@heymanns.com

Dr. Jens Gaster, Hauptverwaltungsrat, Europäische Kommission, DG XV/ Referat Urheberrecht, 200 rue de la Loi, 1149 Bruxelles, Belgien, E-Mail: Jens.Gaster@DG15.cec.be

Margaret Haines, Chief Executive, Library and Information Commission, 2 Sheraton Street, London W1V 4BH, Vereinigtes Königreich, E-Mail: margaret.haines@mail.bl.uk

Dr. Harald Heker, Justitiar, Börsenverein des Deutschen Buchhandels e.V., Großer Hirschgraben 17-21, 60311 Frankfurt a. M., Deutschland, E-Mail: rechtsabteilung@boev.de

Prof. Klaus-Dieter Lehmann, Generaldirektor, Die Deutsche Bibliothek, Adickesallee 1, 60322 Frankfurt a. M., Deutschland, E-Mail: lehmann@dbf.ddb.de

Tomas Lidman, Riksbibliotekarie, Kungliga Biblioteket, Sveriges nationalbibliotek, Humlegarden, Box 5039, 10241 Stockholm, Schweden, E-Mail: tomas.lidman@kb.se

Wim Luijendijk, Vice-President EBSCO International, Inc., General Manager EBSCO Europe, Box 204, 1430 Aalsmeer, Niederlande, E-Mail: wluijend@ebsco.com

Nick Moore, Professor of Information Policy, City University, London, Vereinigtes Königreich, E-Mail: nickm@city.ac.uk

W. Robert Müller, Geschäftsführer der Buchhändler-Vereinigung GmbH, Großer Hirschgraben 17-21, 60311 Frankfurt a. M., Deutschland, E-mail: mueller@bhv.de

Dr. Karl Wilhelm Neubauer, Ltd.Bibl. Dir., Bibliothek der Universität Bielefeld, Universitätsstraße 25, 33615 Bielefeld, Deutschland, E-Mail: neubauer@mail.ub.uni-bielefeld.de

Sandy Norman, Information Manager, The Library Association, 7 Ridgmount Street, London WC1E 7AE, Vereinigtes Königreich, E-Mail: NormanS@LA-HQ.org.uk

Dr. Ing. Thomas Rakow, Projektleiter Electronic Publishing, Springer Verlag, Tiergartenstraße 17, 69121 Heidelberg, Deutschland, E-Mail: rakow@springer.de

Prof. Dr. Gert Rickheit, Rektor der Universität Bielefeld, Universitätsstraße 25, 33615 Bielefeld, Deutschland, E-Mail: rickheit@lili.uni-bielefeld.de

Prof. Bruce Royan, Director, SCRAN Project, Abden House, 1 Marchhall Crescent, Edinburgh EH16 5HW, Vereinigtes Königreich, E-Mail: brue@scran.ac.uk

Maria Śliwińska, M.A., Deputy Director, Nicholas Copernicus University Library, Gagarina 13, 87-100 Torun, Polen, E-Mail: M.Sliwinska@bu.uni.torun.pl

Dr. Gert Staal, Director, SilverLinker Business, SilverPlatter Information B.V., Nieuwe Herengracht 49, 1011 RN Amsterdam, Niederlande, E-Mail: gert_staal@silverplatter.com

Dr. Hans-Georg Stork, Projektleiter, Europäische Kommission, DG XIII/E4, Elektronisches Publizieren und Bibliotheken, EUFO 1280, rue Alcide de Gasperi, 2920 Luxembourg, Luxemburg, E-Mail: Hans-Georg.Stork@lux.dg13.cec.be

Dr. Christine Thomas, Referentin, Bundesministerium für Bildung, Wissenschaft, Forschung und Technologie, Heinemann-Str. 2, 53175 Bonn, Deutschland

Volker Thurner, Lehmanns Fachbuchhandlung, Hardenbergstraße 11, 10623 Berlin, Deutschland, E-Mail: thurner@lehmanns.de